P9-DWJ-974

Herbs, Health and Cookery

Herbs, Health and Cookery

by
Claire Loewenfeld
and
Philippa Back

GRAMERCY PUBLISHING COMPANY · NEW YORK

Copyright © MCMLXVII, MCMLXV by Claire
Loewenfeld

All rights reserved.

This 1982 edition is published by Gramercy Publishing
Company, distributed by Crown Publishers, Inc., by
arrangement with Hawthorne Books, Inc.

Originally published in England as *Herbs for Health and
Cookery.*

Manufactured in the United States of America

Library of Congress Cataloging in Publication Data

Loewenfeld, Claire.
  Herbs, health, and cookery.

  Includes index.
  1. Herbs. 2. Cookery (Herbs) 3. Herbal
cosmetics.
I. Back, Philippa. II. Title.
TX819.H4L6 1982   641.3'57   82-3043
                            AACR2

ISBN: 0-517-105659

h g f e

$\mathcal{P}$reface

Our practical work with herbs over many years, at Chiltern Herb Farms, has provided us with the experience on which this book is based.

Many requests have come to us for a book of herb recipes. We feel health and cookery can and should go hand in hand. To many people, healthful eating conjures up tasteless lettuce leaves and expensive meats. We endeavor to explode this idea with tasty, inexpensive, and easy-to-make dishes, all using herbs.

The enjoyment we have had in compiling this book and trying out every recipe will, we hope, be apparent to our readers and will help to promote their interest.

Contents

*I*ntroduction to the *A*merican *E*dition

The use of herbs in cookery has been enthusiastically adopted by most American cooks today, but little has been published in this country about the magical effect of herbs on health. Herbal teas instead of sleeping pills, a "tisane" of lemon balm instead of pep pills, and fennel sauces to take off weight—these are a few of the delightful prospects offered by Claire Loewenfeld and Philippa Back.

It is fascinating to learn that elder-flower tea can relieve a cold, that a fennel pack will soothe inflamed eyes, and that an infusion of thyme may be an effective pain killer for a toothache!

Certain of the herbs recommended by the English authors will be hard to come by in this country, but others, such as marigold blossoms, blackberry leaves, and even the golden rod, grow wild all around us.

For those on special diets, there are herbs which may be used in a salt-free diet, and others which are recommended for gastric complications—and sweet cicely is urged for use in desserts as a pleasant way to reduce sugar intake.

Not the least of the book's attractions is its guide to which herbs may be used generously or even lavishly in cooking, and which must be used sparingly. There is also an entire section on using herbs for cosmetics.

The recipes in the cookery section range all the way from savory dips and appetizers through desserts and bedtime snacks, and they have the double attraction of being both mouth-watering to read about and easy to follow.

It is difficult to translate certain food terms, because in some cases there is no exact equivalent. "Double cream," for example, is very thick sweet cream, of the same consistency as our sour cream. What we use for whipping cream is called in England "full cream" or sometimes "thick cream."

The British (and the French, too) call the eggplant an aubergine, but their eggplants are tiny by comparison with ours, so that when a recipe calls for "2 medium eggplants," we would use only one of our small to medium eggplants.

European yeast is quite different from American yeast products. It is safer to use American recipes for pizza dough and bread to be sure of results.

Bacon products are quite different, too. "Gammon" is more like our ham; "fat pork" has not been smoked or salted and so has a quite different flavor from our fat salt pork; and when a "rasher of bacon" is called for, it usually means a slice of what we call Canadian bacon.

There is similar confusion about "cream cheese." In England, the term usually means a kind of cottage cheese made with whole milk, blended with cream. But today Philadelphia cream cheese is sold in England; and in certain dishes it's *our* kind of cream cheese that is meant.

Two separate tables or charts (to be found on pp. 13–15) have been drawn up to serve as instant translators when puzzling British food terms or measurements are encountered in the recipes. The equivalent cup or spoon measures (translated from ounce measures) given in the second of the two tables should be regarded as approximate. For real accuracy in measuring such ingredients as sugar, flour, and herbs, a household scale with both gram and ounce weights is recommended for weighing them. But in herb cookery many measurements must be made "according to taste" anyway, since the flavor and potency of each herb vary due to soil or climatic conditions, to say nothing of the difference between fresh herbs and dried herbs or herb extracts. But this kind of cookery is adventurous and fun, especially when, as the authors suggest, you can pluck flower petals or fragrant leaves from your own garden to give humdrum dishes tantalizingly different flavors.

Betty Wason

A *S*hort *I*ntroduction to *H*erbs

WHAT IS IT that attracts people to herbs? Is it the graceful look of the growing herbs, their lovely scent, their quaint and sweet-sounding names and the charm of the herb garden? And yet, the actual purposes for which herbs are meant, and have been used since time immemorial, their preserving properties and the magic they mean for good health and good eating, have almost been forgotten.

We owe most of our culinary traditions to the Romans, who when they came to Britain, brought with them about 400 different herb plants for both culinary and medicinal use and without which they felt they could not live. The Romans, in turn, owed their knowledge of herbs to the Indians, Egyptians, and Greeks. Among the herbs which they brought with them were many we use today, such as parsley, onions, lovage, sage, chervil, thyme, and many more. They boasted that they had no need of doctors, as their knowledge of herbs for food and treatment was sufficient.

From then onwards, herbs have a long history of many "ins" and "outs." Forgotten during the Dark Ages, reintroduced and cultivated by the monks in the early Middle Ages, an important item in the still-rooms of the old manor house, they were well known and much used by many generations until the nineteenth century, when the Industrial Revolution started the mass production of synthetic substitutes for herbs and flavorings.

Now herbs are coming into their own again. This reawakening of interest in the use of herbs does not appear to be a quaint revival, but seems to have its own historical necessity. Since the Industrial Revolution and the "Chemical Age," so much has been done to food in the name of preserving, processing, "beautifying," slashing prices, "assuring a long shelf life" that the original flavors, natural colors, and tempting scents have vanished. We are meant to be tempted through the eye, the nose, and the palate and to use them as instruments for the judgment of the goodness of our food; and the eye, the nose, and the palate cannot in the long run be deceived by coaltar dyes, sulphur preserving agents, and sodium glutamate "flavoraccenting" agents. A strong instinct for survival has recalled herbs to restore flavor where it has been lost.

However, once the palate regains the taste for herbs, it becomes necessary that they be available all the year round. Ways and means had to be found to *retain* the herbs' full flavor and color when drying them. Freshly cut, they are mainly available for those with a garden and even for those only during certain periods of the year. If the flavor and color of herbs are well looked after, most of the nutritional values can be retained; they are bound up together with volatile oils, minerals, trace elements, and the many important substances such as bitter principles, tannins, secretins, organic acids, etc., which give herbs their distinct flavor, and their digestive, disinfectant, antibiotic, or preserving qualities.

A similar development may be observed with herbs used for health, and this is more fully discussed in Part 1. The experience of drugs having undesirable side effects has increased interest in the safer but probably slower noticeable influence of herbs on minor ailments and improving health in general.

AMERICAN EQUIVALENTS OR SUGGESTED SUBSTITUTES

When recipe calls for   *use*

bacon products
   fat pork — unsalted fat from pork
   rasher of bacon — slice of Canadian-style bacon
   streaky bacon — sliced bacon
   gammon — ham (picnic butt is most like gammon)

castor sugar — fine granulated or superfine sugar

condensed tomato puree — tomato paste
cornflour — cornstarch

cream and milk products
   cream cheese — cottage cheese made from whole milk, blended with cream (In some cases, Philadelphia cream cheese may be used.)

   double cream — In some (but not all) recipes, use dairy sour cream. (Double cream is the same consistency as our dairy sour cream, but it's sweet.)

   full or thick cream — heavy (whipping) cream
   single or thin cream — light cream
   creamy milk or Jersey milk — whole or homogenized milk
   curd — pot cheese
endive — chicory
flour — Unless specified otherwise, use all-purpose flour

icing sugar — confectioner's sugar
minced meat — ground meat
semolina — Cream of Wheat breakfast cereal or farina

silverside — top round steak

TABLE OF EQUIVALENT MEASURES

ENGLISH	AMERICAN EQUIVALENT

Spoon measures

1 tablespoon (English)	= 4 teaspoons or 1⅓ tablespoon
Dessertspoon	= 1 tablespoon

Liquid measures

1 pint (English)	= 20 fluid ounces or 2½ cups (American pint is 16 fluid ounces or 2 cups.)
3 pints (casserole size)	= almost 2 quarts
¾ pint (English)	= a little more than 2 cups
½ pint (English)	= 1¼ cups
gill	= ¼ English pint (10 tablespoons, or ½ cup plus 2 tablespoons)
teacup	= ½ cup

Bread crumbs

fine dry 3¼ ounces	= 1 cup
fresh or slightly stale 1½ ounces	= 1 cup
4 ounces	= ¼ of pound loaf

Butter

½ ounce	= 1 tablespoon
1 ounce	= 2 tablespoons
4 ounces	= ½ cup or ¼ pound (1 stick)

Almonds

blanched, whole 5½ ounces	= 1 cup
grated (shredded) 2 ounces	= ⅓ to ½ cup

Bacon

2 ounces, Canadian style	= about 2 thin slices
5 ounces	= about 10 thin slices

ENGLISH	AMERICAN EQUIVALENT

Cheese

Cheddar—4 ounces	= cup grated
"cream" (cottage), 8 ounces	= 1 cup
2 ounces	= ¼ cup
Parmesan, grated—4 ounces	= 1 cup
2 ounces	= ½ cup

Flour

all-purpose 1 ounce	= 3½ tablespoons
2 ounces	= 7 tablespoons
4 ounces	= 1⅞ cups sifted

Gelatin, unflavored

| 1 ounce | = 2 tablespoons (2 envelopes) |

Meat (Ham)

| diced 2 ounces | = ¼ cup |
| 8 ounces | = 1 cup |

Oil   2 ounces = ¼ cup

Raisins

| 1 ounce | = 2 to 3 tablespoons |
| 6 ounces | = 1 cup |

Rice

| 8 ounces (½ pound) | = 1 cup |

Spices, Ground

| ½ ounce | = 2 tablespoons |

Sugar

castor or fine granulated

2 ounces	= ¼ cup
8 ounces	= 1 cup
confectioner's or icing 1 ounce	= ¼ cup
2 ounces	= ½ cup
brown 2 ounces	= 6 tablespoons
1 ounce	= 3 tablespoons

Vegetables

Potatoes	1 pound	= 3 medium
Onions	1 pound	= 3 large
Tomatoes	1 pound	= 3 to 4 small
Spinach	5 ounces	= about 4 cups loosely packed

PART ONE

HERBS FOR HEALTH AND BEAUTY

Chapter 1

Uses and Health Properties of Individual Herbs

SINCE TIME began, herbs have been used for maintaining health and as remedies. Many herbs were found to have digestive properties, and from this some of the flavoring customs may have sprung, e.g., fennel with oily fish. As remedies, herbs were used up to the nineteenth century. During the Industrial Revolution, science began research on our remedies, and many of the herbs and plants were chemically synthesized, but there was no endeavor to find the individual reasons for the effects of herbs on health. In other countries some research on the substances which make herbs so useful for health has been carried out recently; some of this was used when compiling this book, as in this country litle research has been carried out on the qualities of herbs.

Modern drugs have sometimes unpleasant side effects; this may be due to the synthetic nature of the drug, or to the fact that only certain substances of a plant may have been extracted and then concentrated; in this way the balanced effect of the plant may be lost. The known use of whole herbs—or infusions made of them—is safe and has no unexpected or even undesirable consequences. Unless they are used in increased or concentrated quantities—other than suggested in this book—they may be taken without fear. However, for those people who are used to strong stimulants, the effect may be delayed or even unnoticeable. In the following descriptions of the health properties of individual herbs, it is clearly stated which effects have been well known for generations and have often been experienced.

Some herbs are mentioned in this book for their health qualities only; sometimes the health properties of those which are mainly used for cookery are given. The latter are described in more detail in Part Two, "Twenty-four Herbs in a Chest," and are printed in the following section in italics to distinguish them from the herbs included for their health qualities only. All these herbs are meant to be used, not just as an herbalist's treatment, but as wholesome, pleasant, and often health-restoring additions to the daily diet.

ANGELICA (Angelica archangelica)

This gigantic plant with large scented leaves and thick stems is used mainly for flavoring, especially in confectionery, but it also has health properties. Angelica tea resembles China tea in flavor. The bright green stems are often candied or crystallized. The scented leaves are an excellent addition to potpourri.

BASIL (Ocimum basilicum)

The leaves of this most excellent flavoring herb were used at one time as a snuff for nasal colds, and were said to clear the brain and deal with headaches. The leaves have been allowed to permeate in wine for a digestive tonic, and have also had the reputation of stimulating milk in nursing mothers. The herb causes perspiration and aids digestion, the leaves mixed with salad oil being recommended for constipation. Like all strong tasting herbs it was considered to be antiseptic, which probably explains why it was often used with meat and fish. It has been prescribed as a sedative and against gastric spasms; it has acted at times as an expectorant, a laxative, and a carminative; and, by stimulating perspiration, it is supposed to reduce a temperature.

BAY LEAVES (Laurus nobilis)

The sweet bay, from which the bay leaves come, is the true laurel and the only one of this genus which is used for human consumption. The leaves were used for wreaths for poets and heroes in ancient times and to decorate houses and churches at Christmas, and were once considered a cure for many illnesses. Bay leaves have been used for flavoring, preserving, and marinading, their preserving qualities being useful for this purpose. Bay leaves stimulate the appetite. They were at one time used for rheumatic complaints (externally) and as a protection against insects.

BERGAMOT, RED (Monarda didyma)

This old-fashioned perennial flowering plant is a useful tisane, well known in Europe and in America. It is also called Oswego tea. The American colonists used it instead of ordinary tea when boycotting British tea at the time of the Boston Tea Party. Red bergamot provides a delightful tea; when served hot it induces good sleep and has a soothing and relaxing effect. The leaves may also be added to China or Indian tea, wine drinks, and lemonade. Bergamot milk is an excellent nightcap. From July to September bergamot has flowers of several colors, but scarlet flowers belong to the variety used for bergamot tea.

BORAGE (Borago officinalis)

This plant of special beauty has had since the early days of the Greeks the reputation of making men merry. In fact, its exhilarating effect accounts for the Greek proverb "I Borage bring always courage," and for its nickname, "Herb of Gladness." It is the juices in borage which give a cucumber-like coolness to wine or any alcoholic drink. Borage leaves are added to many drinks not only for the flavor but for the purpose of dispelling depressed moods without side effects. The chopped leaves and the lovely, blue, star-shaped flowers are also used in salads.

CELERY AND CELERIAC LEAVES (Apium graveolens)

They contain a variety of vitamins, mineral salts, and many active principles which make them important for health, quite apart from their much-liked flavoring qualities. They are also reported to have a hormone which has an effect similar to that of insulin. They are an excellent seasoning for certain types of invalids, such as diabetics, or for anyone on a salt-reduced diet.

CHAMOMILE (Matricaria chamomilla)

The flowers of the true chamomile have been one of the most important medicinal herbs. It later lost some of its importance in England due to the fact that the two chamomiles, the true chamomile and the Roman chamomile (Anthemis nobilis) became confused. The important healing blue oil is mainly found in the true chamomile, which may be recognized by the flower. This has a yellow receptacle which is hollow and markedly conical from the beginning. It also has a lovely scent which distinguishes it from the similar looking mayweed and other flowers of the same family. It flowers from May to October, and the flowers may be picked all the time whenever they arrive. They are dried for tea, but should be touched as little as possible. Chamomile tea is drunk much on the continent, mainly in France, as an aid to digestion after heavy meals, and has a soothing, cleansing, disinfecting, anti-spasmodic effect, particularly in the case of intestinal pain. It has also a soothing and healing effect on any part of the mucous membrane and on the skin, and that makes it not only a useful tisane but a most helpful herb for cosmetic purposes.

CHERVIL (Anthriscus cerefolium)

This most graceful, delicate-flavored herb, which may be cut early in the year if sown in the autumn, is much liked in spring. The luscious green leaves are traditionally used in all spring soups and sauces because they have blood-cleansing and diuretic qualities, and are considered to have a specially stimulating effect on the glandular system. The juice of the leaves has been used as a cleansing treatment in spring and has also been considered to be a good digestive. All this made it one of the traditional Lenten herbs. As it also increases perspiration, chervil has been used for fever, jaundice, gout, skin troubles, and gallstones. Lastly, finely chopped and warmed chervil has been known to be applied to bruises and painful joints.

CHIVES (Allium schoenoprasum)

Chives, being the mildest type of onion, are also antibiotic in a mild way. They have the reputation of stimulating the appetite and strengthening the stomach, and they are also supposed to have a beneficial effect on the kidneys and to lower blood pressure. They are useful in an invalid diet, and salads, omelettes and other egg dishes, and soups may be offered with plenty of chives during convalescence.

DANDELION (Taraxacum officinale)

A wild herb, though undesirable in the garden, it is of such high nutritious value that it should be used, particularly in spring. It is good in salad or in combination with spinach. Its freshly pressed juice is also useful. Full of useful minerals and vitamins, it is considered helpful to the function of the gall bladder. Dandelion salad in spring is also considered a blood cleanser, owing to its diuretic and digestive qualities. All these qualities make it one of the most valuable herbs, as long as young leaves can be found. A tea may be made of fresh or dried dandelion leaves, which is helpful to digestion, liver, and gall bladder. The roots are used to make a coffee substitute.

DILL (Anethum graveolens)

Dill is a rather special herb for flavoring, and there are some countries in which dill is an indispensable herb. This may be due, not only to its aromatic and pungent flavor, but also to the fact that dill is excellent for digestive purposes. Dill has always had the reputation of being helpful in the case of flatulence and tummy-ache, and for promoting good sleep. Though dill also sharpens the appetite, its seeds used to be chewed before a meal to still hunger pains, as was done with fennel seeds as well. Chewing dill seeds was also supposed to remove bad breath, an interesting suggestion which may be worth an experiment. Dill is rich in minerals and is thus an important addition to our food. It had the reputation of stimulating milk production in nursing mothers. The juice of the plant is astringent and was used externally for piles. From a modern point of view, dill is a good flavoring for diabetics and for those on a low-salt diet, because the salts contained in it are no burden to the system in general.

ELDER FLOWERS AND ELDERBERRIES (Sambucus nigra)
The elder tree gives us in profusion the honey-scented elder flowers and black berries so useful in autumn and winter. The tree has been closely connected with legend and folklore, and it was believed to be unlucky to uproot elder trees. To this we owe many elder trees in the countryside, from which we may collect the flowers, which, apart from being used in fritters, have medicinal and cosmetic properties. They contain volatile oils, vitamins, and many other substances. They increase perspiration and are diuretic, and so are supposed to purify the blood. Elder-flower tea, like lime-flower tea, is useful in the case of colds and may be taken as an alternative to aspirin, particularly if mixed with lime flowers and chamomile. Apart from this medicinal use, the flowers make refreshing summer drinks, and their pleasant, sweet, distinctive flavor may be added to many sweets, such as milk dishes, jellies, and jams. Elder-flower water, an infusion, is safely used for eye and skin lotions and is a mildly astringent stimulant. Thus elder flowers are an excellent addition to the bath. Little bags made of elder flowers through which the hot tap runs are very useful. Facial steam baths made of elder flowers clear and soften the skin and are good against freckles and pigmentation.

The elderberries may be cooked with jam or made into a juice. They have medicinal properties of a different kind. They have the reputation of cleansing the bloodstream, and elderberry juice is good for chills during winter and for people who suffer from pains originating from sciatica and neuralgia.

FENNEL (Foeniculum vulgare)
Fennel is a relative of dill. Both are fish herbs, and a number of their qualities serve the same purpose. Fennel also aids milk production in nursing mothers, has a sedative effect, and stimulates the appetite. In the same way as dill it acts as an anti-flatulent and is good for indigestion. It has a reputation as an expectorant and is used against catarrh. Fennel is said to reduce overweight, so a tisane made with fennel could be worth experimenting with for those who have to watch their weight. Amongst the many herbs expected to be

helpful to the eye, fennel is one of the most useful. Compresses steeped in fennel tea may be placed on the eyes. Bathing the eyes with fennel is good for inflamed eyelids and watering eyes. It may even strengthen the eyes and improve the sight. For cosmetic purposes a facial pack made of fennel tea and honey is recommended against wrinkles.

HIBISCUS FLOWERS:
AFRICAN MALLOW;
KARKADÉ

A delicious thirst-quenching ruby-colored tisane, called Karkadé in its African homeland, is made of the flowers. They give it the beautiful color and a slightly tart, lemony flavor. Two or three flowers may also be added to rose-hip tea to improve the red color and the flavor of this drink. This tea is drunk much on the continent, and is generally a useful summer drink. It is excellent either hot or iced, and may also be used for punch.

HORSERADISH (Armoracia)

The roots of the horseradish grow in most well-worked soils and are more difficult to eradicate from a garden than to grow. The root has a delicious hot pungency and is at the same time cooling. This makes it an excellent flavoring.

Horseradish belongs to the plants which have antibiotic qualities. It contains, in fact, substances which are hostile to bacteria, and is therefore not only most useful for preserving food to which it is added, but also for keeping the intestinal tract in a sound condition. It is stimulating to appetite and digestion, helps the liver to function, has a strong diuretic effect, and is an excellent seasoning for diabetics.

HORSETAIL (Equisetum arvense)

This wild-growing herb looks like a minute version of the gigantic trees of prehistoric times. It contains a considerable quantity of silicic acid, which is useful medicinally, as well as for cleaning and scrubbing all fine metals. In fact, the plants used to be sold in German-speaking countries for scouring. Owing to its content of silicic acid the herb has an astringent and strengthening effect on the tissue, and an infusion of it is excellent for curing brittle nails. The green barren shoots, looking almost like minute Christmas trees, may be collected from May until late summer. They are used for tea. They should not be bruised or broken and should be dried carefully so as not to lose their color.

HYSSOP (Hyssopus officinalis)

The herb has a refreshing aromatic scent and its tea is used as an expectorant. It has a slightly bitter and minty taste and is, therefore, a good flavoring when finely chopped in salads or as an addition to game, meats, soups, and stews. The flowers and tops have also been used in some continental sausages. Hyssop is useful with meat and fish, such as eel, or for rubbing into poultry before roasting. It has been suggested that hyssop "cuts grease." Fruit cocktails, particularly those made with cranberries, may be flavored with a few leaves at the bottom of the dish. It also may be added to pies made with fruit, such as apricots or peaches. One-quarter teaspoon of hyssop sprinkled over the fruit before the top crust goes on is quite enough. Hyssop was mentioned in the Bible for cleansing purposes. It is also an ingredient in the French liqueur Chartreuse.

JUNIPER BERRIES (Juniperus communis)

The shrub juniper, regarded as a magic plant in the past, is connected with many legends concerned with evil spirits, devils, etc., but also with holy legends from the Bible. Its strong, aromatic scent emanates from all parts of the shrub, and the berries are slightly bittersweet, fragrant, and spicy in flavor. They are used for gin and for all spirits which used to be thought good for the stomach. They are part of certain blends of kitchen spices, such as for beef and for game, especially venison. The Laplanders make a tea from juniper berries which is used in all continental countries and in Scandinavia. They are also used for a conserve which is served with cold meat. The substances contained in the berries are stimulating for the appetite and the digestion—in fact, all functions of the body. They are blood cleansers, and their diuretic effect makes them useful for the functions of the kidneys. They also have disinfectant, antibiotic substances. During the nineteenth century, schoolrooms in Switzerland were not well aired, as fuel was short, so the air was sweetened by putting juniper berries on red-hot burning coals. Research has found that, during the burning of the sugar in the berries, a gas is produced which has a disinfectant effect. This explains why they are used to clean the air in an invalid's room.

Meat when smoked with juniper berries receives a special flavor.

The berries need three years to ripen. They are first green, then blueish, and eventually black, and should not be used before they are ripe. In marinades for game and as a flavoring for sauerkraut their preserving qualities come to the fore.

LADY'S MANTLE (Alchemilla vulgaris)

Lady's mantle has a reputation for healing, and has been used against bleeding, but its universal reputation has been connected with female ailments. Its active substances are not all fully understood, but the tea made of its leaves has been considered to be of importance to all women. It has been said that lady's mantle clears inflammations of the female organs. It has also been suggested for use against skin disturbances and against freckles.

LEMON BALM (Melissa officinalis)

Lemon balm, which is growing profusely in many gardens and is often considered a weed, has many virtues, medicinal as well as flavoring. The lemon-scented leaves have an anti-spasmodic effect and, as they at the same time stimulate the heart and have a calming effect on the nervous system, provide an excellent tea to be used as a nightcap.

Lemon balm also has the reputation of securing a long life, and quite a few reports from the past confirm it. It is also believed to induce perspiration in feverish patients, but for this purpose there is perhaps more help to be found with lime-flower, elder-flower or chamomile tea. Lemon balm is considered effective for earache and toothache. It is also reputed to be used against vomiting in pregnancy. This is very likely to be effective, as vomiting is sometimes due to spasms, against which this tea is particularly useful. It also has a good reputation against bad breath. All the effects are mild, and lemon balm may therefore be used for delicate people and over long periods. It is as such one of the most useful daily drinks.

Externally lemon balm has been used for treatment of gout and rheumatism, and has been considered a wound herb for its cleansing and pain-killing effect. Cosmetically, washing with melissa tea or infusion is good for all kinds of skin conditions. Lemon-balm leaves are useful in potpourri and herb cushions.

LIME FLOWERS (Tilia europaea, *or* cordata, *or* platyphyllos);
THE LIMES

The flowers of the limes may be collected mainly from three varieties of the lime tree, and are used to make a delicious and health-giving tisane. They are dried and used together with the large oblong leaf-like bracts. The flowers contain properties which are mildly sleep inducing and help to get rid of mucus. A tea made of lime flowers soothes the nerves, aids digestion, and allays spasms, and it is also useful in cases of chills and colds, and may be used as a pleasant alternative to aspirin, as it also reduces temperature. Lime-flower tea (tilleuil) is used in France as an after-dinner drink, and its calming and anti-spasmodic qualities help to provide a good night's sleep. Together with equal parts of chamomile and elder flowers, it is excellent against colds and flu, because it increases perspiration. Lime flowers are also a cosmetic help against freckles, wrinkles, and impurities of the skin, and they are believed to stimulate the growth of hair. Lime trees take a long time until they bear flowers. The flowers should be collected during June and July. They should not be heaped up or pressed down, but dried carefully on trays in a low temperature.

LOVAGE (Levisticum officinalis)
This is not only an herb with a very different kind of flavor—because it is reminiscent of yeast and similar to a yeast extract—but it has also an unusual health reputation. In many places it has been considered a love potion (though its name may be traced to its geographical origin and has really nothing to do with love) and, as it has a reputation as a deodorant, this may be responsible for its being considered useful to lovers. The herb used in salads and cooking and as a tea stimulates the digestive organs. It has a diuretic and general cleansing action. It is at the same time antiseptic. Czechoslovakian girls used to carry lovage in small bags hanging from a ribbon round their necks when they went to meet their boy friends. It has been used as an addition to bath water, and been placed externally on wounds as an antiseptic and antibiotic. It has been used against flatulence, and is reported to stimulate the milk production in nursing mothers.

MARIGOLD (Calendula officinalis)
The flowers of the marigold have medicinal value, already mentioned in the twelfth century. Apart from their use with salads and rice, and as a substitute for saffron, marigold contains, along with bitter principles, a coloring substance, calendula, which is like carotene, and very small quantities of volatile oil.

The flowers, soaked in oil or in ointments for the treatment of wounds, have an excellent effect on old or badly healed scars, such as those which are left behind from chicken pox in children. Marigold oil is also good for tired feet. It is used for any kind of skin eruption or small ulcers. An old herbal reports that only to look at marigold will "drive evil humour out of the head." It is, probably the lovely sub-color which does this trick.

SWEET MARJORAM (Origanum majorana)

Marjoram is a well-known flavoring herb and is discussed as such on page 138. Its disinfecting and preserving qualities have made it useful for adding to sausages and other meat preserves. Marjoram, particularly the wild marjoram or Origanum vulgare, contains thymol, which is a powerful antiseptic both internally and externally. Marjoram at the same time stimulates the appetite. Marjoram also has the reputation for increasing white blood corpuscles, and this speeds healing of infections. It is supposed to improve the blood circulation. It has been noticed that it acts as an anti-inflammatory agent in the mouth, and an infusion of it is useful as a mouth wash. It acts on mucous membrane, and therefore powdered marjoram has been used as a snuff to help with nasal congestion. Externally, bunches of warm marjoram herb may be placed on the affected parts to relieve rheumatic pains; marjoram oil has been painted on swellings of rheumatic joints.

THE MINTS

The various mints have certain health properties in common. Spearmint (Mentha viridis or Mentha spicata) may be used, for instance, as an infusion for bathing the face, which gives to it a fresh and healthy complexion. Fresh leaves used as compresses in case of headaches have been found useful. Externally, mint rubbed on places affected by gout or rheumatism will help to relieve the pain. Peppermint (Mentha piperita) has medicinal value, particularly as a tea. The tea is, in fact, a good pick-me-up. Peppermint tea relieves pain, cramps, and nervous palpitation, and is a great help in settling the stomach after vomiting. It deals not only with a tummy-ache but also with a general upset, and it has at the same time pain-killing and anti-spasmodic effects. It stimulates production of bile and the functions of the liver, and is altogether helpful with liver and gall bladder trouble. Oil made of peppermint is antiseptic. It is often used for flavoring toothpaste. It not only eases headaches or neuralgic pains, but has an almost anesthetic action.

MUGWORT (Artemisia vulgaris)

Mugwort has the reputation on the continent of helping in the digestion of poultry, such as goose or duck, or fat meat and fish. It thus has become an indispensable seasoning for these foods, and it is difficult to find out now whether it was first known to improve the digestibility of fat food or whether its bitter substances and volatile oil created a flavor which goes particularly well with poultry and meat. Before hops were used, mugwort was also used for flavoring beer—this explains the name—and it may be found in digestive spirits, such as vermouth and absinthe. It's a useful seasoning for diabetics, and a tea of mugwort was once used against rheumatism. It grows wild, but can be grown on any kind of soil. During July to September the high flower shoots—when in bud—are the parts to be collected before they fully open.

NASTURTIUM (Tropaeolum majus or minus)

Nasturtium is one of the popular garden flowers, the leaves of which may be eaten on bread and butter, but it is also one of the few herbs for which some modern health use has been discovered. It has antibiotic qualities and is therefore used in some countries as a kind of herbal penicillin. This quality is probably due to its extraordinary content of vitamin C. Modern research has discovered that the highest vitamin C content is found in the leaves of the plants before they flower in July. As nasturtium will grow in any garden, it is a valuable vitamin addition to the diet, and in cases of an infection, a cold, or a sore throat coming along, it is advisable to increase the intake of nasturtium. It may be dried for winter use, provided that the color can be retained. As it is also a pleasant substitute for pepper, it is important for people with ulcers, and it adds to the appetizing value of a diet prescribed without salt and pepper. However, the quantity of nasturtium should be somewhat restricted, and it should be used with a certain caution. In salads, on cream cheese, or on sandwiches, altogether not more than a third to two-thirds of an ounce should be eaten at one time, or one ounce per day at various meals during the day.

NETTLE (Urtica dioica or Urtica urens)

Nettle is another tenacious weed, disliked by people for its sting, but the young leaves of the stinging nettle have especially curative values. They improve the quality of the blood because they contain iron and also a high content of the previously mentioned silicic acid. In fact, nettle is rich in many minerals and plant hormones. Because of its outstanding qualities, it could and should be used almost daily as a flavoring, added in small quantities to salads and vegetable dishes. A small quantity of dried nettles is hardly noticeable in food, but can on the other hand help with salt-reduced and diabetic diets, as nettles contain a salt which is not a burden to the system. Therefore, nettle is both a flavoring and a medicinal herb. Nettles must be picked with gloves and scissors, but all young shoots, even on older plants, are suitable for food. Nettles are best picked in

spring, but it is possible to find young shoots at any time of the
year. Boiling water takes the sting out of nettles, but they lose it
also when dried. They are only valuable dried if they retain their
green color fully.

PARSLEY (Petroselinum)
Parsley is such a generally used herb for flavoring that it is probably
right to assume that many a family gets some parsley each day,
and this as a habit is more than justified from a health point of
view. Parsley is one of the few herbs which are rich in vitamins A
and B and (most of all) in vitamin C. As such, a small quantity
every day is of help, as vitamin C belongs to those vitamins which
are not stored in the body but should be replenished every day.
Though parsley's contribution is necessarily small, it is of importance
as a regular source. It is considered to have an anti-flatulent, anti-
spasmodic, and anti-fermentative effect. As it counteracts these three
factors, it is useful daily for those who have a tendency toward
these three conditions. It also stimulates the digestive glands and
therefore improves the working of the whole digestive system.
All this points to the frequent and daily need for parsley. Parsley
tea has a reputation as a remedy for rheumatism, obviously due
to its diuretic qualities. Externally parsley water or infusion is
believed to remove freckles or moles.

ROSE GERANIUM (Pelargonium graveolens)
This is probably thet most popular of the many sweet-scented
geraniums. The lovely scent of the leaves is reminiscent of roses,
but has a slight suggestion of spice. The fresh or dried leaves
give a delicate flavor to many sweets, jams and jellies, and fruit
cups. They are also used in baking at the bottom of a cake tin
and their delicate flavor is added to custards, cooked fruit, puddings,
and ice cream. One of the smaller leaves in the bottom of a finger
bowl will give a fragrance to the water. The leaves flavor other
herb teas, as well as make a tea of their own. For hot drinks use
one crushed leaf in the bottom of a cup. Rose-geranium leaves may
also be used either at the bottom of jam jars or at the top for sealing.
The dried leaves are a delightful scented addition to potpourri.

ROSE HIPS:
FRUITS OF THE WILD DOG ROSE (Rosa canina),
SHRUB ROSE (Rosa rugosa), and
SWEET BRIAR (Rosa rubiginosa)
The fruit of the wild and shrub roses are the small red-orange

oblong berries which are left after the flowers have wilted. These colorful berries, an ornament for the bushes, are a nutritious and important fruit, a rich source of vitamin C as well as vitamins A, E, B, and P. Rose hips were reported to be twenty times richer in vitamin C than oranges and sixty times richer than lemons, and were collected during the Second World War as an important vitamin C source; but they are not only health-giving as a vitamin source; they also provide a tisane of long-standing reputation. Rose-hip tea, made of pips and pods, is reputed to help the work of gall bladder and kidneys. Their diuretic quality, too, makes them useful as a daily tea, particularly for people who like to eat uncooked fruit and salads. When rose-hip syrup is made commercially, the vitamin C is extracted and mixed with syrup, thus providing babies with a readily taken vitamin C food.

In many countries a colorful orange-red rose-hip puree is made, which is served with desserts. It makes the excellent rose-hip sauce, which may be used instead of custard or chocolate sauce, providing all its health-giving qualities.

ROSEMARY (Rosmarinus officinalis)

The popularity of rosemary, which has increased recently, probably due to contact with Mediterranean cookery, should also be partly due to its influence on health. When used as a flavoring it acts also on a weak digestion, and is helpful in the case of flatulence; but apart from its qualities as a digestive, it stimulates the circulation and various other functions. It widens the tissues and increases the supply of blood to those parts of the body to which it is externally applied. This has been found helpful in the case of nervous head-aches. Greek students have been reported to have worn wreaths of rosemary round their heads when going to an examination. If a brain worker feels tired and if, through the external application of rosemary, blood is rushed to his head, it is most likely that the brain cells will be freshly nourished, tiredness will be dispelled, and the brain will start working anew. Experiments with this have supplied confirmative experience. Rosemary sprigs put into wine and allowed to permeate have been found to be a good stimulus for the heart, and this may also be due to the reasons given above.

Rosemary also has a wide reputation of stimulating the growth of hair when used as a hair wash or a rinse. This general stimula-tion of functions is one of the important qualities of rosemary. Externally, it is also reputed to improve the skin when used for washing or as a bath addition, and for hair and skin alike rose-mary has definite cosmetic functions. Rosemary kept in oil for some time produces an effective liniment in cases of gout and rheumatism.

SAGE (Salvia officinalis)

Sage has probably one of the oldest reputations for health among herbs, particularly in England, and this matches without doubt its popularity as a flavoring herb. The Arab proverb, "How can a man die if he has sage in his garden," shows the importance which scholars of all civilizations applied to sage. Sage tea, which was once a daily drink, was considered to be one of the reasons why "A man could not die." It was considered a fine tonic, and was also used as a remedy for colds, rheumatism, and fevers. It acts as a disinfectant, preventing colds, and as an expectorant in the case of lingering cough, and it is supposed to stimulate the circulation of the whole digestive system. Its healing powers—expressed in the Latin name *salvere* (to save)—illustrate its use as a universal remedy for all ills. The fact that it has been mainly used to flavor rich meats, such as pork and mutton, and fat fish, is probably due to the fact that it helped as a digestive. Its main health use, however, is a gargle and mouth wash in the case of a sore throat. Red sage particularly has been considered to be an excellent disinfectant gargle in the case of a throat infection because of its astringent qualities; it also keeps the teeth white. Sage was believed to increase wisdom by strengthening the memory, and this is probably the explanation for the use of sage tea until old age. More details on sage tea for a gargle are given in the chapter on teas. It has also excellent cosmetic properties when the herbs are added to a facial steam bath. As a steam bath it has an astringent effect on the skin and also therapeutic qualities in the case of a severe head cold. If sage is steeped in oil, the same astringent qualities are available for use on the skin.

SALAD BURNET (Sanguisorba minor)

Salad burnet, with its luscious green leaves, may be used as a tonic. It may be used with salads, or in drinks; a tea (page 49) may be made of it as well. It is mildly diuretic. Salad burnet is a useful ingredient as a bath addition; when added to a facial steam, it will strengthen and improve the skin.

SOLIDAGO;
GOLDEN ROD (Solidago virgaurea)

Golden rod has a reputation of being an excellent wound herb and of being helpful in the case of kidney and bladder troubles. Its old name was "Heathen Wound Herb," and it was originally imported from the Midle East, where it was being used by the Saracens. It was once very expensive. It not only has the effect of speeding up the healing of wounds, but as a tea it is helpful with the functions of kidney and bladder; it even has had the reputation of dissolving kidney and bladder stones. It has also been used as a disinfectant and as an ointment, probably connected with its use as a wound herb.

SORREL, FRENCH SORREL (Rumex acetosa *and* Rumex scutatus)

The young green slightly acid-flavored leaves of sorrel contain vitamin C; therefore they are a useful herb for salads and soups, particularly in spring, and are considered to have blood-cleansing and blood-improving qualities. They are also supposed to be diuretic and helpful for kidney stones. They should, however, not be used too regularly, because part of the plant contains oxylic acid, which may be damaging to health if taken in excess. As a supplier of vitamin C they are not therefore so generally useful as nasturtium, which may be taken over longer periods. Sorrel, attractive in flavor and useful for health, should be eaten in moderation.

SUMMER SAVORY (Satureia hortensis)

Summer savory (in fact all the savories—there is a winter savory which is coarser and stronger in flavor but remains in the garden for the whole of winter)—has a strong volatile oil as a main constituent. Savory has above all a strong digestive effect, and this may be the reason why it was originally used with beans of all kinds, as on the continent its flavor has been considered inseparable from all kinds of beans, from broad beans to runner beans. It not only increases the flavor, but it also helps with the digestion of beans, which have a tendency to cause flatulence with some people. The origin of this combination was definitely a digestive one. The volatile oil of savory has been infused as a digestive medicine. Summer savory has also been used for aromatic baths, and its strong aromatic scent has a strengthening effect. The leaves have been crushed and used on bee stings to relieve pain and swelling. Summer savory has also an old reputation of preserving sight and hearing, but it would need research and experimenting with this to be certain.

SWEET CICELY (Myrrhis odorata)

Sweet cicely has the old reputation that it cures flatulence and that it is helpful with mild digestive troubles. It has also been recommended for coughs. But its main up-to-date contribution to health is that it is a definite sugar-saver. It is a sweet, slightly anise-flavored herb which grows easily and is available throughout the greatest part of the year. It can easily be dried, or obtained commercially green-dried; fresh as well as dried it helps to reduce the tart flavor of many fruits, and even spinach. If cooked, particularly when dried, with fruit and fruit pies, it reduces up to about half the sugar needed. White sugar is today disliked by many people: by the figure watchers, by mothers for their children's teeth, and because it is bad for health for people in general owing to the excessive way in which it is often used. Experiments made with, for instance, fruit tarts such as plum tart or pies, or stewed plums, have been most successful. In the case of those who are interested in a slim figure, it is certainly better to reduce the sugar by sweet cicely than by tablets. Here is a new function for a little-known herb which may be strongly recommended.

THYME (Thymus vulgaris)
LEMON THYME (Thymus citriodorus)
A valuable volatile oil, thymol, is contained in the leaves of thyme, and is to a large extent responsible for its very old and often confirmed reputation. Though thyme is a very strong herb and may therefore only be used in small quantities, it has been considered to be good for indigestion and flatulence, and for minor intestinal afflictions. Its main quality, however, is that thyme has, owing to its volatile oil and other constituents, strongly antiseptic and disinfectant qualities. It has been considered a sedative and has been used in bronchitis, whooping cough, and other persistent coughs. Its strong scent has made it useful for deodorants, gargles, perfumes, and soap, as a pain-killer for toothache, and in liquid dentifrices. Thyme has always been an important part of an herb cushion, which helps people to go to sleep or sweetens the air in an invalid's room. It was also used for scented lotions and sachets, and as a moth preventative in cupboards and wardrobes. It has been used in potpourri, where the strong scent of thyme and lemon thyme are most useful.

Lemon thyme has a still stronger scent and is more used for perfumes, but it also has an attractive flavor, which—if used in small quantities—gives to fruit salad or any fruit dessert a taste reminiscent of brandy or kirsch. It has been added to herbal tobacco. Its strong and perfumed qualities have, at the same time, a strong influence on health, the details of which still wait to be discovered.

VALERIAN (Valeriana officinalis)

The root of the valerian is probably one of the best herb sedatives. Valerian tea, made of the dried root, is not only the strongest herbal sleep-inducing remedy but has a general calming effect on the nervous system. It is really an excellent tranquilizer and particularly so in all nervous troubles which arise suddenly, when an infusion of valerian roots may be used with success. Though it is not "everyone's cup of tea" and its smell can be upsetting, it has been used as a spice, and even as a perfume in the sixteenth century. Valerian may be found wild and cultivated; the roots are ready to be collected in the autumn of the second year. The tea is best made in the cold way, and instructions will be given on page 50. Valerian tea should not be taken uninterruptedly; after a while a break should be made; but it is most useful in times of strain and tiredness.

VERBASCUM
COMMON MULLEIN (Verbascum thapsiforme)

The common mullein, known to many people as a garden plant, is not only tall and beautiful in the garden, but it is also of great medicinal value. The bright yellow flowers, either freshly picked or carefully dried so that they retain their yellow color, make an extremely health-giving tea in the case of chest troubles, particularly with a long-standing cough, or in fact for any surplus mucus in any part of the body. This tea acts as an expectorant, and will at the same time help to counteract inflammation of mouth, throat, or any bronchial part. It is, however, necessary that the flowers should be bright yellow, as the healing qualities are connected with the coloring matter, and if the slightest discoloration takes place during picking, drying, or storing, the flowers are less effective or useless.

THE VERBENAS:
VERVAIN (Verbena officinalis)
LEMON VERBENA (Lippia citriodora)

Both verbenas are used to make health-giving teas. One is the native vervain known by the Druids, called verbena tea; it has an old reputation as a slightly bitter tisane in France, where it is used as a digestive, and is considered to be useful in nervous exhaustion and as a sedative tea. As it is slightly bitter and soothing, both these qualities offer the explanation for its effect.

Lemon verbena is not a native plant: it came originally from Chile. The scent and taste of the leaves is that of lemon, and its fragrant tea, popular in Spain, is more attractive than the other verbena tea. Lemon-verbena tea has also the reputation of having a sedative effect, particularly on the bronchial and nasal regions. It can be grown in poor dry soil and taken indoors as a house plant when the bad weather starts. The delicious scented young leaves may be used in fruit drinks, salads, jellies, and instead of lemon rind in sauces, and may be made into a tea blended with mint and drunk hot or iced.

WOODRUFF (Galium odoratum *or* Asperula odorata)

This is one of the sweetest herbs of the woods, growing particularly among beeches, with its scent only noticeable after the leaves have slightly wilted and dried. Woodruff used to be put into drawers and wardrobes to keep the moths away, and to impart its perfume. It was also a strewing herb and was stuffed into beds among the linen. Woodruff has become famous as a flavoring for wine in May, which is the time it flowers; and before or during flowering it has the strongest flavor. Its fragrancy has the same reputation as borage, and its exhilarating effect, dispelling depression, was soon recognized as a help for festive occasions. It increases the effect of good wine, and has the reputation of relaxing and at the same time uplifting. Suggestions for its use in drinks are found on page 301, and its use as tea is found on pages 51–52 and 55.

YARROW (Achillea millefolium)

Yarrow is mostly found wild; and it may be collected during its flowering period from June to August. The parts used are the leaves and the flowers, which, after the plant has been cut, may be pulled off the stem. The herb has a rather special, spicy scent, and while flowering it has astringent qualities. Yarrow has, like chamomile, a great number of health properties. Owing to its bitter substances it belongs to those herbs which are good for the whole of the intestinal tract. It stimulates appetite and is anti-flatulent and helps with intestinal troubles, such as colitis or gastric trouble. It is helpful in the case of fermentation and constipation, as well as for trouble with liver or gall bladder. It stimulates both the functions of the kidney, and thus has a diuretic effect, and those of the circulation, and thus has an influence on the heart functions. Yarrow is also reported to have a regulating influence on the period and to have a wound-healing effect. It is supposed to help with gout and rheumatic pains, and is reported to have a favorable effect on a beginning diabetes. For all these purposes a tea made of yarrow is the best way of taking it. Its most effective use, however, is a cosmetic one: yarrow is particularly good for greasy skins, and cleans and beautifies the skin. For this purpose it may be taken internally as a tea and as food, and externally as facial steams and face packs. An infusion of yarrow may be used externally for a warm bath addition. As food, freshly extracted yarrow juice is used, of which two teaspoons may be taken with cold water. Young leaves or flowers of yarrow may also be chopped finely and mixed with salads early in the season or eaten between bread and butter; however, not too much of it should be taken during one day.

Chapter 2

*D*irections for *T*eas and *O*ther *H*erb *M*ixtures

THE BEST WAY to extract the value of the herb as a whole—other than using herbs chopped or whole for food—are herb infusions or teas. It is advisable to make an infusion of an herb with boiling or, in some cases, cold water. Such teas are wholesome and often health-restoring drinks, refreshing and cooling in summer, and warming in winter. Some of them are reputed to have specific therapeutic, others cosmetic, values for internal and external use, such as bath additions, etc. Some allow types of both uses.

Most of these tisanes may be used instead of ordinary tea, as a helpful addition to the daily diet. They are not necessarily meant to be treatment but to be used as first cups of early morning tea or as nightcaps. Sometimes the herbs are used with water as a tea or tisane, sometimes with milk for a highly recommended bedtime drink. The word "tisane" applies to herb teas only. It is frequently used in England, though it originated in France, where herb teas were and still are being used daily.

There are many teas which may be made from different herbs and used for many purposes. These may appear overwhelming at first to the reader who has no experience with herbs; therefore a selection of the most useful teas and herb mixtures for day-to-day use follows at the end of this section (page 54).

Often herbs have been used to add an additional flavor to either hot or cold China tea; a sprig of mint or lemon thyme is often used in iced tea. However, many refreshing and delicious drinks may be prepared by using herb leaves, flowers, or seeds without necessarily combining them with ordinary tea.

The flavors of these teas are usually most delicate and may be very easily impaired by using badly dried or badly packed herbs with their flavors mingled. Each herb should be packed strictly separately in an airtight container.

The herbs' delicate flavors are also easily affected by metal; therefore great care should be taken in using only earthenware, china, porcelain, glass, or unchipped enamel. There are also other pitfalls. Too long steeping can ruin the flavor of any delicate herb; therefore it is best to steep the leaves a short time, using more of the herb if a stronger infusion is desired. One teaspoon of leaves in the non-metal teapot gives a basic measurement per cup. This results in a delicate and subtle flavor. There are, however, teas which require boiling for 10 minutes to bring out the full flavor and for each herb this is mentioned specially.

If dried leaves are used for the preparation of an herb tea, one teaspoon of herbs for each cup and one teaspoon for the teapot is generally considered adequate. Any deviation from this is specially mentioned in each recipe. Dried herbs for teas have a certain concentration, and, if well-dried, produce a definite flavor. Though for most recipes the quantity given for a green-dried herb is the same as for the fresh herb, for teas, however, the question of concentration is of special importance, and therefore it is really necessary to use three times as much of fresh herbs for making tea. If fresh leaves are used, the flavor is less concentrated, as they still contain all their moisture: three teaspoons of the herb for each cup is suggested. The fresh leaves should be bruised by being crushed in a clean cloth before infusion. The same applies to a tea made from aromatic seeds, where one tablespoon seeds per pint of water is suggested; the seeds should be crushed well before boiling.

METHODS OF PREPARING HERB TEAS are very simple, and the results are subtle, soothing, and often very refreshing, all at the same time. Here follow three basic methods of preparing herb teas:

    (a) *Teas Made from Dried or Fresh Leaves or Flowers*
      1. Warm china or glass teapot.
      2. Place green-dried or fresh, crushed herb leaves in teapot.
      3. Pour boiling water over herb leaves.
      4. Allow to steep 5–10 minutes only.
      5. Strain.

    Note: If a stronger infusion is desired, use more leaves at the beginning of the preparation.

Herb leaves may be put into thin muslin or paper bags. In some countries herb teas are available in bags similar to the tea bags used in this country for ordinary tea. It is difficult to judge the quality of the herbs if supplied in tea bags; if suitable strainers are used, it would be advisable to use whole or shredded leaves or whole flowers, the quality of which can be seen.

    (b) *Iced Herb Teas*
      1. Place crushed fresh herbs or dried herbs in an earthenware container.
      2. Pour boiling hot water over the herbs.
      3. Allow to steep for 5 minutes.
      4. Strain and cover container.
      5. Place container in a refrigerator to cool.

(c) *Herb Teas Made from Seeds*

1. Bruise seeds slightly, possibly with a pestle in a mortar, to bring out oil.
2. Pour boiling water into enamel saucepan placed over a strong heat.
3. Add bruised seed.
4. Simmer gently 5–10 minutes.
5. Strain quickly and serve hot.

Teas Made of Herbs

ANGELICA TEA. Angelica tea should be served hot as a digestive tonic. The leaves may be used fresh, or dried, if the color of the leaf in drying remains light green as in its natural state. If the leaves are left whole it is difficult to measure them by teaspoon; therefore the equivalent of a teaspoon per cup has to be estimated.

ANISEED TEA belongs to the seed teas; 1 teaspoon seeds should be used per pint of boiling water. (See above for method.) After being strained, the tea should be served hot. Aniseed tea has a soothing influence and induces sleep; it is therefore suitable as a nightcap.

It has an anti-flatulent effect, and one cupful after meals is recommended, unless seed tea is available (page 49). Aniseed may also be used with hot milk. Its aromatic flavor makes it a pleasant bedtime drink.

BASIL TEA was once famous for its sedative effect, particularly against gastric spasms and flatulence. It has been also used in the case of a cough and for stimulating perspiration to reduce temperature. For this purpose one teaspoon of cold tea every hour was recommended. Its strong scent was used against head colds, and it may be used as a part of a facial steam bath to clear the head. The tea is made of leaves in the same way as other leaf teas.

BERGAMOT TEA. Red bergamot is a pleasant tea which, served hot, induces good sleep and has a soothing and relaxing effect. It is also called Oswego tea. Bergamot leaves make an excellent addition to China or India tea, as well as to wine drinks and lemonade.

To make tea:

To bring out the real flavor of bergamot tea, one teaspoon bergamot per cup should be simmered for 10 minutes in an enamel or stainless-steel saucepan. Bergamot tea may be sweetened with honey, if desired.

An excellent nightcap may be made with milk:

Bergamot milk:
　One tablespoon shredded dried bergamot leaves. One-half pint milk.
　Pour the boiling milk over the leaves. Allow to draw for at least 5
　　minutes. Strain and serve hot. This may be sweetened with honey,
　　and a little lemon may be added.

In Europe the dried red flowers, retaining their strong red color, are
used as a sedative and relaxing tea called "Gold Melissa."

BILBERRY TEA. Bilberries (Vaccinium myrtillus) may be carefully
dried and then chewed raw in cases of dysentery, or made into
a tea for the same complaint.

To make tea:
　Soak 1 tablespoon of dried bilberries for some hours. Pour 2 pints of
　　boiling water over the berries. Bring to the boil.
　Remove from the heat and allow to draw for 10 minutes. Strain and
　　serve hot without sugar.

Bilberry-leaf tea (see Wild Herbs in Spring, pages 55–59).

BITTER TEA is made of a mixture of three herbs:
　　Wormwood (Artemisia absinthium)
　　Centaury (Centaurium umbellatum)
　　Blessed thistle (Cnicus benedictus)

Equal parts of these three herbs will provide a tea which is most
helpful for lack of appetite due to stomach disorder. It should
be served hot.

BLACKBERRY LEAF TEA. The leaves of the blackberry shrub are valuable if gathered in spring; an infusion or tea may be made for
gargling and taking internally. They are an excellent addition to
a mixture of other wild leaves. (See page 55.)

BORAGE TEA. The excellent exhilarating qualities of borage, found
when it is used in drinks such as in claret cups, may also be experienced if borage leaves are used for a hot tisane or an iced tea,
made either with dried or fresh leaves. Those who do not like
alcohol will feel the encouraging effect of borage when using it
this way. Borage flowers may also be added to this tea, and are
said to improve the functions of the heart. The leaves may be
added to many other drinks shortly before serving.

CARAWAY TEA. Caraway seeds are part of seed tea; they have a carminative, that is, an anti-flatulent, effect. In the case of flatulence, one cupful after meals of either caraway or seed tea is recommended. The boiling water should be poured over 1 teaspoon bruised caraway seeds per cup and allowed to steep for 20 minutes and be strained.

CENTAURY TEA (Centaurium umbellatum) is known to be a good tonic and a help in dyspepsia.

CHAMOMILE TEA. The chamomile flowers—and a very little of the leaves of the true chamomile (Matricaria chamomilla)—have a pleasant flavor; and a tisane is much drunk in France as an aid to digestion after heavy meals. It has a soothing action on the gastrointestinal tract and all mucous membranes.

An infusion made of it is excellent for a mouth wash after dental treatment, or for a sore mouth of any description, for a gargle, and for rinsing inflamed gums, or for a sore throat. It is excellent as part of the herbs used for a facial steam for a heavy cold, as well as an eye bath in the case of inflamed eyelids.

To make tea:
   For drinking as well as for infusions:
   1 teaspoon chamomile flowers per cup of boiling water. Do not steep
      the flowers longer than 3–5 minutes. Strain quickly.
   As a drink chamomile tea may be sweetened with honey, if desired.

Chamomile has excellent cosmetic qualities.

COLTSFOOT TEA (Tussilago farfara). Rich in vitamin C and helpful for catarrh and cough.

COWSLIP TEA (Primula veris), made from flowers quickly dried and also from roots if available, is a good bedtime tea, as a sedative effect has been observed. This tea may also be used as an expectorant in the case of colds and as a bath addition.

CYSTITIS TEA. This is a mixture of the following herbs which are helpful in cystitis:

   Equisetum (Horsetail)   ⎫ in
   Sage leaves   ⎬ equal
   Uva Ursi (Bearberry leaves)   ⎪ parts.
   Mallow (Sylvestris)   ⎭

   One tablespoon mixed herbs per cup of water. Bring to the boil and
   boil for 5 minutes. Take one to three cups per day.

DANDELION TEA. As dandelion has diuretic and digestive qualities, and improves liver and gall-bladder functions as well as rheumatic conditions, a tea made from fresh or dried dandelion leaves is most helpful. The tea is made like other leafy herb teas. The roots, when roasted, are used as a coffee substitute and have the same effect as the tea.

DILL-SEED TEA. Dill has many helpful qualities, and its richness in minerals and volatile oil has provided many suggestions for the use of dill seeds. In particular it has been used for insomnia, and whether dill is used in the baby's water or is boiled in wine as a nightcap for adults it serves this purpose.

The tea, made of one teaspoon crushed dill seeds per cup of boiling water and served unsweetened and hot as other seed teas, has been found effective for hiccoughs and vomiting.

ELDER-FLOWER TEA is useful in the case of colds and as an alternative to aspirin. Mixed with lime flowers and chamomile in equal parts it is very helpful in the case of flu and chills, if taken hot in bed, for it increases perspiration. A teaspoon per cup of tea and an extra teaspoon for the pot makes a very pleasant sleep-inducing tea.

Ordinary tea may be flavored by adding one-third of elder flowers to the quantity of tea leaves used.

Elder-flower drink:
> Refreshing summer drinks are made with cold water or milk. Half a jug filled with elder flowers to which boiling water is added should be strained when cold and slightly sweetened.

An infusion made of elder flowers and water may be used for an eye bath or eye compresses and also has cosmetic qualities.

Hot elderberry juice:
> 1 pint of juice, 8 oz. sugar. Wash and drain the berries; they need not be stalked. Heat them slowly in a stone or earthenware jar, covered by a lid in a slow oven. From time to time drain the juice which will develop.
> Put the remaining berries in a cloth (tied to the legs of a reversed kitchen stool). Place a bowl underneath and allow to drip overnight. Squeeze the cloth well. Boil 1 pint of juice with 8 oz. of sugar until ¼ of the liquid has evaporated (about ½ hour). Pour in dry hot bottles and seal well.

One to two tablespoons of elderberry syrup diluted with a glass of hot, not boiling, water is an old remedy for colds and coughs and is also recommended for people suffering from sciatica and neuralgic pains.

ELDER-LEAF TEA (see Wild Herbs in Spring, page 55).

EYEBRIGHT TEA. This small delicate flower grows in abundance in late summer and autumn. As a tea it improves digestion in general.

FENNEL TEA. Fennel seeds have the same quality as dill seeds and may be used for the same purpose. As fennel also has a reputation as an expectorant and against catarrh, and as fennel is said to reduce overweight, a tisane made of either fennel leaves or crushed fennel seeds may be useful for both purposes and worth experimenting with. Fennel tea can be most helpful for treatment of the eye: compresses steeped in fennel tea placed on the eye, and bathing the eyes with a fennel infusion for inflamed eyelids and watering eyes, have been found effective. The tea is also reputed to improve the sight. Fennel and fennel tea have also cosmetic qualities.

HIBISCUS TEA. The lovely red flowers of the African hibiscus, also called Karkadé, give a beautiful burgundy-colored tea with a slightly tart lemony flavor. This tea is thirst quenching in summer and warming in winter. Not exactly a medicinal tea, it is a delightful summer drink without stimulating substances, but is also very useful when used for punch, alcoholic or non-alcoholic.

One heaped teaspoon of hibiscus flowers are used per half-pint of water. If the flowers are placed in warmed and dried teacups the usual teaspoonful for the pot should be allowed. After pouring the boiling water over the flowers, the tea should be allowed to steep for 5-10 minutes and then be strained. This tea is most attractive in a glass teapot because of its lovely color. It has the flavor of a tea to which lemon juice has been added and should be sweetened with honey for those who find this too tart. It is equally good hot or iced.

Karkadé punch:
  Hibiscus tea to which sugar, 1/3 stick of cinnamon, and 1 or 2 cloves are added.

Two or three hibiscus flowers added to rose-hip tea will give it a beautiful burgundy color and a lemony flavor.

HORSETAIL (Equisetum), a plant without flowers, with no special attractions, wilts soon after picking. It contains a great deal of silicic acid, which makes the herb astringent and antiseptic: it has been used in folk medicine for mending tissues, particularly for tears in the mucous membranes.

The tea made of it is diuretic and is often found in mixtures for bladder and kidney teas. It has also cosmetic qualities, such as strengthening and toning the skin and improving hair and nails. This tea was much used on the continent, particularly by the famous Kneipp, who had great success treating people with hydrotherapy and with herbs in the nineteenth century.

Equisetum tea:
> For making the best use of the herb's properties, 1 teaspoon of the herb per cup should be soaked for several hours, then be boiled in the soaking water for 10–15 minutes and be allowed to steep for another 10–15 minutes before straining.

HYSSOP TEA is an expectorant and good in the case of a pernicious cough. In the case of intestinal catarrh, also catarrh of the bronchial tract and asthma, it is a useful remedy. It has also been considered a vermifuge. It is made like any leafy herb tea and is served hot; the herb is also used to flavor cocktails.

JUNIPER BERRIES. Juniper berries provide an excellent tea for liver and kidney conditions, though it is not advisable to take juniper-berry tea during a chronic inflammation of the kidney.

The berries, if chewed, have a cleansing effect on the whole system. They are antiseptic and also reduce excess fluid in the tissues. In fact, juniper berries stimulate all functions of the body.

Juniper-berry tea:
> 1 teaspoon or 12–18 crushed berries are used per cup; pour boiling water over them and allow to draw for 10 minutes. Strain. To be taken in the case of stomach and intestinal trouble; also in the case of trouble with the respiratory tract; sweetened with 1 teaspoon honey.

A similar infusion in larger quantity is suitable as a bath addition.

Juniper syrup:
> Boil 1 lb. of juniper berries with 6 pints water until tender. Crush and bring again to the boil and pass through a sieve. After it has cooled, add honey until a liquid syrup is obtained. Put into containers with a wide opening and close well. One teaspoon before meals stimulates the appetite and the circulation.

LADY'S-MANTLE TEA, made of lady's-mantle leaves, has been considered a protection for the female organs. At the same time it is said to improve the functions throughout a woman's life, thus preventing female disorders. It has, in fact, been called "a woman's best friend." The tea has also been considered of importance during pregnancy, and immediately afterward. It is supposed to have a regulating effect on the monthly cycle, and has been particularly recommended to be taken from the fortieth year onward. It has been suggested that operations could be avoided if this tea were used in time and over long periods. The tea has been recommended also for the treatment of wounds, and an infusion of the herb is helpful against inflammations of the skin and acne.

LEMON-BALM TEA is one of the most useful herb teas, probably in a class with chamomile and peppermint tea, the most widely used herb teas. The leaves have an anti-spasmodic effect and at the same time stimulate the heart; and, as they also have a sedative effect on the nervous system, they provide an excellent tea to be used daily. Lemon balm does not actually induce sleep, but promotes it because it removes spasms and tension which may prevent sleeping. The tea is equally useful as an "early cup of tea," when it helps to counteract over-tiredness left over from the evening before, when it might otherwise develop into a headache or migraine. It is reputed to prolong life, and there are various reports of those who drank it every day and reached unbelievable years of age. It is supposed to help the brain worker to overcome loss of memory and depression; and it has the reputation of sharpening the wit and understanding.

It is made like all leaf herbs with a teaspoon per cup, but must be allowed to steep for at least 10 minutes, if not longer. It is one of the teas which do not deteriorate from longer steeping.

LIME-FLOWER TEA, similar to chamomile tea, is one of the most popular daily teas drunk for pleasure or for its medicinal value in France. It is a delicious tea which promotes perspiration, and it therefore belongs to those teas which, as a pleasant alternative to aspirin, are useful in cases of chills and colds. At the same time, the tea is mildly sleep inducing. It soothes the nerves, aids the digestion, and allays spasm. It is used as an after-dinner drink, is calming, and helps to provide a good night's sleep. In its quality to combat chills, it is one of the teas which, with equal parts of chamomile and elder flowers, should be taken in bed to increase perspiration; it is also part of the herbs to be used for a facial steam in the case of severe head colds. Its cosmetic qualities are mentioned on page 61.

LIME-LEAF (see Wild Herbs in Spring, page 56).

LIVER TEA is a mixture of the following herbs, which are helpful to the functions of the liver.

> ½ oz. peppermint leaves (2 parts).
> ½ oz. dandelion leaves (2 parts).
> ¼ oz. rosemary (1 part).
> ¼ oz. blessed thistle (broken) (1 part).
> ⅛ oz. wormwood (½ part).

LOVAGE TEA. An infusion made of lovage has a distinctive celery flavor and is more similar to a broth than a tea. It may be served, therefore, as a relaxing savory broth with a little herb or sea salt added, or it may be tried as a tisane sweetened with a little honey. This herb is also considered a deodorant, and it stimulates, as a tisane, the digestive organs, as well as having a diuretic and cleansing action. It is at the same time antiseptic. All this seems to point to the internal and external qualities of a deodorant. Lovage tea is also reported to stimulate the milk production in nursing mothers. It may be worth while to experiment with its deodorant qualities internally as a tea and externally as a bath addition. It has also cosmetic uses.

LOVAGE SEEDS have the same quality as the herb; they grow in pairs and look similar to caraway seed. Apart from being used for flavoring and cooking, they have been used in the past for a cordial.

Lovage cordial:
> Freshly harvested seeds and a good quality of brandy should be used for lovage cordial.
> 1 oz. lovage seed.
> 1 pint brandy.
> 4 oz. sugar.

1. Crush the seeds slightly in a mortar with a pestle (or they may be tied in a clean muslin cloth and crushed with a wooden mallet).
2. Add the crushed seeds to the brandy.
3. Then add the sugar and stir well.
4. Put in a cool, dark place for 2 months, shaking the container occasionally.
5. Then pass the cordial through a paper filter.
6. Re-cork and serve at room temperature when desired.
   Note: It will yield 1 pint.

MARIGOLD TEA. A tea made of marigold petals is soothing for intestinal conditions, such as colitis, and promotes perspiration. It helps the body to make better use of vitamin A and has also cosmetic properties.

MARJORAM TEA. The fresh leaves of sweet marjoram may be infused, and the tea then served hot or iced. The pleasure of taking it is increased by blending it with any of the mints. Its health-giving qualities are those mentioned in the description of this herb in Herbs for Health and Beauty.

MELISSA TEA (see Lemon-balm tea, pages 44 and 54).
The refreshing lemony flavor of melissa tea is subtle when whole leaves are used, while shredded leaves are stronger in flavor.

THE MINTS. The various mints all supply refreshing teas made from either fresh or green-dried leaves. Spearmint, apple mint, or any garden or wild mint, gives a refreshing drink for cold summer evenings if boiling water is poured over some freshly picked green leaves. In a glass teapot this tea shows its jade-green color. It may be sweetened with sugar and lemon juice if desired.

Peppermint tea:
  The most used and probably most attractive of the mint teas is peppermint tea. It is excellent as a daily tea, as it is not only most helpful as a pick-me-up, but it will also deal with any discomfort after a meal, settle the liver, and be a perfect substitute for coffee, especially for those whose gall bladder does not function satisfactorily. It is most helpful for an upset stomach, and, with a few chamomile flowers added, it will settle cramps and relieve pain, particularly after vomiting. More details about its medicinal properties are given in Herbs for Health and Beauty (page 26) and details about its cosmetic properties on pages 62, 65, 68, and 69.
  Peppermint tea made of whole leaves has a subtle flavor, while a stronger flavor is found with shredded leaves. It may be used instead of ordinary tea; but, after a period of taking peppermint tea regularly, a break should be made before using it again.

Peppermint milk:
  It may be taken as a refreshing pick-me-up or as a helpful warm nightcap; and it is most useful against cramping pain in the abdomen, also soothing and refreshing.
  1 tablespoon fresh or green-dried peppermint.
  ½ pint boiling milk.
  Pour boiling milk over peppermint and allow it to draw for 5–10 minutes; then strain and serve hot.

MUGWORT TEA. Mugwort was originally used for flavoring beer and may still be found today as a part of bitter liqueurs. A tea made of mugwort leaves was once used against rheumatism. At the time of the Greeks and Romans it was used as a gynecological medicine. Only the buds are used for making tea, and it may be made like any leaf tea.

NETTLE TEA *or* BROTH. The medicinal qualities of nettle may be found in nettle tea. As boiling water takes the sting out of nettles, it may be made out of fresh or green-dried leaves.

PARSLEY TEA. Parsley, which is good to use daily because of its content of vitamin C, makes an excellent tea, a hot tonic of diuretic qualities which helps to reduce excess fluid in the tissues. It has an age-old reputation for relief of rheumatism, particularly in England.

Parsley is also used internally for cosmetic reasons.

RASPBERRY-LEAF TEA (Rubus idaeus) is well known as a helpful herb before or during confinement, and for female disorders. It has an astringent and stimulant effect. The leaves should be dried without stems.

Raspberry-leaf tea:
One teaspoon of leaves per teacup of boiling water. Allow to draw for 15 minutes.

ROSE-GERANIUM TEA is a delicate rose-flavored drink and may be served hot or iced. The tea may also be blended with various mints; and rose-geranium leaves may flavor other herb teas in the same way they give their delicate flavor to sweets and fruit cups. For hot drinks, one crushed leaf should be used in the bottom of a cup.

ROSE-HIP TEA is made from the complete fruit of roses: the pods and pips, after tops and tails have been removed. The hips may be picked in late autumn, and should be dried carefully so that they retain their red color. They may, however, be obtained commercially dried and with pods and pips in a balanced proportion.

Rose-hip tea is excellent for daily use and may be taken over unlimited periods. This drink is served twice daily at the famous Bircher-Benner Klinik in Zurich. The tea has the reputation of being helpful to the functions of kidneys and gall bladder. It has diuretic qualities and is important for all those who wish to slim on a diet containing plenty of salads and fruit.

Color and flavor of rose-hip tea may be much improved by adding a small quantity of hibiscus flowers, because they provide not only a beautiful burgundy color but a lemon flavor, which makes it unnecessary to use lemon with the tea.

To make tea:
  2 tablespoons rose hips (pods and pips in balanced proportion).
  Soak rose hips in water in a small container for 12 hours. Bring 3 pints of water to the boil in an enamel or other non-metal saucepan. Add the rose hips, and then simmer gently for 30–40 minutes. Strain.

The tea may be kept covered in a china or pottery jug for 1–2 days and re-heated when needed. If desired, a few more hips may be added for re-heating. Sweeten with brown sugar or honey if desired.

ROSEMARY TEA. The fresh or green-dried leaves, young sprigs, and flowering tops may be infused to make rosemary tea. This is a stimulant for the heart in the same way as rosemary wine (page 29). An infusion made of the same parts of rosemary is useful for the growth of hair and has many cosmetic functions. The tea may also be blended with lavender flowers. It may be served hot or iced.

RUE TEA (Ruta graveolens). This was once a well-known tea in country districts and considered a remedy against dizziness and female disorders.

SAGE TEA was in general use in England before China and Indian tea became known. Many country people still believe that it ensures long life, and the proverb "How can a man die with sage in his garden" was one quoted at the Arabian universities. It is a wholesome drink in spring, served hot or iced. The tea may be blended with any of the mints. It has also been considered a valuable tonic, and was used for colds, rheumatism, and fevers. It is disinfectant and is supposed to stimulate the circulation of the digestive system. It was particularly used for a persistent cough; the reputation that it is the best gargle in the case of a throat infection came originally from the continent, but this has been confirmed, though it is particularly the red sage that has been used for this purpose. Sage leaves are also an important part of the infusion made for a facial steam in the case of severe colds. The astringent qualities make sage tea useful all round, internally and externally. The leaves also flavor drinks, wine cups, and cocktails, or apple juice for the non-drinker. Its cosmetic properties may be found on page 54.

SALAD-BURNET TEA (Sanguisorba minor) is a pleasant tea which may be made from fresh or dried leaves. Served very hot it is helpful to the kidneys. It is useful as a tonic, and may also be served iced. The herb was originally used to flavor wine, especially claret, and has been reputed to have exhilarating qualities. It has the reputation of having a cleansing effect on liver, gall bladder, and kidneys, and is supposed to stimulate the secretion of bile and the glandular system altogether. It has also been used as a bath addition and for cosmetic purposes.

SEED TEA is a carminative (an anti-flatulent) tea. It is made of three seeds which were mentioned before:

> Caraway seeds
> Fennel seeds   in equal parts.
> Anise seeds
> Crush the seeds with a pestle. Pour boiling water over the seeds. Allow to steep for 20 minutes. Then strain.
> This is a very pleasant, warming drink. In the case of flatulence, drink one cupful after meals.

Other variations of the seed tea are used to stimulate the milk production in nursing mothers. For this purpose either fennel tea, caraway tea, or dill tea may be taken, or the following mixture:

> 2 oz. anise seeds.
> 2 oz. dill seeds.
> 2 oz. marjoram.
> One teaspoon of this mixture is used per cup; otherwise the same method as for seed tea should be used. Two to three cups may be taken per day.

SOLIDAGO TEA (golden rod, Solidago virgaurea). This old wound herb, which was helpful because it has anti-inflammatory qualities, has also been found helpful with the functions of kidney and bladder. The upper part of the herb in flowering should be dried and broken apart.

> Boil the herb for 1 minute. Allow to steep for 10 minutes. Then strain.
> In cases of dropsy or inflammation of bladder and kidneys, two to three cups may be drunk daily, and diuretic qualities will be experienced.

SUMMER-SAVORY TEA. Summer savory has an old reputation of preserving sight and hearing, and it would be interesting to experiment with these qualities by making a tea of it. An infusion of it has at one time been used as a digestive medicine. It also has been used as an aromatic bath addition. Proceed as with any other leaf herb tea, but steep a little longer.

SWEET-CICELY TEA. Sweet cicely's reputation that it cures flatulence and is helpful with mild digestive troubles may be tested by infusing the herb and making a tea out of it. Its main use is to flavor and to act as a sugar saver; and the anise-like sweetness of it provides a tea that need not be sugared.

THYME TEA (GARDEN *and* LEMON THYME). Fresh or dried leaves may be infused. Served hot the tea has all the medicinal qualities of thyme (page 32) and in particular is useful for its antiseptic and disinfectant qualities. Thyme tea may be blended with sage and served hot. Lemon-thyme tea is more fragrant.

To make tea:
  3–4 sprigs of fresh thyme, or 1 tablespoon of green-dried thyme (leaves and flowers). Pour 1 pint of boiling water over it. Draw for 10 minutes to make a tonic tea.

VALERIAN TEA. Valerian tea is made of the dried root of Valeriana officinalis, which is a slightly different plant from the decorative valerian found in so many gardens. It provides the best herbal sedative. The tea made of it has strong sleep-inducing qualities and a general calming effect on the nervous system. Its flavor and smell may not be liked by some people, but others get quickly used to it and can take it regularly without difficulties.

  The tea can, like other infusions of roots, be made with boiling water, using a teaspoon of root per cup, but it is infinitely more effective when made in the cold way.

Cold valerian tea:
  Soak 1 level teaspoon valerian root in one cup of cold water; cover and stand in cold place for 12–24 hours. Strain and drink approximately 1 hour before retiring.
  If too strong, use half of this cup and dilute with water. Add water to the remaining half-cup and use this the next day.
  It is advisable to soak this tea every evening or every second evening to have a regular supply for a period of 2–3 weeks; then a break is indicated. After this valerian tea may be taken again.

VERBASCUM TEA is made of the bright yellow flowers of the common mullein, which can be either grown in the garden or obtained dried. The flowers must be bright yellow when dried because their medicinal value is bound up with their yellow color. They provide a pleasant tea which gives dramatic relief to cases of persistent cough and bronchial conditions and which relieves the respiratory tract of mucus.

It is prepared in the same way as other leaf or flower teas, but should be allowed to steep until the tea becomes yellow. During an acute cold or in the case of chest troubles or cough, two to three cups per day may be taken.

VERBENA TEA. Vervain, which is the Verbena officinalis, is a native plant of very old usage. It makes a slightly bitter tisane used in France and in England as a digestive and is considered soothing in nervous exhaustion. It may be used as a sedative nightcap. It also is a good digestive, but is not as pleasant as lemon verbena.

LEMON-VERBENA TEA. Lemon verbena produces a fragrant tea with a scent and taste of lemon. It is often confused with the other, less attractive, verbena tea. Lemon-verbena tea may be blended with mint, and may be taken hot or iced. It has a sedative effect, particularly on the bronchial and nasal regions.

The delicious scent of its leaves—fresh or green-dried—may be used in fruit drinks.

WOODRUFF has always been a famous herb in Europe because it provides the most delicious flavoring for wine in May. It is at its best when it flowers. It is reputed to have the same exhilarating effect as borage—perhaps even more so. It therefore not only increases the effect and flavor of good wine, but, as it is reputed to be relaxing as well as uplifting, it is also useful when used as a tea. Woodruff tea has additionally the reputation of relieving headaches and migraines. As it is made of one of the herbs which have an anti-spasmodic effect, woodruff tea is also soothing and calming. In Scotland it was taken to increase perspiration in order to ward off colds. It is also considered diuretic and tonic and helpful to the functions of gall bladder and liver. It has been credited with blood-cleansing qualities in spring; and it is reputed not only to improve the quality of sleep but also to increase the length of sleeping time. All these qualities make it a useful nightcap or a morning cup of tea.

It is best picked during May when it flowers, but needs to wilt and dry to give off its particular fragrance. If the leaves can be picked and dried so carefully that they retain their green color, they are excellent to use throughout the year for making tea or flavoring wine or fruit drinks. As the leaves are best dried whole when they stand like a ruff around the stem, the equivalent of a teaspoon per cup or glass will have to be estimated. If used green-dried for drinks they should first be soaked in a little wine. For tea they should be infused in boiling water. Woodruff leaves may be added to China tea, which will give this subtle tea a special fragrance.

Woodruff tea:
1 teaspoon per cup, but not more, should be used. The tea should never be boiled but may draw for a long time (up to 1 hour) in hot, but not boiling, water.

YARROW TEA has, like chamomile tea, many uses. It may be made of yarrow leaves and flowers and is good for the digestion. The milky juice of the plant is rich in minerals and vitamins.

The tea made of dry yarrow is also effective and may be taken during those seasons when fresh yarrow is not available. It is prepared as the leaf or flower tea. That is, a teaspoon per cup is used with boiling water. A similar infusion may also be used for cosmetic purposes as a pack, for washing, and as a bath addition. Yarrow is particularly useful in spring and in combination with dandelion.

Facial Steam for a Cold

An infusion made of the following mixture of herbs produces a steam which is most helpful for inhaling in the case of a persistent catarrh of the upper respiratory or bronchial areas.

Ingredients:
A handful of whole or shredded sage leaves.
A handful of whole or shredded peppermint leaves.
A handful of whole lime flowers.
A small handful of chamomile flowers.

Method:
1. Place the herbs in an unchipped enamel bowl or heatproof glass or earthenware bowl (not metal).
2. Have all equipment ready to make sure that the first steam is not lost.
3. Expose neck and chest and then pour two to four pints of fast boiling water over the herbs.
4. Immediately bend over the bowl and cover yourself with a large bath towel in tent fashion.

5. Inhale the steam—lift corner of bath towel if the heat becomes uncomfortable.
6. Carry on for 10 to 15 minutes, as long as there is sufficient steam and you feel comfortable.
7. Wash face and all exposed parts with cold water immediately.
8. Stay indoors, preferably in bed, for at least one hour.

Note: Only one facial steam per day should be taken for a cold, and one every other day when strain is felt.

To this basic herb mixture for a steam, in the case of a cold, may be aded smaller quantities of basil, elder flowers, lavender, verbascum flowers.

A similar steam with some further additions may be used for cosmetic purposes.

Herb Mixture for Abroad

When traveling abroad—particularly in southern countries—people have often experienced digestive upsets. One of the authors has been asked repeatedly, after lectures, whether herbs could be helpful in this connection.

She then made up a mixture of hers—called "Mixture for Abroad" —which she used herself with success. She also had satisfactory reports from other travelers. The mixture may be used sprinkled over food regularly, if carried in a small glass container in a pocket or handbag. It will add flavor and act as a disinfecting protective in the case of unfamiliar bacteria which the body is not equipped to resist.

When mixing the herbs consult the Guide (page 119) for proportions, and taste the flavor at the end so that there is not one overpowering herb and the mixture remains a pleasant overall herb flavor.

*Fennel herb *or* fennel seeds (ground in electric blender).
*Basil.
*Mugwort (if available).
Borage.
Nettle.
Salad burnet.
*Dill.
*Tarragon.
*Lovage.

*Marjoram.
Nasturtium.
*Rosemary.
*Sage.
Grated horseradish (if available without vinegar).
*Celery leaves.
*Thyme.
Hyssop.

    * Essential herbs (may be obtained commercially).

Juniper berries may be added to this mixture, or should be chewed during the same period.

Start eating four berries per day; this may be increased by one each day to 15, and then decreased by one each day down to four.

A Selection of the Most Useful Day-to-Day Teas and Mixtures

PEPPERMINT TEA	Settling after-dinner digestive; instead of coffee for liver and gall-bladder sufferers; pick-me-up for fatigue.
CHAMOMILE TEA	Digestive, after-dinner tea. Healing gargle and infusions.
LIME-FLOWER TEA	Pleasant after-dinner drink. Alternative to aspirin for colds.
ELDER-FLOWER TEA	Pleasant summer drink. Alternative to aspirin for colds.
HIBISCUS TEA	Ruby-colored, thirst-quenching, stimulating summer drink.
ROSE-HIP TEA	Most wholesome daily tea, rich in vitamin C and helpful to kidneys.
MELISSA TEA (lemon balm)	Relaxing, anti-spasmodic, and yet stimulating morning and evening drink.
SAGE TEA	All-round wholesome tea; also for colds, coughs, and gargling.
VERBASCUM TEA	Dramatic relief for coughs.
HERB MIXTURE FOR FACIAL STEAM	For colds in the head and the bronchial tract and for beauty.
PARSLEY TEA	Tonic, with diuretic qualities for rheumatism.
RED BERGAMOT TEA and RED BERGAMOT MILK	Sleep-inducing nightcap. Pleasant—relaxing.
VALERIAN TEA	Sedative and sleep-inducing tea before retiring; tranquilizer (not a pleasant flavor).
SEED TEA	Anti-flatulent drink after meals.
MIXTURE FOR ABROAD	For digestive upsets abroad.

Wild Herbs for Health in Spring

There are a number of wild herbs which have been used in many countries over centuries.

For those who are interested enough to collect some of these herbs and experiment with them, here are some suggestions. Quite a number of these herbs may also be found in one's own garden.

The wild herbs are grouped together according to the purposes for which they are used. There are, for instance, certain herbs which are useful to circulation and have, at the same time, a soothing influence on the nerves of exhausted or strained people.

Herbs Stimulating and Herbs Soothing

To this group belong the leaves of the *wild strawberry*. They may be dried. The famous herbalist and hydrotherapist, Kneipp, reports on his experience that the leaves and roots stimulate the liver and have a general soothing effect. A tea made of them also acts favorably on intestinal catarrh.

Blackberry-leaf tea (Rubus fructicosus). The leaves of the blackberry shrub are gathered in spring, and, as they contain a number of curative substances, they have been used in folk medicine for gargling and particularly for skin troubles. For a valuable spring drink, blackberry leaves should be mixed with equal parts of the leaves of *wild strawberries* and *woodruff* with a pinch of *thyme* added. This provides an aromatic tea equally good for an early cup in the morning or for a drink in the evening. This tea is thirst quenching and diuretic.

Spring Tea:
   3 parts of:
      Blackberry leaves
      Wild strawberry leaves
      Woodruff leaves
      and a pinch of thyme

The leaves of the elder tree contain in spring a number of curative substances and when dried produce *elder-leaf tea*, which is diuretic, improves the circulation, and has a cleansing effect; it is helpful after physical or mental strain and is also considered mildly sleep inducing. The dried leaves and young tips may also be chopped up and added to soups, or externally placed on inflammations.

An excellent means to stimulate the circulation is found in the herb *centaury*. Tea made of this herb stimulates the glandular system and the liver, and improves the circulation. The tea should only be allowed to be steeped in water which is not boiling. Centaury tea made from one teaspoon per cup should be allowed to draw for 10 minutes. It provides a drink for the early morning, when it has a soothing effect on the nerves and a cleansing effect on the kidneys. It has been considered one of the best teas for cosmetic purposes because it improves the skin.

Wild chicory growing near meadows provides leaves and roots which, when gathered in spring, may be taken either as a pressed fresh juice or be dried for tea. They improve the functions of liver and gall bladder as well as the general circulation, if taken as freshly expressed juice, one teaspoon four times a day, or as a tea. Chicory is most effective when complemented by the simultaneous use of woodruff.

A soothing tea is made of the leaves of the lime tree. The young leaves of the tree, picked in spring, freshly chopped, and allowed to steep in hot, but not boiling, water for about half an hour produce *lime-leaf tea,* a tea to relieve cramping pains and other nervous conditions.

The leaves of the *wild raspberry* and its flowering sprouts have a calming effect and are useful for skin rashes. A tea made from the fresh or dried plant and the chopped or pounded leaves may be used externally on the skin.

The *hops* are one of the most famous nerve-soothing herbs and have been used for more than one thousand years. The young sprouts of the wild hop in spring provide a pleasant tasting tea which is said to relieve restlessness, palpitations, insomnia. Should beer in which hops are used be liked for similar reasons?

The leaves of the *walnut* and its male as well as female flowers may be prepared like the tea made of lime-tree leaves, and an infusion made with two teaspoons of the chopped leaves in hot, but not boiling, water is helpful in a way similar to lime-leaf tea. The young freshly chopped walnut leaves have cosmetic properties against the loss of hair and skin troubles.

Spring Fatigue

Another group of herbs can help to combat spring fatigue and to cleanse and renew the system. *Nettle, dandelion,* and *yarrow* are useful at this time of the year, as are the leaves of the lime tree. Young leaves of nettle are rich in minerals and vitamin A. A few tablespoons of freshly pressed juice made of young leaves, or in a morning beverage, or leaves served freshly chopped on bread or on cereals are excellent, and may be given to children if they can be made palatable by adding them to the right kind of food.

A cup of nettle tea in the morning and at night is excellent for liver, gall-bladder, and intestinal troubles. Only honey should be used to sweeten it.

Dandelion increases elimination and perspiration. It is activating and helps the body to get rid of winter deposits. The leaves and roots should be gathered before flowering in order to make a freshly pressed juice; two to three tablespoons may be taken daily early in the morning. Finely chopped leaves and roots may be added to salads, soups, or bread and butter. The effect of dandelion is often improved by the addition of yarrow as finely chopped raw plant, added to soups. Yarrow tea may be taken internally and used externally for healing wounds or as compresses for skin impurities.

Spring and the Figure

During springtime people become more figure conscious than at any other time of the year. Some feel heavy and bulky and may be more aware of the weight they carry around; lean people may wish to add to a shape with which they are not happy.

Certain herbs help to regulate the glandular system and are helpful in improving the functions and the shape of the body as well as that of the mind. To the group of regulating herbs specifically for people who are underweight belong in particular *nettle, dandelion, centaury, yarrow,* and *blackberry leaves.* The value of these herbs for spring has already been discussed. Furthermore, there are *watercress* for salads, as well as *berry leaves.* These leaves collected in April and May before the fruit forms contain substances which have this regulating effect on the glandular system; they may be made into tea.

Among the herbs particularly useful for the figure watchers concerned with overweight is *wood sorrel,* useful to elimination by the way of the kidneys. These leaves should be added to soups and salads.

They have to be used in moderation, as their flavor is very sour, but they may be used in combination with nettle and spinach by adding them in small quantities to spinach puree or a spring salad.

The fresh plant may also be expressed to make a juice, which should be taken with three parts of water. A handful of fresh wood-sorrel leaves should be steeped in two pints of boiling water and allowed to cool to be taken as a tea.

The leaves of the *coltsfoot* may be used in a similar way. They are rich in vitamin C. It is suggested not only to collect the flowers from March to May, but also the leaves from May to July. Both should be carefully dried so they won't lose their color. The tea made of them has a spring-cleaning effect, as it is diuretic and considered to be an expectorant, cleaning the respiratory tract. Coltsfoot is also used for cosmetic purposes.

The leaves of *ribwort plantain* may be collected from the beginning of May to the end of August before the plant goes to seed. They should be dried well, as they easily become dark and then are no longer useful for making tea. Some fresh juice may be expressed from the flowering plants and the root, straight after picking, and a few spoonfuls of this, as well as the tea made from the dried plant, are useful in the case of obesity.

The leaves of *fumitory* may be picked from May to July. When dried they make a tea useful for liver and gall-bladder trouble, some times connected with overweight. In ancient medicine they were recommended against depression, sometimes allied to the same condition.

The crushed leaves of *wormwood,* together with the flowers, may be used to make a tea which helps all functions of the obese.

Horsetail tea (equisetum), mentioned before, is most useful for obesity because of all its special substances and particularly its minerals. It is, however, necessary to find the equisetum in fields, rather than to pick the kind which grows near water or marshes.

Improving the Mood

The sluggishness which is often felt in spring, and for which these various herbs are suggested, often produces certain disturbances of mood. People are often exhilarated by the advent of spring, but the opposite feeling may occur, as any disturbance in the physical functions is more strongly felt during spring than at any other time of the year and may lead to contrasting moods.

For the consequent depressions and changes of mood certain herbs can be helpful. There are, for instance, the *barberries,* with their bright yellow flowers, often found in gardens and hedges. Later on in the year their berries can be made into an excellent juice or stewed to provide a sweet rich in vitamins; but it is not well known that the root of the barberries is a help against liver and gall-bladder troubles. The root may be boiled, and the whole plant, added to a tea made of it, will help the flow of bile.

Also the roots of *fennel* may be dug up, as they contain volatile oils similar to those of the seeds. The tea helps in cleansing the mucous membranes and the intestinal tract, has an anti-spasmodic effect, and improves the general feeling of well-being. Fennel is not only found in gardens, where it is grown as an herb, but can be found wild, particularly near the coast.

Fresh *wood-sorrel* leaves, mentioned before, made into a tea, provide a drink which is not only refreshing but thirst quenching and of a stimulating and cleansing nature. It therefore is a suitable drink to improve spring moods. The juice serves the same purpose.

Chapter 3

*T*he *N*atural *W*ay to *B*eauty

HERBS HAVE been used for cosmetic purposes almost since the beginning of time and, infused with water and mixed with oil, they have been the main constituents of cosmetics.

Until the chemical industry started substituting the properties of herbs, these were the only beauty aids, and after a century of chemicals there is a tendency nowadays to return once more to a natural way to beauty.

Only a few years before her death, Helena Rubinstein, who probably had the greatest influence on beauty aids and who started as a chemical student at the beginning of the century, returned to herbs and produced her new "Herbessence" collection. She issued ten beauty preparations—after years of research—in all of which herbs play a major part. Thus from the Egyptian ladies who perfumed their hair with marjoram to the present day "Herbessence," cosmetics have come full circle.

Herbs have many functions, both internally and externally, as the beauty of the skin is so much dependent upon the proper working of all body functions. Therefore the use of herbs in food is of equal importance to the external beauty of the skin as their use *on* the skin. Among the many herbs are those that improve circulation, have a tonic effect, can fade freckles and pigmentation, refine and whiten skin; some are cooling and astringent; others smooth out wrinkles, help blemishes. Others repair tissues, heal wounds, improve existing scars, and soothe pain.

Herbs can provide a natural approach to beauty if the appropriate individual herbs are carefully dried, and leaves, flowers, and seeds skillfully blended. Such mixtures are often based on centuries-old traditions of many countries. By infusing these fragrant herbs in hot water, the inherent qualities of the essential oils, with their magic effects on beauty, as well as their full aroma are made available.

Chemical extractions, which mostly utilize only part of the plant, can interfere with the effect of the whole plant as such. Preservatives and coloring additives, often used in the cosmetic industry, can be damaging. If herbs are used in infusions, etc., the chemical aids become unnecessary and no changes in the essential qualities of the herbs take place.

The use of herbs has a psychological effect. The natural herb scents produce a feeling of relaxation and comfort, and the volatile oils a stimulating influence on the nerves. Both of these qualities create an atmosphere which helps to make full use of the effects of "herbal" cosmetics.

The beauty aids for which herbs are particularly useful are:

> Facial steam
> Face packs
> Compresses
> Bath additions
> Herb pochettes (as a bath addition)
> Eye compresses
> Eye bath
> Nail bath
> Hair rinses

Herb preparations which rely on the scent for their effect:

> Herb cushions
> Herb potpourri

Herbs Used for Cosmetics

According to their effect, the herbs are divided into activating herbs and reducing herbs.

The activating herbs:

LIME FLOWERS — One of the best cosmetic herbs: slightly bleaching (good against freckles); improves circulation, helps to smooth wrinkles. Good for compresses; antiseptic and stimulating in facial steams. Demulcent and mucilaginous properties. Also stimulates growth of hair.

CHAMOMILE — Healing, soothing, disinfectant, anti-inflammatory effects, or astringent in cases of aging skin, but not a tonic. If combined with yarrow—tonic; for blond hair.

PEPPERMINT	In facial steams, antiseptic, disinfectant, stimulating circulation. Also good for compresses.
FENNEL HERB AND SEEDS	Antiseptic tonic, smooths wrinkles, helpful for the eyes. Addition to packs with honey and for creams.
ROSEMARY	Stimulates growth of hair. Healing, warming, increasing blood supply to certain places.
ELDER FLOWERS	One of the best cosmetic herbs. For centuries used to cure sunburn, and remove freckles and wrinkles. As a lotion: to soften, whiten, and cleanse the skin. Helpful for the eyes.
YARROW	For greasy skins. Used for tisanes, facial steam, face packs, and as a hair tonic. For compresses on chapped hands.
NETTLES	Improving skin and hair. Used for packs, bath additions, hair rinse and oil.

The reducing herbs:

MARIGOLD PETALS	Excellent healing properties against acne; helps old and new scars, inflammation, and rough skins; used in ointments and oil.
SAGE	Cooling and astringent for packs and facial steams. Good for hair rinse.
LADY'S MANTLE	Used by the Arabs as a cosmetic herb. Astringent and restoring beauty to the skin. Infusion against inflammation and acne. Taken as tea and used for compresses. Freshly expressed juice for freckles.
EYEBRIGHT	Infusion for eye bath in case of tired eyes and for inflammation of the eyelids. Also for eye compresses.
VERBENA	Cleansing and strengthening effect on the eyes; helps with inflammation of the eyelids.

HORSETAIL   Owing to its high content of silicic acid has good astringent, antiseptic, and tonic properties. Strengthening tissues, hair, and nails.

COLTSFOOT   Infusion used as compresses for dilated facial veins (thread veins).

LOVAGE   Infusion to be used as a bath addition or shredded leaves in a muslin bag under the hot tap for a bath as an herbal deodorant and against impurities of the skin. Tea taken internally also acts as a deodorant and increases effect of the bath addition.

SALAD BURNET   An herb used for cookery which grows throughout the winter and may be used as an addition to the facial steam or to the bath; it beautifies the skin and strengthens the body.

Cosmetic Suggestions

Facial Steam for Beauty

This is the beauty aid with the most immediate effect. The skin of the face will always improve with the help of the humidity and the temperature of a facial steam. The effect may be much improved with the addition of either a mixture of herbs or some specific herbs for specific purposes. It is recommended particularly for any skin with large pores or impurities.

A general mixture of dried herbs for improving the skin of face and neck:

Sage (whole leaves if available)*
Peppermint (whole or shredded)*
Basil (small quantity)
Chamomile flowers*
Lime flowers*

---

* Essential herbs for a facial steam. The others are helpful as an addition and provide also good specific effects from each herb.

Elder flowers
Marigold petals
Nasturtium flowers
Cornflowers
Lavender flowers
Verbascum flowers
Nettle leaves (if available)
Fennel
Yarrow (if available)
Salad burnet (if available)

Warning: Facial steams are not indicated and, in fact, should not be used at all on very dry skin, because it is usually too thin and too sensitive to heat, particularly if there are any dilated red veins visible in the face. Also the steam is not good for people with heart trouble, difficulties in breathing, and for the asthmatic.

Method of facial steam. Cover the hair and clean the face as normally done in the evening. Place approximately two handfuls of the herbs in a bowl; bring two pints of water to a boil and pour over the herbs. Hold the head above the bowl at a distance of 8 to 12 inches. Cover head and bowl with a big bath towel, and perhaps cover this with a thin rug so that the steam cannot escape through the pores of the cloth, but remains to act on the face. After 8 to 10 minutes, provided you feel comfortable that long, you emerge red and steaming from underneath the cloth. The affected parts—face and neck—should be washed with a wet wash-cloth, steeped in cold water, and the face allowed to cool down. Do not go out until one hour after the steam bath.

The steam may be taken once per week for cosmetic purposes. People suffering from acne will probably find that any black spots will come out easily after the steam, but one should be careful not to press or cause any inflammation. After the steam bath, some face packs are indicated.

Natural Face Packs

Method: A pack is usually made out of some material such as yogurt, curd, fuller's earth *, a clay powder *, mixed with the help of an infusion or an herb tea into a thick paste. This paste should be applied thinly to the face with a broad brush. The surrounding areas of the eyes and lips should be left uncovered or be covered with wet cotton pads. The pack has to be applied when you are lying down in an outstretched resting position, pos-

---

* Available from drugstores or health-food shops.

sibly with the legs higher than the face; after 10 to 15 minutes, remove paste and wash face with warm water. Finish with a cold compress on the face.

Eggs have several uses in face packs—egg yolk is particularly suited for dry skin on the face. For this purpose it is suggested to use:

The mayonnaise pack. Stir egg yolk well with drops of pure olive oil and add lemon juice. Add some fennel. Allow the pack to remain on the face for 10 to 20 minutes; then wash off with warm water, previously boiled.

A *white of egg pack* should not be used too often, as it may be too astringent. Beat white of egg to a firm froth and add a few drops of lemon. This mixture can be painted with a soft brush on to face and neck. After 10 minutes, wash off the pack with cold boiled water. The pack is tonic, refreshing, but not suitable for dry skin. With some finely chopped or green-dried *yarrow* added the pack helps large pores and greasy skin.

Oil pack—for the middle-aged skin (40 to 50 years). Warm pure olive oil in a small bowl standing in boiling water. Soak in it a layer of cotton as large as the face, and place it on the face. Protect the eyes beforehand with pads of cotton soaked in water. Remove when cold, and clean face with soft paper tissues. Finish with alternative compresses dipped in a warm infusion of *chamomile flowers* and *yarrow* combined, *peppermint,* or *sage,* to be followed by a compress made of cold water.

Fennel pack. For the aging skin, a pack made of curd, yogurt, or clay powder, with a strong infusion of fennel seeds or herb, plenty of honey, and some fennel herb helps to enliven the skin, to smooth wrinkles. Acting as a tonic, it is also antiseptic and allays irritation of the skin.

Linseed herb pack. Boiling linseed into a thick slimy consistency makes an excellent facial pack which contains oil and vitamins D and E; combined with chamomile it has an anti-inflammatory effect.

Yogurt herb pack is valuable for bleaching and clearing the skin. Some clay powder mixed with yogurt to which a strong infusion of *fennel* (for the case of wrinkles) or *yarrow* (for a greasy skin) and some honey is added may serve several purposes.

Curd herb pack. Add to curd a little milk and honey, a few drops of lemon, and a small quantity of an infusion of *sage* or *horsetail* for a thick paste for large pores. It also refreshes the skin.

Wild herb packs. Dandelion, nettle, cowslip, and *daisy* are of great benefit to the skin, particularly in spring. Nettle and dandelion contain so many health properties, including vitamins, minerals, and plant hormones, that they have a strong cleansing effect, improving the content of the blood, etc. For their effect on the functions of the body see pages 62, 68, 72, and 73.

The skin is much improved by the tonic and astringent qualities of the wild herbs. As nettle and dandelion supplement each other, they may be used together in equal parts. The young leaves of nettle and dandelion should be gathered, if possible, in the morning, finely chopped up, crushed, and simmered lightly for 10 minutes to provide a thick mash. The skin of the face should be prepared beforehand with warm compresses before the actual herb pack is put on. The herb mixture should be spread on a piece of thin muslin, and this can go as a pack or compress straight on to the face. The eyes must be protected by wet cotton pads. After the herb pack has been on for 15 minutes, it should be washed off with lukewarm water to which some lemon juice has been added. This pack may be applied every second morning, and if this is done for two weeks in spring, the result will be surprising. The skin will become clear and fresh, small wrinkles will disappear. The pack also has a healing influence on spots which have a tendency to become inflamed.

Nettle pack. The same method may be used for nettle leaves and sprouting tops alone.

Yarrow pack may be made from fresh sprouts and buds in the same way.

Elder-flower packs are useful to improve the skin when mixed with yogurt, buttermilk, whey, or any of the dairy produce which has undergone fermentation. The action of the elder flower is improved by the lactic bacteria. Elder flowers may be added to yogurt or cream cheese for facial packs or other face packs such as clay powder, etc. The packs may also be made with an elder-flower infusion. These face packs are stimulating and tonic rather than soothing; they clear and soften the skin and are good against freckles and pigmentation.

Elder flowers should be mixed with yogurt, etc., into a thick paste and be allowed to permeate; then either put straight on the face with a brush or packed in thin muslin and used like a compress. Elder-flower tea should be drunk in combination with the use of elder-flower packs.

Blackberry-leaf pack. Collect the leaves when young and tender; they should be dried without stalks for tea. Chop fresh leaves, boil with a little water into a pulp-like mash, wrap in muslin, and apply warm on the face or any parts which are affected by skin troubles. The packs should be left for 20 minutes before retiring. Blackberry-leaf tea supports the effects of the face pack.

Valuable additions to packs:

Lemon	Contains vitamins C and P. Astringent, bleaching; also for hand creams.
Cucumber Juice	Bleaching, clearing, astringent.
Yeast	Excellent for a pack for greasy skin. May be dissolved in milk, yogurt, or buttermilk; mixed with fuller's earth or clay powder.* After drying, pack will peel.
Honey	Tonic; honey and eggs.

Compresses

They have the advantage of producing a layer of humidity over the skin which acts like a moisturizer, particularly for dry skin, which does not only need fat but also moisture. Compresses may be made with water, but very often are much improved by use of herb teas for general or specific purposes. Before use of compresses, the face should be cleaned thoroughly.

For people who do not suffer from too dry a skin or dilated veins, alternative compresses with hot and cold water are most useful.

Prepare two bowls, one with warm and the other with cold water. Instead of the warm water, an herb tea may be used. Particularly for greasy skin, *yarrow tea* is recommended. Provide two soft pieces of lint, which should be folded into triangles and placed in the prepared bowls. First place the piece of lint from the warm herb tea bowl on to the face. It should be as warm as is comfortable. Place the cloth around the nose so that it is free for breathing. This allows the face to relax, particularly when the body is stretched out in a comfortable position. Close the eyes. If the face has become warm under the compress, take it off and add immediately the compress from the cold water bowl. The first cold compress should only remain on the face for 10 seconds, approximately a third of the time of the warm compress. Then the warm compress is replaced and is followed by the cold again. This should be repeated according to

---

* Available from drugstores or health-food shops.

the time available, but at least three or four times. The last compress should always be a cold one. This brings a great deal of fresh blood to the skin of the face, and the functions of the skin become stimulated.

Cold-water compress. This is suitable for many types of skin. Place soft pieces of lint big enough to cover the face, possibly two layers of lint, in cold boiled water or in a cooled infusion of *sage*, *lady's mantle*, or *peppermint*. Leave for 10 minutes on the face. If the skin is dry, oil carefully beforehand, using only a little oil. These compresses are a tonic for the skin and reduce large pores.

Coltsfoot compress (for dilated veins). For those people for whom alternative or cold-water compresses are not possible because they suffer from dilated thread veins in the face, another type of compress made from an infusion of coltsfoot is helpful. Use a teaspoon fresh chopped or green-dried coltsfoot leaves per cup, pour boiling water over, and allow to steep for 10 minutes. When the infusion has become lukewarm, dip one or two cotton pads into it, place on the affected parts, and allow the humidity in the cotton to be soaked up by the pores. After removing them, do not wash the part, but use a little oil or cream on it.

This may be done twice a day. No lotions containing alcohol should be used. It is also possible to make compresses dipped into an infusion of *chamomile* and *yarrow* combined.

More about the treatment of dilated facial veins on page 73.

Dandelion compress. The young shoots of dandelion leaves—before they go into flower—provide an effective cosmetic compress, improving the circulation of the face and with it removing impurities of the skin. Chop young dandelion leaves finely, add boiling water, and allow to simmer for 5 minutes. Dip a clean cloth (of linen, cotton, or lint) into this infusion, and put this compress on the carefully cleaned face. As soon as the compress starts to become cool it should be renewed.

In the case of dilated veins, the procedure must be altered. The finely chopped leaves are simmered with boiling water and allowed to cool until the liquid is lukewarm. Dip the compress into this lukewarm infusion and allow it to remain on the face for 20 minutes.

Bath Additions

The effects of a full warm bath can often be much improved by the addition of herbs. Particularly at the end of winter, with spring coming, people get the urge to join in the renewal of nature and add herbs to their bath. When people feel tired, the skin looks grey and wilted. This is the best time to start refreshing baths at home which cost little and make one feel younger. Water belongs to the oldest and cheapest cosmetics, and the addition of cultivated or wild herbs, added over a period of perhaps six weeks, may be as good as any spring cure in a distant place. An hour's rest in bed after such a bath will improve the effect.

A soothing effect on the nervous system can be expected with the addition of *chamomile, valerian, rosemary, horsetail,* and *pine needles. Peppermint baths* can be a great help to people suffering from skin troubles (also with an addition of *horsetail*). It is best to try out which herbs in general are best for baths, and this may vary with different people, but mixtures may be used; a mixture of *lovage, chamomile, peppermint, rosemary, fennel, sage,* and *yarrow* has an excellent effect.

For a full bath, about 10 ounces of dried herbs made into an infusion and allowed to stand for about 10 minutes would be an excellent addition, particularly in spring. Some people like to add bran, which contains fats, oil, and vegetable hormones, and gives a velvety look to the skin in connection with the effects of the herbs. In commercial cosmetics, the Herbessence bath oil provides a kind of "beauty bath" similar to one for which the various herbs are used.

Elder-flower water is usually used for skin lotions because it is a mildly astringent stimulant and is therefore very good to be added to the wash water or as a bath addition. Small additions of sea salt are stimulating and strengthening, and increase the blood circulation.

FOOT BATHS. For a foot bath the addition of an infusion of *horsetail* and some sea salt is helpful, particularly to feet which have to stand a great deal of strain; finishing with cold water improves the effect. After such a bath, the feet should be rubbed with oil in which *marigold petals* have been soaked.

ALTERNATIVE BATHS FOR FEET AND LEGS. Two pails or tubs which allow the legs to be immersed in the water up to the knees are necessary. Fill one with warm water and add a strong infusion of *lime flowers* or *rosemary.* Fill the second with cold water, of which the worst chill is taken off. Immerse the legs in the tub filled with the water which is as warm as it can be borne for 5 to 10 minutes. Then dip legs in the cold tub for 10 seconds (counting up to 20); then back into the warm tub for another 5 to 10 minutes, finishing with another 10-second dip in the cold water. Only two changes should be made. Dry by rubbing the water into the skin, and then go for a walk or to bed.

BATH ADDITIONS OF WILD HERBS. The wild herbs recommended for spring compresses, etc., are also suggested to be added to a bath particularly during spring. They are *dandelion* and *nettle* with the addition of small quantities of *cowslip* and *daisy* if available. It is best to dry these herbs with care so that they retain their color before use—of cowslip, only flowers and roots should be dried. After drying, chop up the herbs, mix them well, and infuse a large quantity, approximately one pound, in 6 to 8 pints of hot water for about 30 minutes. Drain and pour the infusion into the tub, which should be filled up with warm water. The bath should have a temperature of 95–100° F. or 35–37° C., and should last not more than 10 or 15 minutes. This bath could be taken every second day in the evening for about two weeks, not long before retiring, but not too soon after a meal. The effects should be felt from the third bath onward.

For those who have difficulties in going to sleep, the addition of an infusion of *valerian* will improve the night's sleep. A brushing massage of arms and legs under water in the direction of the heart, while cool water is being slowly added, will add to the effect. A further strengthening bath addition is a mixture of conifer sprouts from pine, fir trees, larch, juniper. Boiling water should be poured over the young sprouts while they are fresh, and the resulting infusion added to the bath.

Blackberry leaves. The leaves, picked in spring without stalks, should be dried and then crumbled, and about 10 ounces mixed with 6 pints of water at a temperature of 115° F. or 45° C. After allowing to draw for three minutes, strain and add to the warm bath water.

Pochettes

Smaller additions to a daily bath may be achieved by packing the herb in question into a small bag of a porous material. Hang this "pochette" underneath the hot tap and allow the hot water to pass through this bag when filling the bath. The pochette may also be allowed to stay in the bath to increase the effect. This method, which is simpler than making a special infusion, is particularly suited to *lovage,* which may be used as a deodorant bath addition. Although the pochette may be hung up and dried and used for several baths, it is advisable to fill a new pochette whenever one feels that the infusion becomes weaker.

Herb Mixtures for Improving Eyes, Hair, and Nails

Eyes

Eyebright cleans the eyes, improves the sight, and, as a compress, improves inflammation of eyelids.

Elder-flower water—an infusion—is a mild astringent and stimulant and may be safely used for eye compresses or eye baths.

Fennel tea—compresses steeped in fennel tea placed on the eyes, or bathing the eyes with fennel, help inflamed eyelids (conjunctivitis) and watering eyes, strengthen the eyes altogether, and help to improve the sight.

Chamomile may be used for eye compresses for inflammation of the eyelids.

Verbena has a cleansing and strengthening effect on the eyes and is used for inflammation of the eyelids.

An infusion should be made of either of these herbs and used for compresses in cases of tired eyes or for inflammation of the eyelids or for an eye bath.

An herbal eye bath can be prepared from a larger number of herbs. An infusion of these herbs is useful for either eye baths or eye compresses.

This mixture consists of larger parts of:

> Eyebright
> Chamomile
> Fennel

and additions of carefully dried:

> Cornflowers   } They should not lose their bright colors
> Marigold petals { in drying.

smaller parts of:

> Lovage
> Horsetail
> Summer savory
> Verbena
> Lady's mantle
> Yarrow

and still smaller parts of:

> Thyme
> Rosemary
> Mugwort (if available).

Method:

Use one heaped teaspoon of this mixture per cup of boiling water. Allow to steep for 5 minutes; strain. Use either as an eye bath or for eye compresses.

For compresses, cut two to three layers of white lint for each eye. Soak in the lukewarm infusion and place over each eyelid. Try to lie down and relax and repeat the freshly soaked compresses for 5 or 10 minutes. Finish with a cool, clear-water compress. Even three minutes of compresses are better than none at all.

Hair

HERBAL HAIR RINSE. A special flower and leaf mixture has a stimulating effect on the glands and tissues of the scalp and stimulates growth and healthy development of the hair.

The hair rinse should consist of the following herbs, cultivated and wild mixed:

Cultivated	*Wild*
Lime flowers	Nettle
Chamomile	Horsetail
Fennel	Yarrow
Sage	
Rosemary	

The basis of the mixture should consist of equal parts of lime flowers, chamomile, and fennel, and smaller parts of all the other herbs. If the hair rinse is used for blond hair, the largest part should be chamomile, while for dark hair less chamomile but more rosemary is indicated.

Method:

Place two heaped tablespoons of the mixture in a china jug and pour over two pints of boiling water; cover and steep until the right temperature for rinsing; strain. Wash hair in the usual way. Rinse with clear water until all soap or shampoo is removed; then rinse again and again with the infusion.

The scalp may be massaged with yolk of egg before washing, or a whole egg beaten can be used for a dry scalp before or after washing. The same herbs mentioned for hair rinse may also be steeped in oil, allowed to stand in the sun (for a few weeks whenever there is sun), and then applied to the scalp and massaged with the fingers of both hands before washing. This stimulates growth, prevents dandruff, and makes the hair strong and shiny. The scalp may also be massaged with oil in which *nettles* have been steeped. The hair has to be well rinsed after washing to remove all oil.

Nails

Many people suffer from brittle or splitting nails. A warm oil bath should be taken twice per week for 10 minutes each, alternately with baths of *horsetail infusion*. The high content of silicic acid helps to strengthen the nails. The baths should continue over several weeks or months, as nails cannot improve quickly. It is helpful to drink horsetail tea during the same period.

Herbs for Specific Conditions

Dilated Veins [thread veins]

Those people who have a tendency to dilated veins, which are often increased by the use of coffee and alcohol, can be helped by drinking more herb teas instead of coffee; particularly *chamomile tea, coltsfoot tea,* or *yarrow tea.* People who have this tendency should never allow extreme temperatures to touch the face, but should protect the skin by the use of oil or creams from extreme weather conditions.

Facial steams, alternate compresses, and cold compresses, as well as alternately splashing the face with warm and cold water, which is normally so helpful to the skin, cannot be used. Instead, *coltsfoot* compresses are suggested (page 68). Strong massage of the face is also not indicated, but to wash the face with milk and leave the milk to dry in for a few minutes before washing the face again is useful.

Acne

Young people often suffer from acne. Although they sometimes grow out of it, it often gives them a difficult time. The facial steam with herbs is particularly good for this condition. Apart from the herbs suggested as a general mixture for facial steam, special additions of *chamomile, lady's mantle,* and *yarrow* are advisable; 10 minutes after the steam is finished, when the skin is soft and the pores are open, it is possible to carefully move two fingers in small circles with a thin sterile paper tissue to get some of the blackheads or inflamed spots out. They should not be touched at any other time. It is also useful for this condition to make a pack with fuller's earth or clay powder mixed with *yarrow tea* or *coltsfoot tea* into a paste. At the same time, one cup per day at least of yarrow tea should be drunk, and there are certain foods which are useful to be eaten in large quantities while suffering from any skin condition and in particular from acne.

Beauty from Within

During a period of using packs, compresses, and steams for the purpose of dealing with certain skin conditions, it is advisable to eat an uncooked salad daily in larger quantities than usual (page 86) to which as many herbs as possible are added for flavoring. Little salt and no spices should be taken. If salt is used at all, it should be sea salt. It is further recommended to eat a lot of *parsley*, which is good for the skin because of its content of vitamin A. Apart from daily use in salads and cooking, it may be eaten daily on bread and butter.

The external effect of *dandelion*, for instance as face packs, may be supplemented by its use as food at the same time. The freshly picked, tender, finely chopped leaves may be dressed with oil, lemon juice, and perhaps some milk or yogurt, and a small portion added to a salad. As these leaves have a tendency to be bitter, they should only be used finely chopped in combination with other herbs and possibly lettuce or other green salad leaves.

Yarrow salad and *yarrow tea* supplement the use of yarrow in packs for greasy skin; *coltsfoot tea* the use of coltsfoot in packs for dilated veins; *blackberry-leaf tea* and *elder-flower tea* should be taken in conjunction with the packs made of the same leaves and flowers; and *horsetail tea* should be taken as a supplement while using nail baths.

Strawberries, bananas, and tomatoes are used sometimes for packs, but are better taken as food in as large quantities as available.

Sweet-scented Herbs

Herb Potpourri

Past generations liked large china bowls of potpourri (dried flowers, mostly rose petals) in their drawing rooms. Many detailed recipes distinguished between wet potpourri and dry potpourri, but all advised additions of fixatives, powders, or salts; but, as time went on, the scent of the rose petals became musty and eventually was overpowered by the scent of the fixatives. Sometimes scented toilet waters or perfumes were even added, which gave the potpourri bowl an unnatural scent, different from the scents of nature.

Experiments with the scent of herbs and the new ways of drying flowers to retain their bright natural colors allow a new kind of potpourri. The delightful, lasting, and natural scents of this pot-pourri come from the unspoiled and well-preserved, entirely natural scents of flowers, sweet-scented herbs, and spices.

The colors are provided by the brilliant, well-dried flower petals. The new way of keeping such potpourri in a contemporary living room is in a clear glass bowl, with a clear lid firmly enclosing the scents, if desired, but allowing the eye to enjoy the colors.

This new potpourri bowl should be kept in a dark cupboard of the living room to be taken out and the lid removed when the room is occupied. The air is filled with the sweetest scent, cleansing the atmosphere, and the eye can enjoy the colors. When the room is emptied and the occupants retire for the night, the lid is replaced, and the bowl can go back into the dark cupboard. In this way a potpourri may be enjoyed for its scent and color for a long time.

The following herbs, well mixed, provide the kind of scented leaf mixture which will give most of the scents needed:

Green-dried	Peppermint leaves	Lemon-balm leaves
	Sweet-cicely leaves	Red bergamot leaves
	Sage leaves	Lovage leaves
	Basil leaves	Tarragon leaves
	Rosemary leaves	Marjoram leaves
	Angelica leaves	Rose-geranium leaves
	Lemon-thyme leaves	Lemon-verbena leaves

The flower mixture consists of:

Lavender flowers	Nasturtium flowers
Elder flowers	Cornflowers
Verbascum flowers	Lime flowers
Chamomile flowers	Marigold petals

The following spices may be used for scent:

Cloves (whole)
Cinnamon sticks (broken)
Nutmeg (best freshly ground by an electric blender)
Coriander (best freshly ground by an electric blender)
Cardomom (best freshly ground by an electric blender)
Aniseed (half ground)
Orange, grapefruit, and lemon peel (dried and crushed in a blender)

The bowl is best started with layers of brilliant flowers, such as verbascum and cornflowers, with the addition of marigold petals. Then a layer of herb mixture and a layer of flower mixture follow. In between the layers some of the spices and some dried and ground orange, grapefruit, and lemon peel may be placed. The top layer but one should be scented herbs, such as tarragon, rosemary, rose geranium, lemon thyme, and lemon verbena, with crushed bay leaves.

The very top layer should be well arranged with rose petals, chamomile flowers, lime flowers, lavender flowers, and whole dried flowers such as cornflowers, small roses, pansies and yarrow, and one or two angelica leaves to give an attractive and colorful pattern to the top.

Herb Cushions

Herb cushions have been used in the past to soothe people and make them go to sleep more easily. In the course of years, herb cushions have been requested by all kinds of people—especially chronic invalids or old people. The cushions usually have two functions to perform—one is to soothe the nerves of those who have difficulty in getting to sleep, often through problems arising from surroundings, such as hospital wards, or people who, being invalid, have become over-sensitive to smells which surround them.

Originally, the all-lavender cushion probably fulfilled both these functions, because it has a soothing effect on the nerves and also provides a clean and attractive scent; herb cushions may, however, be filled with a mixture which has a refreshing, clean scent and at the same time a soothing and sleep-inducing quality.

The herbs which should provide the basic needs of an herb cushion are:

Peppermint	
Sage	(Used in three equal main parts.)
Lemon Balm	
Lavender	(About half of the above-mentioned herbs.)

and half again of:

Dill	Woodruff
Marjoram	Angelica
Thyme	Rosemary
Lemon Thyme	Lemon Verbena
Tarragon	Red Bergamot

A small addition of valerian, if available, should add to the sleep-inducing quality of the cushion, but it should not be enough to make it a predominant and unpleasant-smelling addition.

It is not necessary to use all the herbs mentioned above, but those which are underlined are most helpful.

It is best to use a porous material for the herb cushion; porous linen, for instance, is excellent. If the herb cushion is used regularly, it is better to enclose the herb mixture first in muslin or hessian and make another cover of coarse linen or another loosely woven material which can be changed and washed without disturbing the herb mixture.

However useful the gift of such an herb cushion may be for an invalid or for an old person, it will be equally useful and attractive as a scented and soothing—even elegant—addition to any bedroom. Sachets or cushions of lavender have always been used in drawers—made of such an herb mixture they not only scent all drawers containing clothes or linen, but they also keep the moths away.

Chapter 4

*E*veryday *S*uggestions and *R*ecipes for *H*ealthy *E*ating

THE DAILY SALAD

I<small>T HAS THE</small> highest health value of any dish in the daily diet. Some schools of thought on diet consider a 50 per cent intake of *uncooked* fruit and vegetables important. This is suggested not only to provide adequate vitamins and minerals from foods which are left as near as possible to their natural state, but also to balance the proportion of the important uncooked food to cooked food, which should be about half each.

Nowadays it has been recognized that salads have become an essential dish of the first order. The 50 per cent intake can be easily achieved if an uncooked fruit porridge is taken, possibly twice a day, with the addition of an uncooked daily salad for lunch or the evening meal. This is important for the figure watchers, as they can be certain that half of their food will hardly add to the calories; and for everyone it becomes a daily vehicle for the intake of the important vitamins and minerals as well as a delicious appetizer or *hors d'oeuvre.*

A small regular intake of these important nutrients is better than large quantities at greater intervals. If the salad is kept small and eaten before the cooked course as an *hors d'oeuvre,* or instead of soup, it not only increases the appetite and the enjoyment of the food, but decreases the quantity of the not so healthy food by providing part of the meal. Thus a small daily salad regularly is more helpful than large salads occasionally.

What the Salad Should Contain

The daily raw salad should consist of almost all parts of the plant; it is important that roots, leaves, and fruit are represented in it. The flower part may be optional.

> *Root vegetables* such as:
> Raw grated carrots
> Raw grated beetroots
> Parsley roots
> Radishes, etc.

are important and indeed, available throughout the year.

The leaves are represented by all kinds of green salad leaves such as:
Lettuce
Endive
Watercress
Mustard and cress
Corn salad.

The fruit is usually:
Tomato
Cucumber *or may be*
  Avocado pear
  Zucchini
  Red pepper

The flower is represented by:
Raw grated cauliflower
Raw grated broccoli.

Serving the salad:

The uncooked salad, combined in the way suggested, is best arranged in a way that the vegetables are not all mixed up, but laid out separately like flower beds or strips on a shallow dish, making use of the tempting colors and allowing people to choose more of some and less of others. This is helpful for those who are being gradually converted to eating more salad, and, above all, for children.

The salad bowl should be preferably a wooden one, with salad servers to match. After each use, rinse bowl with cold water. This method of cleaning keeps the faint flavors in the wood, and in time the wood develops a fine patina. If any cleaning of the bowl is desirable other than cold water, some warm oil should be used. This is also the best cleaning for wooden salad plates, which are excellent; if rinsed in water and then cleaned with warm oil they will remain beautiful and useful. Wooden forks and spoons do not bruise salad leaves as much as stainless steel or silver.

Mix the dressing in a small glass or china bowl, or cup, particularly if some of the dressing or the basic oil and lemon mixture is to be kept for another day.

SALAD DRESSINGS

Mixing green leaves and raw vegetables in a large container with a dressing is a very old custom, originally an Arabian one. It has gone a long way through Greek, Roman, and European kitchens, and many outstanding seasonings and dressings have been used.

Salad dressing has two functions: One is to complement the flavors of a salad and the other is to add to its health value. It is still not sufficiently realized how important the salad dressing is; more important when the vegetable parts of the salad are not cooked. If "what is healthy could just as well be enjoyable," and "what is enjoyable will be eaten," it is well worth while taking trouble over the salad. Make it a daily habit, an essential addition to your menu, providing only a relatively small number of calories.

Vegetables have to be thoroughly cleaned for the purpose of an uncooked salad, and chopped, sliced, or grated.

Oil

The important health value of the salad dressing is found in the fact that the oil, cream, and/or other fatty substances which are used in every salad dressing provide the necessary lubricant which helps to absorb the fat-soluble vitamins, particularly vitamin A. Without this the vitamin A contained in carrots, tomatoes, etc., can never be utilized by the body.

It is furthermore important that the oil in the dressing should be the cold-pressed sunflower oil or corn oil. Although the controversy over whether one kind of fat can be made responsible for certain conditions is by no means closed, there is no doubt that these oils can keep the balance of saturated and unsaturated fats in order and help to prevent troubles arising from disturbing this balance. The dressing and in particular the oil in it, helps to cover the exposed surfaces caused by grating, chopping, or cutting, so that the vegetables do not go on losing important nutrients.

Many of the existing salad-dressing recipes are suggested with olive oil and vinegar. Olive oil often has a special flavor, and it is difficult to find a brand that is not too strong for some palates. People have frequently taken a dislike to salad dressings because of the predominant flavor of some olive oils. Apart from the health factor, the unflavored sunflower oil or corn oil is often preferred. The lack of flavor in the oil helps one to enjoy better the flavors of the salad and the herbs. It will not only have advantages for heart and circulation, but it will furthermore not be a fattening "fat," in fact, the unsaturated fatty acids will help to maintain a slim figure.

Lemon juice and vinegar

Lemon juice is preferable to vinegar, even to wine vinegar, and has an enhancing effect on the other ingredients; it will improve the flavor of the herbs, while the vinegar has an overpowering tendency. Lemon juice has not the habit-forming qualities of vinegar, whereby more and more is needed or wanted for a dressing until the palate is blunted for the more delicate flavors. It also adds vitamin C to the salad.

Dairy additions
Useful additions to the salad are yogurt, buttermilk, and skimmed milk, as they add some of the acid normally contained in vinegar and lemon juice and some milk protein at the same time; they are not only very tasty, but also a health-giving addition.

Seasonings
In the suggestions here, certain seasonings are omitted from the salad dressings, such as cayenne pepper, chili powder, chopped capers, curry powder, freshly ground black peppercorns, mustard, Tabasco, or Worcester sauce; they all have a tendency to overpower the herbs, and, though they may be good at other times, they certainly should not be combined with the dressing of a health salad.

Dressings which are more complicated, and have many ingredients, should not necessarily be used for raw daily health-giving salads; they are best for special salads offered for a party or as a summer luncheon dish. Recipes for these are given in Part Three, Chapter 2, pages 179–85.

Herbs
The salad should be dressed, and this is where the herbs play their important part. They make all the difference to the salad as a whole, as they not only will improve its flavor and make it more wholesome, but, used wisely, will ring changes and increase the appetite for the salad, even if the herb mixture remains more or less the same. The herbs may be individually combined and varied with the various vegetables.

The housewife with a little time on her hands can try out endless variations of herbs in the dressing. The section on Basic Dressings is followed by a table with suggestions for herbs and dressings to be used with a number of vegetables; also the guide (page 119) should be consulted for proportions. Green-dried *bouquet for salads* consists of all the herbs suitable for salads combined in the right proportions; an addition of this is always safe and will not spoil a salad.

Basic Dressings
The simplest and most wholesome salad dressing is the French dressing, the basic one that may be used for all salads; it may be varied by using different kinds of herbs with different vegetables.

The French dressing:

Ingredients per person:
1 tablespoon sunflower *or* corn oil
1 teaspoon lemon juice

Some grated onion *or* garlic
 (optional)
1 teaspoon fresh *or* green-dried
 herbs

Mix all these ingredients well together, stirring vigorously to break up the oil.

Mayonnaise:

Ingredients:
1 egg yolk
1 cup (10 oz.) oil

Lemon juice according to taste

All ingredients must be of the same temperature. Whisk yolk; add oil drop by drop, whisking continually. The oil should not be too cold or too warm, or the mixture becomes too thick.

The above quantities are sufficient for 6 to 8 portions, or even more, if more oil is added. The mayonnaise will keep for days in a cool place and may be used for various dressings.

Mayonnaise dressing:

Ingredients per person:
1 tablespoon mayonnaise
1 teaspoon lemon juice

Some onion and garlic (if liked)
1 teaspoon fresh *or* green-dried
 herbs

Mix all these ingredients thoroughly but with a light hand.

Yogurt dressing (for those on a low-fat diet):

Ingredients per person:
2–3 tablespoons yogurt
A few drops of lemon juice

Some onion and garlic if liked
1 teaspoon fresh *or* green-dried
 herbs

Whisk all ingredients well together.

Yogurt and cream dressing:

Ingredients per person:
2 tablespoons yogurt
2 tablespoons cream

Few drops of lemon juice
1 teaspoon fresh *or* green-dried
 herbs

Whisk all ingredients well together.

Cream dressing:

Ingredients per person:
2 tablespoons cream   Some onion and garlic if liked
1 teaspoon cream cheese *or* yogurt   1 teaspoon fresh *or* green-dried
1 teaspoon lemon juice   herbs
    Whisk all ingredients well together.

Almond-puree dressing (for those who should avoid animal fat and protein):

Ingredients per person:
1 tablespoon nut purée *or* almond   Onion and garlic if liked
   purée   1 teaspoon fresh *or* green-dried
3 tablespoons water   herbs
1 teaspoon lemon juice
    Add drops of water to nut purée until it becomes whitish and of a creamy consistency; add remaining water and mix all ingredients together slowly and thoroughly.

Further simple dressings:

1. Ingredients:
4 tablespoons cream   1 teaspoon fresh *or* green-dried
1 tablespoon lemon juice   herbs
    Whisk cream well and add slowly the lemon juice, constantly stirring.

2. Ingredients:
3 tablespoons oil   1 tablespoon lemon juice
   (preferably sunflower oil)   1 teaspoon fresh *or* green-dried
                              herbs
    Add drops of lemon juice to the oil, constantly stirring.

3. Ingredients:
4 tablespoons cream   2 tablespoons apple juice
1 tablespoon lemon juice   1 teaspoon fresh *or* green-dried
                              herbs
    Add lemon juice slowly to the cream, constantly stirring.
    Add apple juice.

Vinaigrette (for a light diet, without egg, and using sunflower oil only):

Ingredients:
4 tablespoons sunflower oil   ½ chopped onion
2½ tablespoons lemon juice   1 hard-boiled egg, chopped
2 tablespoons water *or* vegetable   1–2 chopped gherkins, parsley, *or*
   stock   chives
Salt   1 tablespoon diced tomatoes
    Whisk all the ingredients together.

Suggestions for Herbs Used in Salad Dressings

Quoted by kind permission of the author from Ruth Bircher's *Eating Your Way to Health,* Faber and Faber, translated and edited by Claire Loewenfeld.

Raw Vegetables	Method	Dressing	Herbs
Cabbage lettuce	Use whole leaves	French dressing	Chives, onion
Lettuce (thinnings)	Use whole leaves	French dressing	Chives, onion
French endive	Cut in ½-in. strips	French dressing or mayonnaise	Chives, onion parsley*
Cos lettuce	Use leaves whole or shredded	French dressing or mayonnaise	Sweet basil, marjoram†
Lamb's lettuce	Use whole leaves	French dressing or mayonnaise	Onion
Cresses	Use whole leaves	French dressing or mayonnaise	Onion
Spinach	Shred	French dressing or mayonnaise	Peppermint
Cabbage: white savoy, sprouts, sauerkraut	Shred finely	French dressing or mayonnaise	Lovage, savory, thyme
Tomatoes	Slice *or* dice	French dressing or mayonnaise	Basil, thyme, dill
Cucumbers	Slice finely	French dressing or mayonnaise	Dill
Fennel	Slice finely *or* chop	French dressing or mayonnaise	Onion, chives
Pepper	Shred finely	French dressing or mayonnaise	Chives
Large black or white radishes	Slice *or* grate	French *or* cream dressing	Chives
Small red radishes	Grate *or* slice	French *or* cream dressing	Chives
Celery	Shred finely	French *or* cream dressing	Onion, chives
Baby summer squash *or* zucchini	Slice finely *or* grate roughly	French dressing or mayonnaise	Dill, basil
Carrots *or* young rutabaga, *or* other roots	Grate finely	French *or* cream dressing	Marjoram, lovage

* A small quantity of chives, parsley, and onion may be added to every raw salad.

† For proportions, see Guide, page 120.

Raw Vegetables	Method	Dressing	Herbs
Celeriac	Grate finely	Cream or French dressing	Basil, thyme
Beets, uncooked	Grate finely or roughly	Cream dressing or mayonnaise	Lovage, thyme, caraway seeds
Cauliflower	Separate florets, grate stalks	Cream dressing or mayonnaise	Basil, marjoram, walnuts
Chicory	Cut in ½-in. strips, shred	Cream or French dressing	Tarragon, marjoram
Jerusalem artichokes	Grate	Cream dressing	Thyme, lemon balm
Kohlrabi	Grate or chop finely	Cream or French dressing	Thyme, lovage
Red cabbage	Shred or grate finely	Cream or French dressing	Some grated apple, caraway seeds, lovage

SALAD RECIPES

Apart from the daily raw salad—its combination and dressings are discussed on pages 79–81—there are some salads which are especially recommended for healthy eating, either because of the reasons mentioned before, or because they contain young wild herbs or vegetables with special significance for certain troubles.

Wild Herb Salads

Tender young dandelion, sorrel, and nettle leaves may be served as a salad in a dressing of sunflower oil, lemon juice, and, if liked, a little finely chopped onion; onion green, parsley, and chives may be added. The leaves are usually tender until the plant starts to flower. Later they become hard and have less value. The wild herbs should only be collected on ground which has not been chemically treated.

The dandelion leaves are most useful because of their bitter principles in the case of trouble with liver and gall bladder.

Salad Made from Wild Herbs

This salad is made of three wild herbs and is of cosmetic importance because it contains yarrow.

Ingredients:

Equal parts of yarrow, plantain,   1 medium boiled cold potato
  and watercress   Salad dressing—consisting of lemon
A little garlic   and cream, *or* No. 2 of lemon and
½ oz. cucumber   oil, *or* No. 3 of lemon, cream, and
Fresh chopped or green-dried   a little apple juice (page 185)
  chives and parsley

Method:

1. Select and clean herbs.
2. Wash them carefully and allow to drain.
3. Cut yarrow and plantain into fine strips; leave watercress whole
   and arrange in a bowl.
4. Grate cucumber and grate potato on to greens in the bowl.
5. Add herbs and salad dressing.
6. Mix well.

Italian Dandelion Salad (*serves 4*)

Ingredients:

½ clove of garlic   A little salt
8 oz. young dandelion leaves   1 teaspoon each fresh chopped or
2 tablespoons sunflower oil   green-dried tarragon, chervil, and
1 tablespoon lemon juice   salad burnet

Method:

1. Rub the inside of a wooden salad bowl with a cut clove of garlic.
2. Tear the dandelion leaves into small pieces and place in salad
   bowl.
3. Gradually stir the oil with the lemon juice till blended; then add
   the herbs and stir well.
4. Pour over dandelion leaves.
5. Add the salt and toss the salad thoroughly with wooden salad
   servers.

Note: If liked, ripe black olives may be added to the salad. The
salad may be served with herb bread (page 290) or hot garlic bread.

Potato Salad with Dandelion (*serves 4-6*)

A main-dish salad, made more valuable by the addition of dandelion.

Ingredients:

1½ lbs. boiled potatoes
1 large chopped onion
1 clove garlic
1 teaspoon each fresh chopped or green-dried chervil and parsley
½ teaspoon each fresh chopped or green-dried lovage and sage
1 sour apple (peeled and diced)
4 tablespoons oil
2–3 tablespoons lemon juice
2 tablespoons hot stock
Some grated celeriac *or* chopped celery
A large quantity of young dandelion leaves (approx. 5 oz.) cut into fine strips

Method:

1. Peel potatoes while hot and cut them into thin slices.
2. Keep them hot on a saucepan with boiling water.
3. Chop onions finely.
4. Grate or mince garlic.
5. Chop herbs or reconstitute green-dried herbs in lemon juice.
6. Make a dressing out of oil, lemon juice, and the hot stock.
7. Add the herbs and the apple to the dressing.
8. Mix all ingredients well with the warm potatoes and celery.
9. Add strips of dandelion leaves and mix well.
10. Allow to cool.

Potato Salad with Sorrel

Instead of dandelion leaves, add finely cut strips of sorrel and reduce lemon juice to 1 to 2 tablespoons.

Three Chicory Salads with Three Different Dressings

[a] Chicory Salad

Chicory is one of the best winter vegetables. It is always fresh, stimulates the appetite because of its slightly bitter flavor, can easily be digested, is rich in vitamins, and contains bitter principles which are particularly valuable with liver and gall-bladder conditions. It is especially helpful to diabetics.

Ingredients:

8 oz. chicory, finely cut up
1 tablespoon sunflower oil
1 tablespoon sour cream
1 tablespoon tomato juice

1 teaspoon each fresh chopped or green-dried chives and lemon balm
Lemon juice (according to taste)
½ teaspoon each fresh chopped or green-dried tarragon and chervil

Method:

1. Wash chicory well and cut into small pieces.
2. Make a dressing out of all the other ingredients.
3. Mix with the chicory.

Note: The salad may be made without sour cream, just using sunflower oil and a little more lemon juice.

[b] Chicory Salad with Fruit and Herbs Dressed with Nut Mayonnaise

Ingredients:

8 oz. chicory
1 apple
1 banana
Nuts
Slices of orange
Sweet cicely and lemon balm

Nut mayonnaise:
1 tablespoon sunflower oil
1 teaspoon nut purée
2 tablespoons yogurt
1 teaspoon lemon juice
A little horseradish
Chives

Method:

1. Cut chicory and banana in slices.
2. Dice apple.
3. Chop nuts.
4. Mix with a dressing of nut mayonnaise and add herbs.
5. Decorate with orange slices.

Method for nut mayonnaise:

1. Add the sunflower oil drop by drop to the nut purée.
2. Add yogurt and lemon juice.
3. Mix in a little finely grated horseradish and plenty of chives.

[c] Chicory and Grapefruit with Cream-Cheese Nut Mayonnaise

Finely cut chicory and cut-up grapefruit may be served in the following dressing:

Ingredients:

Juice of 1 lemon
½ teaspoon nut purée
1 tablespoon curd *or* cream cheese

Juice of 1 orange
½ cup yogurt
Grated horseradish

Method:
1. Add lemon juice drop by drop to nut purée and then add cream cheese, orange juice, and yogurt.
2. Add horseradish according to taste.
3. Mix with chicory and grapefruit.

Fruit and Vegetable Salad with Nut Mayonnaise

Ingredients (salad):

1 orange	1 piece of celery *or* celeriac
1 apple	1 tomato
2 slices of pineapple	3 walnuts

Ingredients (nut mayonnaise):

2 tablespoons nut purée	Dash of yeast extract, diluted
2 tablespoons water	½ teaspoon fresh chopped or green-dried marjoram
1 tablespoon sunflower oil	
1 teaspoon lemon juice	A little grated horseradish
1 tablespoon yogurt	1 clove garlic

Method:
1. Add water in drops to nut purée until it becomes whitish and emulsifies.
2. Add the oil, lemon juice, and yogurt slowly and gradually with a few drops of yeast extract.
3. Mix in marjoram, horseradish according to taste, and the squeezed garlic.
4. Dice the fruit and vegetables and serve with nut mayonnaise decorated with nuts.

Fruit Salad with Nut Mayonnaise

Ingredients (salad):
(per person)

Nut mayonnaise:
(per person)

1 apple	1 teaspoon nut purée
1 banana	1 teaspoon sugar
1 orange	Milk
A few raisins	Water
1 teaspoon fresh chopped or green-dried sweet cicely	
½ teaspoon fresh chopped or green-dried lemon balm	

Method:
1. Cut the fruit, mix with herbs, and serve with nut mayonnaise.

Method for nut mayonnaise:
1. Stir nut purée with drops of water until it shows a creamy consistency.
2. Add more water and milk until the required consistency is reached.
3. Sugar according to taste.

Autumn Salad of Carrots, Radishes, and Kohlrabi, with Curd Mayonnaise (*serves 2-3*)

A nourishing yet healthy dressing, especially for those who should avoid animal fat.

Ingredients:
3 small carrots
1 small kohlrabi
1 small radish
1 tomato

Curd mayonnaise:
1 tablespoon sunflower oil
1 teaspoon nut purée
2 oz. curd (cream cheese with the cream taken off and no cream added)
3 tablespoons milk
1-2 tablespoons lemon juice
1 tablespoon grated apple
1 teaspoon chopped onion (if liked)
1 teaspoon chives
Pinch of paprika
3 tablespoons milk

Method:
1. Clean all vegetables thoroughly.
2. Grate them separately on a two-way grater.
3. Serve the vegetables in individual small bowls and decorate with tomato slices.
4. Serve with curd mayonnaise served in a small separate bowl.
   Note: Some parsley, lemon balm, or some coriander seed, improves the flavor of the carrots. A little caraway or paprika improves the radish. A little chopped onion may be added if the raw salad is to be eaten at once and not left for the evening or the next day.

Method for curd mayonnaise:
1. Add the oil drop by drop to the nut purée.
2. Add curd and milk and mix well.
3. Add lemon juice, grated apple, onion, and chives.
4. Add paprika according to taste.
   Note: Curd mayonnaise can be used with any other raw salad.

SAUERKRAUT is pickled cabbage—a valuable raw vegetable, particularly in winter, as it is rich in vitamin C. It is easier to digest raw than when cooked. Therefore, sauerkraut salad is important, particularly in diabetic diets, and may be eaten daily in small quantities as *hors d'oeuvre* or with the daily raw salad.

Sauerkraut may be bought in cans, but the best sauerkraut is made from home-grown cabbage in the autumn (see recipe below).

Homemade Sauerkraut

Ingredients:

4 lbs. cabbage (when shredded)
1 oz. coarse sea salt
Sticks of horseradish (if available)

1 handful caraway and juniper berries *or* mixed sauerkraut herbs and spices containing caraway seeds and juniper berries, dill, fennel, mustard seeds

1. Remove outer leaves and stalks of cabbage.
2. Shred cabbage, preferably using a wooden shredder with two blades, or an electric shredder.
3. Using a large earthenware jar (preferably with straight sides), put layers of cabbage alternately with sprinkled layers of salt, caraway, juniper, etc.
4. Add horseradish pieces from time to time.
5. Press down each layer with fists or a wooden masher until liquid rises and covers the cabbage.
6. Repeat this until the container is full.
7. Cover with a clean cloth, then with a wooden lid or a plate.
8. Put a heavy clean stone on top to press the lid firmly down.
9. Leave for 4 weeks, occasionally ladling out the rising liquid and washing the rim of the jar and the lid.

Note: After 4 weeks the sauerkraut is ready for use and may be eaten raw or cooked. At intervals of one week the cloth, lid, and stone must be washed. If the top layer of sauerkraut becomes soft and discolored, it must be removed.

As long as these instructions are carried out with care, the sauerkraut may be kept until the warm weather.

Sauerkraut and Apple Salad (*serves 3-4*)

Ingredients:

½ lb. sauerkraut
1 apple
½ cucumber

Chopped onion *or* leek
1 tablespoon sunflower oil
Some walnuts

Method:

1. Mix sauerkraut, diced apple, cucumber, and onions, or leek.
2. Mix all ingredients with the oil and with some nuts.

Note: All salad herbs may be added. If the sauerkraut is home-made, it is already pickled with sea salt, juniper berries, dill, fennel.

Apple-Horseradish Salad (*serves 2*)

Horseradish is often used for the preparation of raw salads because it is an excellent seasoning and it contains many plant ferments, which are important for health. For slimming, use yogurt.

Ingredients:

1 eating apple
½ teaspoon freshly grated horseradish

1 tablespoon sour cream *or* yogurt
Lemon juice

Method:

1. Grate apple and horseradish quickly on the same grater and mix with the other ingredients immediately.
2. Serve at once.

Salad Made of Lettuce and Herbs (*serves 4*)

Ingredients:

1 head of lettuce
2 tablespoons sunflower *or* corn oil
1 tablespoon lemon juice

1 teaspoon each fresh chopped or
green-dried chives and dill
Some finely chopped onion and/or
onion green
1 clove garlic

Method:

1. Wash lettuce well.
2. Allow to drain in a basket.
3. Make a dressing of oil, lemon juice, chopped herbs (and onion, if liked).

4. Rub salad bowl with garlic.
5. Prepare salad in a bowl and mix well with dressing.

Green Salad with Nasturtium Dressing (*serves 4*)

Supplies vitamin C and acts as a vegetable antibiotic (see page 142).

Ingredients:

Lettuce, endive *or* corn salad
Nasturtium flowers
Juice of 2 lemons
3 tablespoons salad oil

1 dessertspoon finely chopped fresh
  or green-dried nasturtium leaves
1 teaspoon finely chopped fresh or
  green-dried chervil
Salt

Method:

1. Arrange green salad leaves and nasturtium flowers in salad bowl.
2. Squeeze juice of the lemons into the salad oil in a small separate bowl and stir well.
3. Add nasturtium leaves, chervil, and a little salt, and mix again.
4. Pour this dressing over the salad and toss with wooden salad servers.
5. Serve immediately.

Radish Salad (*serves 4-6*)

This salad is most helpful for people suffering from gall-bladder and liver troubles, contains antibiotic qualities, and has a nourishing dressing, softening its flavor.

Ingredients:
1 large radish (white or black)

Method:
1. Wash and peel radish.
2. Grate coarsely onto a plate.
3. Sprinkle some salt on it.
4. Cover with second plate.
5. Allow to stand for half an hour.
6. Press out between hands and remove liquid.
7. Add special dressing.
   Note: May be served immediately or kept in the refrigerator. It should be dressed before serving.

Salad Dressing for Radish Salad

Ingredients:
6 tablespoons yogurt
3 tablespoons French dressing (sunflower oil and lemon)
3 tablespoons sour cream
1 tablespoon fresh chopped or green-dried chervil
1 tablespoon fresh chopped or green-dried tarragon

Method:
1. Mix all ingredients well.
2. Allow to permeate.
3. Keep in refrigerator until needed.

JUICES AS FOOD *(not as drink)*

Food of the highest quality for everyday health, as well as for the invalid and the baby

Freshly expressed uncooked and undiluted fruit and vegetable juices are one of the most concentrated and most health-giving foods. They cause no disturbance to the intestinal work of the body, as they are the most easily assimilated of all foods. There are now quick and easy ways of liquidizing all foods by mechanical means, such as electric liquidizers or, better still, electric juice extractors; and, as these uncooked juices are rich in vitamins and minerals, they are really an ideal nourishment, particularly for the invalid and the baby.

They are, of course, not meant to be the exclusive food of healthy human beings, who must have some roughage to function properly. However, in all cases when roughage must be avoided, such as in gastrointestinal conditions, for small babies who are not yet adjusted to digesting roughage, for old people whose teeth are no longer serviceable, or for all those who are rushed and strained—mothers, professional, and business people—juices are ideal. In the long run it is, of course, preferable that people should return to eating raw salads and fruit as soon as circumstances permit.

Juices are food and not drink and therefore should not be gulped down, but should be taken by spoon and possibly chewed a little so that the saliva can do its pre-digesting work. They not only provide the extra vitamins and minerals so important for people after operations and during convalescence, but they also strengthen the resistance against disease and infection. The juices should be taken preferably before eating anything cooked—before breakfast, and certainly before a cooked breakfast, and before lunch, dinner, or supper.

All fresh juice must be drunk immediately after preparation because the oxidization from the air destroys valuable substances in a short time. The stone fruit or berries, raw vegetables, leaf vegetables, and herbs should be finely chopped up before going into the juice extractor.

It is not easy to make vegetable juices really attractive, and no food will be enjoyed in the long run if it cannot be made attractive to take. This is where herbs have to play their great part. To make a vegetable juice or cocktail which is really a pleasure needs experience. It is an art to make this kind of juice, adding lemon, cream, cereal cream, and, above all, the right kind of herbs in the right combination.

Fruit juices may be served either unmixed, as in the case of oranges, tangerines, grapefruit, apples, pears, grapes, strawberries, raspberries, red currants, bilberries, peaches, apricots, and plums, or mixed as, for instance, orange and grapefruit, or juices made of soft fruit mixed with apple juice, or peach and apricot, or plum juice with apricot and mashed bananas, etc.

Apple juice. As apples are a fruit which fully ripens in most countries, they are usually available for juice. Quality has been improved, and different varieties are available throughout the year. After the apples have been washed, only the stalk and the top have to be removed; the apple may then be cut into pieces suitable for the type of juice extractor used. It contains vitamins A, B, and C, as well as sodium and other minerals. Owing to the rich content of pectin, the juice is agreeably mild. If we are the happy owners of good apple trees we can make our own apple juice throughout autumn and, often, winter. Lemon balm and sweet cicely combine with apple juice, as does an occasional pinch of lemon thyme.

Orange, lemon, and grapefruit juice are rich in vitamin C. They should, however, be fully ripe and if possible not chemically treated. Orange and lemon peels contain volatile oils and there-fore—if one can be sure that the skins have not been chemically treated—they may be squeezed with their cleaned peels, because the volatile oils can then be utilized. If we only want the pure juice, the fruit should be halved and then pressed on an orange press. Grapefruit juice stimulates the functions of liver, kidney, and glands and is one of the best aperitifs; its tartness is reduced by the use of sweet cicely.

Soft-fruit juices are rich in vitamin A and contain many minerals. If sweetened with honey or brown sugar and if diluted with a little water they are good for quenching thirst, particularly for people running a temperature. When making a freshly expressed juice of soft fruit, it should be first put through a blender then through a juice extractor.

Lemon juice should be immediately added to, or should form the basis for, each fruit juice to retain the color; it also adds vitamin C. Further additions of sugar, honey, cream, cereal cream, and the sweet herbs, such as sweet cicely and lemon balm, are suggested for improving the flavor.

Herbs. Sweet cicely is an excellent addition to take away the tartness of any fruit, particularly if sugar is not liked or is not advisable; and a little lemon balm will also help to sweeten and to give the slight lemon flavor which is so pleasant with every fruit juice. The herbs may go straight into the blender or juice extractor with the fruit.

Nourishing Additions. Cream, yogurt, nut purée, and almond purée add protein and make such juices a full meal. For those who find juices too tart or acid, they can be neutralized by using some cereal cream such as cream of rice or barley, and herbs such as sweet cicely and lemon balm.

Vegetable Juices. If served fresh, these have a high vitamin and mineral content. Each juice has in itself special value and provides special minerals and vitamins. Unmixed vegetable juices can be made of tomatoes, carrots, beets, white radishes, cabbage, celeriac— in fact of most leaf, root, and tuberous vegetables.

In preparing mixed vegetable juices, great care has to be taken to make the juices palatable. Too much of one ingredient may spoil the flavor of the juice. The best mixture is carrots, tomatoes, and spinach in either equal parts, or less spinach if spinach has been found too tart. Tomatoes and carrots, tomatoes and spinach, other mixtures and spinach may be combined according to individual taste. It is, however, important to add less of the green leaf vegetables than one would in a salad because these are apt to spoil the flavor. It is preferable to have a good basis of either tomatoes or carrots before adding green leaves or any other vegetables.

A mixed vegetable juice is often called a vegetable cocktail and is equally good for the invalid and as an aperitif before a low-calorie meal.

Various herbs will improve every vegetable juice, but should be used in small proportions; this has to be tried out for each individual taste. It is practically impossible to give hard-and-fast recipes, as there is variation not only in the individual appreciation but also in the intensity of flavor of each vegetable and herb.

The herbs suggested for flavor and for health are:

Chives	Dandelion	} particularly
Parsley	Young nettle	} in spring
Celery leaves	Some sorrel	

Herbs which will "make" a vegetable cocktail are:

Lemon balm	Sweet cicely
Tarragon	Lemon thyme (pinch)
Chervil	Basil (pinch)

Carrot juice is one of the most popular because it is easy to take, not too tart, and not too expensive. It contains vitamins A, B, and C; minerals such as calcium, iron, and iodine. Its natural content of sugar has energy-giving qualities. Carrots have always been recommended to improve the sight and are important for those who must be aware of night blindness.

It is the first juice on which a baby can be started to add some uncooked vegetables and thus vitamins and minerals to its feedings; as it has not an acid flavor babies are happy to take a few teaspoons every day, sweetened with honey. Pasteurized milk may be added.

Carrots should be well cleaned, scrubbed and scraped if young, or peeled. The juice can be made either by grating on a two-way grater onto a clean cloth and squeezing, or by putting the carrots into an electric blender, and then passing through a muslin or using a juice extractor. Parsley, a pinch of marjoram and lovage, lemon balm, tarragon, and chervil are excellent herbs to add.

Celery or celeriac juice has a diuretic effect and is therefore useful for people with a tendency to rheumatism and for those who want to lose weight. Mixed with a little lemon juice and some cream, it is usually liked very much; it contains vitamins A, B, C, and E, as well as minerals such as calcium and potassium. Chives, parsley, and lovage, and a pinch of basil and thyme improve the juice.

Beet juice is excellent for certain conditions of the liver and improves the hemoglobin of the blood. As beet juice has not an attractive flavor by itself, it is advisable to mix it with some dairy cream or cereal cream and a little lemon juice. Chives, lemon balm, dill, lovage, a pinch of thyme also add flavor.

Tomato juice is an excellent aperitif if herbs are added, such as basil, chervil, tarragon, parsley, celery leaves, or a dash of sweet cicely. The herbs may be mixed all together with the tomato juice or they may be tried out as separate additions. They give a superior flavor to tomato juice compared to any of the commercial sauce additions. Tomato juice contains vitamins A and B, and it is an excellent basis for other vegetable juices, particularly for those which have tart flavors.

Cabbage juice has been recently used as a therapy, particularly in America and Switzerland, as a help against duodenal ulcers. It is advisable to add a third of carrot juice, which doesn't reduce the effect but makes it more palatable. Cabbage juice provides calcium. Parsley, chives, lovage, caraway (pressed through a juice extractor) improve cabbage juice.

Radish juice, expressed from either the large white or black radish, is helpful in the case of gall-bladder and liver troubles, but may only be taken in small quantities. Chives, lemon balm, and sweet cicely, in not too small quantities, and chervil make radish juice milder and easier to take.

Spinach juice is helpful for anemic people, as it improves the hemoglobin of the blood, owing to its iron content, but it is tart in flavor and not easy to take. If wanted for therapeutic reasons, it should be either mixed with a cereal cream or added in small quantities to a vegetable soup. Small quantities may also be added to sweet vegetable juices such as carrot or tomato. Chives are helpful, as are chervil and peppermint.

Mixed Juices.

These combine a variety of nutrients which supplement each other.

Carrot and apple juice. Carrots and unpeeled apple are passed through the juice extractor, and chervil, sweet cicely, and lemon balm should be added.

*Celery, carrots, and apple with lemon balm and pinch of
lovage.*
Beets and apple with lemon balm and sweet cicely.
Cucumber and carrots with dill and chervil.
Tomato and carrots with pinch of basil and chervil.
*Carrots, tomato, and spinach with pinch of basil, chervil,
tarragon.*

When mixing these juices, nettle, dandelion, sorrel, and celery leaves may be added before extracting the juice. Also parsley, chives, onion green may be extracted with the juice for flavor. Chives or any other herbs such as parsley, chervil, a leaf of lovage, tarragon, very little marjoram or thyme may be added, unless specific herbs are suggested.

A little lemon juice and lemon balm are always a welcome addition, and sweet cicely may be used in generous quantities for added flavor and as sweetener to any juices made from vegetables combined with fruit, such as apple.

Some milk or the top of the milk improves and softens the flavor of all vegetable juices, and the added fat of the milk allows the better utilization of part of vitamin A.

Freshly expressed juices are best supplemented by an addition of:

Cereal Cream.

Raw juices which contain acids, such as citrus fruits, or have a tart flavor are best supplemented with one-third of cereal cream, which neutralizes tart fruit flavor and makes some of the juices easier to take, particularly for babies and people with gastrointestinal conditions.

It is best to prepare such a cereal cream beforehand and keep it in the refrigerator to add to freshly expressed juices.

Cream of rice or barley:
1 heaping teaspoon rice *or* rice flakes, *or* barley meal *or* flakes
1 cup (8 oz.) water

Mix cereal with cold water.
Bring to the boil.
Cook for 5 minutes, stirring constantly.
Allow to cool.

Cream of linseed:

1 tablespoon linseed   1 cup (8 oz.) water

Wash linseed in a sieve under running water.
Boil in the water for 10 minutes.
Strain and allow to cool.

Examples:

Orange juice with cereal cream:
Squeeze 1 orange; add some linseed cream; mix well, possibly in a blender.

Black-currant juice with cereal cream:

2–3 oz. black-currant juice (ex-   1–2 oz. rice *or* barley cream
- pressed in a juice extractor)   1 teaspoon lemon juice
Sweet cicely (expressed with the   Honey to sweeten
juice)   Top with dairy cream (if allowed)
2 oz. water (boiled and cooled if
for small children or invalids)

Tomato juice with horseradish:
Peel and grate a small piece of fresh horseradish and add to a glass of freshly expressed tomato juice. Add 1 teaspoon of rice *or* barley cream to soften the hot flavor of the horseradish.

Some fresh or reconstituted green-dried basil, *or* parsley and chives, may be extracted together with the tomatoes.

Horseradish contains some antibiotic substances which are of importance to the diet in cases of inflammation of the intestinal tract.

Juices with Protein—*A Complete Meal*

Some excellent fruit drinks may be made with or without a blender if fresh berries or freshly expressed fruit juices are used, or a concentrated juice such as black-currant juice.

Strawberry milk:

5 oz. milk   A little honey for sweetening
Some fresh strawberries
The same fruit milk may be made with all other berries. If the berries are tart, the milk may be sweetened by the addition of sweet cicely and honey.

Savory curd drink:
A nourishing liquid food, rich in protein, easy to digest:

5 oz. buttermilk
1 tablespoon curd
½ teaspoon nut purée
1 tablespoon concentrated fruit
juice

½ teaspoon grated horseradish
½ teaspoon each freshly chopped *or*
green-dried tarragon and chervil

All these ingredients should be mixed in a blender.

Other variations of such liquid foods are health giving, particularly in cases of chronic conditions of liver or in a post-operational diet.

5 oz. buttermilk
1 tablespoon curd
½ teaspoon nut purée

1 teaspoon tomato puree
Some fresh chopped or green-dried
basil

5 oz. milk
1 tablespoon curd

Some malt
Some fresh chopped or green-dried
sweet cicely

3 oz. milk
1½ oz. orange juice
1 tablespoon curd

1 teaspoon nut purée
1 teaspoon fresh chopped or green-
dried sweet cicely

Juices with Non-Animal Protein and Fat

Fruit-nut milk:

An excellent and valuable substitute for dairy milk and cream; according to analysis, similar to mother's milk.

Ingredients:
3 oz. water
2 oz. orange juice

1 teaspoon nut purée
1 teaspoon honey

Mix well equal quantities of nut purée and honey.
Add water drop by drop, stirring well.
This produces a creamy consistency which, through the addition of water and orange juice, eventually provides a fruit-nut milk.

A generous quantity of either fresh chopped or green-dried sweet cicely, *or* lemon balm, *or* chervil, will add to the flavor and value of these protein foods.

Freshly extracted juices of fresh black-currants, raspberries, or bilberries may be added to the nut purée.

Also vegetable juices flavored with herbs may be combined with nut purée.

For those who should avoid animal fat:

The nut fat becomes such a fine emulsion in the fruit-nut milk that it can be well tolerated even in the case of liver and gall-bladder trouble, provided that these are not in an acute state.

Nut purée made of hazelnuts contains 68 per cent fat.

Nut purée made of almonds contains 59 per cent fat.

Nut purée made of cashew nuts contains 49 per cent fat.

The cashew puree contains somewhat less fat than the almond or hazelnut purée and is therefore suggested for fruit-nut milk if there is a particular sensitiveness to fat.

MEATLESS AND HEALTH DISHES

The following dishes are grouped on their own because they provide—together with Salads and Juices given elsewhere in this chapter—further alternative menus for those interested in healthy eating.

Tomato Soup with Soya Dumplings

Ingredients:

Soup:
1 lb. tomatoes, diced
1 tablespoon sunflower oil
½ onion, finely chopped
1 tablespoon wholegrain flour
1 pt. vegetable stock
A little yeast extract
1 teaspoon each fresh chopped or green-dried basil and parsley

Dumplings:
⅓ oz. butter *or* margarine
1 slice of processed cheese
1 tablespoon whole-grain flour
1 tablespoon semolina
1 tablespoon soya flour
1 teaspoon bouquet for omelettes *or* 1 teaspoon mixed fresh chopped or green-dried parsley and chives

Method (soup):

1. Sauté onion in the heated oil until transparent.
2. Add basil and parsley.
3. Add the diced tomatoes and cook until tender.
4. Sprinkle with flour.
5. Smooth with vegetable stock.
6. Pass through a sieve and season with some yeast extract and a trace of sugar.

Method (dumplings):

1. Work fat with the processed cheese, flour, semolina, soya flour, and herbs into a paste.

2. Form small dumplings, wetting the teaspoons or the hands with hot water.
3. Allow to simmer for 3 minutes in the hot tomato soup.

Health Vegetable Soup

Ingredients:

2 tablespoons sunflower oil
3 small carrots, finely diced
1 small kohlrabi *or* other root, diced
1 stick of celery, diced *or* 1 small celeriac, diced
1 leek, chopped
3 small potatoes, diced
2–2½ pints vegetable broth *or* any stock

A small quantity of yeast extract
1 tablespoon fresh chopped or green-dried parsley
1 tablespoon mixed fresh chopped or green-dried celery leaves and lovage
A pinch of fresh chopped or green-dried summer savory and marjoram
If available, the finely diced root of Hamburg parsley

Method:

1. Sauté all vegetables in heated oil.
2. Add the herbs and sauté.
3. Add the diced potatoes and add vegetable stock.
4. Simmer until tender.
5. Before serving, the soup should be tasted and more herbs added if necessary.

Note: If necessary, the whole of this soup, when finished, may be placed in the blender and serve as a purée, which makes it easier to digest.

Nettle Soup

A health-giving soup, especially in spring. After nettles are cooked, they lose their sting.

Ingredients:

3 oz. young nettle leaves
1 tablespoon butter *or* oil
1 small onion, chopped
¾ lb. potatoes, peeled and diced
2–2½ pints stock

1 teaspoon mixed fresh chopped or green-dried marjoram, basil, sage
1 dessertspoon fresh chopped or green-dried lovage
½ tablespoon butter
2 tablespoons cream

Method:

1. Wearing rubber gloves, pick only young nettle leaves.
2. Select nettles and free from stalks; wash and allow to drip.
3. Cook in saucepan without additional liquid over low heat until tender.
4. Allow to cool, then chop.
5. Sauté onion in fat until golden.
6. Add potatoes and sauté again; add boiling stock.
7. When potatoes are cooked, add nettle and all herbs.
8. Allow to simmer for 15 minutes.
9. Allow to stand in warm place for 15 minutes.
10. Before serving, add butter and cream.

Tomato-Cottage Cheese Spread

Ingredients:

3 oz. curd *or* cottage cheese
3 tablespoons milk
1 tablespoon sunflower oil
1 teaspoon tomato puree

½ teaspoon nut purée
Lemon juice
1 teaspoon each fresh chopped or green-dried chives and basil
A little chopped onion, if liked

Method:

1. Add the oil drop by drop to nut purée.
2. Add lemon juice and all other ingredients.
3. Use as a spread on rye crackers *or* pumpernickel.

Red Radish Spread

Ingredients:

1½ oz. curd *or* cottage cheese
1 tablespoon sunflower oil
1 tablespoon milk
1 bunch small red radishes

Some lemon juice
1 teaspoon each fresh chopped or green-dried celery leaves and tarragon
A little salt (if permitted)

Method:

1. Grate radishes.
2. Mix with all other ingredients.
3. Use on rye bread, pumpernickel *or* rye crackers.

Carrot-Cheese Spread

Ingredients:

2 oz. curd (without cream) *or* cottage cheese
1–2 oz. grated carrot
Some milk
1 teaspoon sunflower oil
1 dessertspoon fresh chopped or green-dried parsley
1 teaspoon each fresh chopped or green-dried lemon balm and sweet cicely
A pinch of fresh chopped or green-dried marjoram
Lemon juice according to taste

Method:

1. Grate carrots finely on two-way grater.
2. Mix with curd, milk, and oil.
3. Season with the herbs and lemon juice.

Note: Best prepared in a blender. Used as a spread on rye crackers *or* pumpernickel.

Spinach Sauté

Ingredients:

½ lb. spinach
1 small onion
1 teaspoon fresh chopped or green-dried onion green
1 tablespoon sunflower oil
Lemon juice

A little vegetable stock
Yeast extract
1 teaspoon fresh chopped or green-dried lovage
1 teaspoon mixed of chopped nettle, dandelion, and sorrel (optional)

Method:

1. Sauté finely chopped onion and onion green in heated oil until transparent.
2. Add two-thirds of the washed spinach and allow to cook for 5 minutes in covered saucepan.
3. Put this spinach, together with the remaining uncooked spinach, into the blender and make into a puree for some seconds.
4. If the spinach has not provided enough liquid for the blender, add some vegetable stock.
5. Before serving, season with some lovage and wild herbs, according to taste.

Chicory au Gratin

Ingredients:

½ lb. chicory
1 tablespoon sunflower oil
1 oz. cheddar *or* Gruyère cheese
Yeast extract

1 teaspoon each fresh chopped or green-dried parsley, and onion green *or* chives
1 teaspoon each fresh chopped or green-dried chervil and fennel

Method:

1. Cut chicory fairly coarse.
2. Heat oil in a flameproof dish and add parsley and onion green.
3. Sauté chicory in this for 5 minutes.
4. Add other herbs and season with yeast extract.
5. Cover with the grated cheese and place under grill for 20 minutes.

Vegetarian Stew

Ingredients:

1 cooked beet, diced
1 large apple, diced
1 cucumber pickled in brine, diced
1 tablespoon sunflower oil
¼ pint vegetable stock
1 tablespoon herb bouquet for soups and stews
   or 1 tablespoon mixed fresh chopped or green-dried parsley and lovage
¼ teaspoon each fresh chopped or green-dried marjoram, thyme, and chervil
Caraway seeds
Lemon juice
Yeast extract (diluted with a little water)
1 tablespoon sour cream

Method:

1. Sauté cooked beet, apple, and cucumber in the vegetable oil.
2. Add vegetable stock.
3. Allow to cook for 5 minutes on low heat.
4. Add herbs, caraway, lemon juice, and yeast extract.
5. Add sour cream.

Strawberry Cream (Milk-protein food)

Ingredients:

3 oz. curd *or* cottage cheese
6 oz. fresh strawberries
  (reserve a few for decorating)
2 tablespoons milk

1 tablespoon brown sugar (or according to taste)
1 teaspoon each fresh chopped or green-dried lemon balm and sweet cicely

Method:

1. Wash and hull strawberries.
2. Pass the berries through a sieve together with the herbs, curd, or cottage cheese and milk, or mix it all in a blender.
3. Add sugar according to taste.
4. Decorate with some of the best fruit.

Note: This is an especially good sweet for everyone. Even children find it delicious, and it does provide vital substances for their growth and well-being.

Banana-Cheese Cream

Ingredients:

3 oz. curd *or* cottage cheese
2 small bananas
1 tablespoon fruit juice *or* syrup

4 tablespoons milk
Linomel*

Method:

1. Mash the bananas with a fork.
2. Beat until frothy.
3. Add the curd and all other ingredients to the banana froth.
4. Stir until smooth.
5. Decorate with Linomel and banana slices.

---

* Available at some health-food stores. Linomel is made of linseed, crusted with pure bees' honey. It is a valuable addition to fruit and cream cheese and tastes very good.

Chapter 5

*H*erbs in *I*nvalid *C*ooking

DURING ILLNESS and convalescence food can play a decisive part in fighting a condition and speeding up recovery. In spite of the special study made of invalid food, the very great help provided by herbs is barely understood. Where we have to restrict certain foods, such as salt, in feeding a patient with heart trouble, or are trying to tempt a convalescent after an operation, far too little use is made of this important aid. The first-class catering trade—the livelihood of which depends upon the flavor of its dishes—may have shelves full of drums or glass jars of green-dried herbs; yet the hospital and nursing-home diet kitchens are not so much concerned with the help which first-class fresh or green-dried herbs can give to the diet in nursing a patient back to health. With some "culinary cunning," to which herbs are of such significant help, so much could be done for the invalid.

However, when the invalid is at home, the housewife or mother can tempt the patient with herbs to encourage eating. This requires skill in presenting food which not only tastes good but is wholesome and helps recovery. Herbs should make invalid food far from dull, even when salt-restricted diets have to be followed. And they provide important minerals, trace elements and essential oils.

The following recipes will show in which way herbs can be used as an instrument for restoring the patient to full health.

Breakfast Frumenty (*serves* 2)

Ingredients:
3–4 heaped tablespoons whole-wheat flakes

Lemon juice and 1 teaspoon honey *or* orange juice

4 tablespoons milk *or* yogurt
2 apples

1 teaspoon each fresh chopped or green-dried lemon balm and sweet cicely
1 teaspoon milled nuts (optional)

Method:

1. Mix wheat flakes with milk or yogurt.
2. Grate the apples into this.
3. Flavor with lemon juice and honey (according to taste) or with orange juice.

Note: Apple is always an ideal supplement to whole cereals, and this is the idea on which the famous Bircher muesli is based. Apples are available almost the whole year. When grating apples on a stainless two-way grater it is difficult to avoid their becoming brown, because the apples oxidate so quickly in contact with the air. Mix them quickly with the prepared wheat flakes and then serve *as quickly as possible.*

This breakfast dish may also be made with strawberries, peaches, apricots, plums, oranges, or pears, cut up finely. Any berries should be mashed with a fork beforehand.

Wheat Breakfast (*serves* 2)

Ingredients:

1½ oz. freshly crushed wheat *or* cracked wheat*
Lemon juice
Water for soaking

4–6 prunes
1½ apples
1 teaspoon each fresh chopped or green-dried sweet cicely and lemon balm
1 pinch fresh chopped or green-dried lemon thyme

Method:

1. Wheat and prunes should be soaked overnight in separate bowls.
2. In the morning, cut the prunes finely and, together with lemon juice, add to the soaked wheat.
3. Then grate apples into it and mix all quickly.

Note: Any freshly crushed wheat will become more digestible when warmed for 15 minutes over steam. Instead of prunes, dried apricots, raisins, or mixed dried fruits may be used. A little light cream (shortly before serving) will improve the flavor.

* Available at health-food shops.

Whole Cereal-Apple Breakfast (*serves* 2)

A valuable breakfast.

Ingredients:

1½–2 oz. cracked whole wheat* *or* freshly crushed whole wheat
¼ pint water
¼ pint milk *or* some yogurt
1 teaspoon honey
1 teaspoon fresh chopped or green-dried sweet cicely

Method:

1. Soak the wheat overnight in water.
2. Add a little water in the morning and cook over low heat, constantly stirring.
3. Allow to cook for 3 to 5 minutes.
4. Sweeten with honey and sweet cicely.
5. Grate an apple into the porridge.
6. Add some fresh milk or yogurt before eating.

Mixed Vegetable Drinks with Milk

The following drinks are a liquid milk-protein food, and are important for post-operational cases and for providing nourishing food to an invalid without being a burden to the digestion. The drinks are best mixed in a blender; the vegetable juices may be varied, and to all of them some freshly chopped or green-dried herbs should be added according to taste or by using the herbs suggested with individual vegetable juices (see page 97). If yogurt or buttermilk is preferred, some of this may be added instead of some of the milk. More details about making vegetable juices are given on pages 96–97.

(a) 2 oz. milk
   1 oz. spinach juice
   ¾ oz. tomato juice
⅓ oz. celery juice
A few drops of lemon juice
Herbs

(b) 2 oz. milk
   1 oz. carrot juice
   1 oz. celery juice
A few drops of lemon juice
Herbs

* Available at health-food shops.

(c) 2 oz. yogurt *or* buttermilk
    1 oz. carrot juice

A little grated horseradish
A few drops of lemon juice
Herbs

(d) Enriched milk-protein food

3 oz. milk
1 tablespoon curd
½ teaspoon nut purée

1 teaspoon tomato puree
Herbs

(e) Beet milk

An excellent milk food for the anemic made palatable by milk.

2 oz. milk
½ oz.. freshly expressed beet juice
¾ oz. apple juice

½ teaspoon honey
½ teaspoon lemon juice
Herbs

Spreads

(a) Cheese spread (oil-protein food)

Ingredients:

1½ oz. curd *or* cottage cheese
½ portion processed cheese
2 tablespoons milk
1 teaspoon sunflower oil

1 pinch paprika
1 teaspoon finely chopped onion
1 teaspoon fresh chopped or green-dried chives

Method:

1. Mix curd, cheese, milk, and oil in blender until creamy.
2. Add paprika, according to taste.
3. Add onion and chives last.

(b) Horseradish-cheese Spread

Ingredients:

1 pkt. soft cheese (gervais, etc.)
2 teaspoons grated horseradish (approx.)
1 tablespoon single cream *or* top of the milk
1 teaspoon fresh chopped or green-dried lovage

A pinch of each fresh chopped or green-dried thyme and summer savory
Slices of tomato for decoration
Fresh chopped or green-dried basil for decoration

Method:

1. Mix all ingredients well together.
2. Spread on rye or other crackers.
3. Decorate with tomato slices and sprinkle with basil.

Diet Cereal Soup (oatmeal reinforced with nut purée)

Ingredients:
2 tablespoons whole oat flakes *or* whole oatmeal
1 teaspoon nut purée
1 teaspoon each fresh chopped or green-dried parsley and lovage
2 teaspoons bouquet for soups and stews
or 2 teaspoons mixed fresh chopped or green-dried chives, celery leaves, basil, and chervil (see GUIDE, page 119, for proportions).
Yeast extract

Method:
1. Start cooking oatmeal in cold water; add parsley and lovage and allow to boil for 10 minutes.
2. Pass through a sieve.
3. Add drops of water to nut purée until it is of a creamy consistency; then add to the soup.
4. Add some unsalted yeast extract and bouquet for soups and stews *or* 2 teaspoons mixed herbs.
   Note: If used for salt-restricted diet, use more yeast extract; otherwise season with salt.

Invalid Chervil Soup

Ingredients:
1 small onion
1-2 tablespoons oil
A good handful of fresh chopped chervil
or 1-3 tablespoons green-dried chervil
1 potato
Hot vegetable *or* yeast stock up to 1 pint

1 teaspoon fresh chopped or green-dried parsley
½ teaspoon fresh chopped or green-dried celery leaves
Lemon juice
1 clove garlic, minced

Method:
1. Heat oil carefully; add finely chopped onion and sauté.
2. Add fresh or green-dried chervil and sauté.
3. Grate raw potato into this mixture.
4. Add hot stock.
5. Allow to simmer on low heat for 5-10 minutes.
6. Add finely chopped parsley and celery leaves.
7. Flavor with drops of lemon juice and the minced garlic.
   Note: This soup avoids flour, as it uses potatoes for thickening and is therefore more valuable for certain diets or for the invalid.

Cooked Carrots

Ingredients:

¾ lb. carrots
1 tablespoon sunflower oil
1 tablespoon fresh chopped or
  green-dried parsley
1 teaspoon mixed fresh chopped or
  green-dried lovage and lemon
  balm

A pinch of fresh chopped or green-
  dried marjoram
1 teaspoon lemon juice
A little yeast extract
Water or vegetable stock
Fresh parsley (if liked)

Method:

1. Clean the carrots carefully; wash and cut into small sticks or cubes.
2. Heat oil in a saucepan.
3. Add parsley.
4. Add carrots and sauté.
5. Add all other herbs, lemon juice, and yeast extract.
6. If necessary, add a little vegetable stock; cook until tender.
7. Add freshly chopped parsley before serving (if liked).

Calves' Liver from the Grill

Ingredients:

1 slice of calves' liver
1 slice of apple
1 teaspoon sunflower oil

Sea salt
Horseradish
1 tablespoon cream

Method:

1. Brush the slice of liver with sunflower oil on both sides.
2. Add the slice of apple.
3. Put under hot grill and grill for 6–8 minutes.
4. When grilling is finished, season with a little sea salt.
5. Serve with grated horseradish mixed with the cream.

Apricot Dumplings with Soya Flour

Ingredients:

3 peeled boiled potatoes
2 tablespoons whole-grain flour
1 tablespoon whole semolina
1 tablespoon soya flour
1 egg

4 fresh apricots
4 lumps of sugar
1 teaspoon fresh chopped or green-
  dried sweet cicely

Method:

1. Grate the peeled potatoes and mix with flour, semolina, and soya flour.
2. Mix with the egg and knead well.
3. Divide the dough into four parts.
4. Take the pits out of the apricots and put a lump of sugar and ¼ teaspoon sweet cicely in each.
5. Roll out the dough and wrap the apricots in pieces of it.
6. Drop the dumplings into boiling water.
7. Allow to simmer for 10 minutes on low heat.
8. Serve with stewed apricots.
   Note: Dessert plums may be used instead of apricots.

Sweet Fennel (Finocchio)

Ingredients:

2 sweet fennel
1 tablespoon sunflower oil
¼ pint vegetable stock
1 tablespoon sour cream
1 teaspoon fresh chopped or green-dried fennel leaves

1 teaspoon fresh chopped or green-dried parsley
½ teaspoon each fresh chopped or green-dried chervil, tarragon, and borage (optional)
Yeast extract

Method:

1. Clean fennel and take away the outer parts.
2. Heat sunflower oil carefully and add the cut-up fennel and parsley.
3. Sauté.
4. Add some vegetable stock.
5. Allow to simmer on low heat.
6. Add sour cream, fennel, and other herbs.
7. Add a little yeast extract.

Baked Rosemary Potatoes

Method:

(*a*) 1. Brush potatoes well under running water to clean.
   2. Halve lengthwise.
   3. Dip surfaces on to rosemary leaves.
   4. Place cut surfaces downwards on a tin which has not been buttered.
   5. Allow to bake in the oven or under the grill until ready.
(*b*) 3. Dip cut surfaces onto rosemary leaves and salt.
   4. Place cut surfaces down on an oiled flat tin.
   5. Brush with vegetable oil and bake at 350° until tender (½ to ¾ hour).

Risotto with Tomato Sauce

Ingredients:

Risotto:
1 teaspoon oil
1 cup rice
½ teaspoon fresh chopped or green-
  dried rosemary
1 pinch of curry
3 cups of water
½ teaspoon marigold petals, if
  available
1 pinch yeast extract, preferably
  salt free

Tomato sauce:
¾ lb. tomatoes
Lemon juice
Garlic, minced
Paprika
½ teaspoon fresh chopped or green-
  dried basil

Method (risotto):

1. Heat the oil.
2. Sauté rice with rosemary and curry for a few minutes.
3. Add the water and marigold petals.
4. Allow to come to the boil.
5. Then put into a slow oven (300° F.) for 25 minutes.
6. Before serving, add yeast extract according to taste.

Method (tomato sauce):

1. Cut tomatoes into quarters and then put through a sieve.
2. Season with lemon juice, paprika, garlic, and basil.
3. Put into fireproof container and warm over a saucepan of boiling water.

Asparagus with Scrambled Egg

Ingredients:

Asparagus:
½-¾ lb. fresh asparagus, or 1 small
  can white asparagus, drained
Paprika
½ oz. fresh melted butter
1 teaspoon fresh chopped or green-
  dried tarragon

Scrambled egg:
2 eggs
1 tablespoon milk
1 pinch of sea salt
Fresh chopped or green-dried
  chives
Chives and parsley for garnishing

Method (asparagus):

1. Clean and trim fresh asparagus; cook in boiling water until
   tender (approximately 8 minutes). If canned asparagus is used,
   simply heat in its liquid 3 or 4 minutes.
2. Drain.
4. Serve on a flat dish.

4. Sprinkle paprika and tarragon in two strips each over the flatly arranged asparagus.
5. Serve with the butter.

Method (scrambled egg):
1. Beat eggs with the milk.
2. Add salt and chives and beat well again.
3. Butter a small shallow container, fill with the eggs, and allow to set in a pan containing boiling water.
4. Garnish with chives and parsley.

Rice Pudding

Ingredients:

½ cup rice
½ oz. butter *or* vegetable fat
1 tablespoon sugar
2 eggs
3 oz. curd *or* cottage cheese
3 tablespoons milk
1 tablespoon raisins

Grated peel of lemon
Sugar in which vanilla pods have been stored
1 teaspoon each of mixed fresh chopped or green-dried sweet cicely and lemon balm

Method:
1. Put rice into boiling water in a saucepan and allow to simmer for 20 minutes, or until cooked.
2. Pour into a sieve and rinse with cold water.
3. Allow to drain well.
4. Beat butter, sugar, and egg yolks until creamy.
5. Add curd and milk and, lastly, rice and raisins.
6. Add lemon peel, vanilla sugar, and herbs according to taste.
7. Add white of egg beaten to a stiff froth.
8. Butter fireproof dish and bake quickly in the oven.

Orange-Cheese Cream

Ingredients:

3 oz. curd *or* cottage cheese
1 orange
1 teaspoon nut purée
1 teaspoon honey
2 tablespoons milk

½ teaspoon fresh chopped or green-dried sweet cicely
½ teaspoon fresh chopped or green-dried lemon balm

Method:
1. Squeeze the orange.
2. Add all other ingredients.
3. Mix well, possibly in a blender.

Cherry Cream

The cherries in this recipe, particularly if made in a blender, are so finely dissolved that they can be tolerated by sensitive people who suffer from liver or gall-bladder conditions. If, technically speaking, the cherries are totally mashed into a puree, all the old restrictions on stone fruit do not apply.

Ingredients:

3 oz. curd
6 oz. cherries
3 tablespoons milk
1 tablespoon brown sugar

1 teaspoon fresh chopped or green-dried sweet cicely
½ teaspoon fresh chopped or green-dried lemon balm
Retain a few cherries for decoration

Method:
1. Stone the cherries.
2. Pass through a sieve, or mash in a blender.
3. Mix cherries well with other ingredients.
4. Decorate with the remaining cherries.
   Note: The curd for this sort of sweet must always be very fresh and should not taste bitter.

Fresh Fruit Mold (*serves 2*)

Ingredients:
¼ pint freshly expressed juice of raspberries, blackberries, red or black currants, grapes
or ¼ pint juice of orange and grapefruit, *or* lemon—half each (strained)
¼ pint water
Sugar according to taste
1 teaspoon fresh chopped or green-dried sweet cicely
½ teaspoon fresh chopped or green-dried lemon thyme
2 tablespoons cornflour

Method:
1. Mix fruit juice with the water.
2. Bring two-thirds of the mixture to the boil.
3. Add sugar and herbs.
4. Smooth cornflour with remaining cold liquid.
5. Add to the boiling juice and boil until clear, stirring all the time.
6. Pour into mold rinsed with cold water.
7. Leave to set.
8. Turn out and serve with thin or whipped cream, if desired.

PART TWO

HERBS FOR COOKERY

Twenty-four Herbs in a Chest

A Guide to the Strength of Individual Herbs

HERBS HAVE individual flavors, varying immensely in kind and strength. Some have to be used in large quantities; others in very small ones. It is practically impossible to give exact quantities for the use of herbs. In no other field do tastes differ quite so much. The palate changes when using herbs and, as it becomes more discriminating, wants either more or less of certain herbs.

The following table is intended to be a basic guide to avoid errors caused by unknown pungencies and is meant to be a warning and encouragement at the same time. It is often suggested by herb books and recipes that it is better to use less rather than more herbs. This is not correct, as erring on the other side may not make the best use of the flavoring qualities of an herb. Even more caution is advised when dealing with dried herbs. Though this warning may be justified when using powdered herbs, it is certainly not a precaution to be used with green-dried herbs, which reconstitute to the size of fresh chopped herbs, and are similar in strength of aroma to the fresh herbs.

Therefore, once the nature of an herb has been fully understood, the actual quantity has to be determined by its individual strength and one's own taste, and this has to be discovered by one's own experience; this table is merely to guide one's first steps. This same approach should be applied when using herb mixtures, unless one feels one can trust a reliable bouquet of a specialist firm, mixed by an expert.

BASIL	.. .. ..	Sparingly.
BAY LEAVES	.. ..	Cautiously, until familiar with flavor.

CELERY LEAVES	..	..	As much as desired to give a celery flavor.
CHERVIL	.. ..	..	Generously.
CHIVES	.. ..	..	According to taste.
DILL ..	.. ..	..	Wisely; sometimes generously.
ELDER FLOWER	..	..	Lavishly.
FENNEL	.. ..	..	Wisely.
LEMON BALM	..	..	Lavishly.
LOVAGE	.. ..	..	Economically, until familiar with flavor.
MARIGOLD	.. ..	..	Lavishly.
MARJORAM	.. ..	..	Judiciously at first—easily over-powers other flavors.
MINT ..	.. ..	..	Generously.
NASTURTIUM LEAVES		..	With caution.
ONION GREEN	..	..	According to taste.
PARSLEY	.. ..	..	Generously.
ROSEMARY	.. ..	..	Economically.
SAGE ..	.. ..	..	With discretion.
SALAD BURNET	..	..	Generously.
SORREL	.. ..	..	Carefully.
SUMMER SAVORY	..	..	Carefully, until familiar with its strength.
SWEET CICELY	..	..	Lavishly.
TARRAGON	.. ..	..	Judiciously—beware of hidden tang.
THYME	.. ..	..	With care.

General Information

Basil (Ocimum basilicum)

Basil, strong and powerful, is king among herbs. It is invaluable in the kitchen, because it can make an impact on so many dishes and gives a sweet, delicate pungency to food. Growing abundantly in India, where it is used a great deal in curries, it also grows wild in the hot Mediterranean sun; there it enhances tomato dishes of every kind and rarely is one served without it. Newcomers to this herb should, however, use it carefully as otherwise it may dominate other flavors.

Common or sweet basil is an annual, growing to about 3 feet high with quadrangular stems and light green leaves of a fair size (3 in.

by 1½ in.), grey/green beneath and spotted with dark oil cells when held against the light. The flowers are whitish and appear in whorls in the axils of the leaves. It is a difficult plant to grow because of its great need for warmth and nourishment. It needs a well-drained light soil and a very sheltered place, possibly sloping to the south. It can only be started after all the frost has disappeared and in many ways it is less risky and does better in pots in a fairly rich soil. Its excellence and the small quantity needed more than compensate for the trouble needed to grow it. Basil may be added to egg, cheese, and fish dishes and to any sausage mixture.

Years ago farmers' wives grew pots of basil to give to their visitors, a gift which was gladly accepted because, apart from the basil's use as a flavoring, the pots were known to keep flies away; for this quality the French still put pots of basil on the tables of their sidewalk restaurants. If basil leaves are allowed to permeate wine, this makes an excellent digestive tonic; and the crushed leaves used as a snuff clear the head in cases of headaches and nasal cold.

Basil is one of the few herbs which increases its flavor when it is cooked. While it may be added liberally on tomatoes for use in sandwiches, in cooking it should be used SPARINGLY.

Pizza Napolitana with Basil
  (page 293)
Spaghetti with Tomato Meat
Sauce
  (page 258)

Stuffed Tomato with Basil
  (page 172)
Genoese Pesto to be used with
  Spaghetti
  (page 257)

Day-to-day dishes for which basil is traditionally used:

APPETIZERS	Tomato juice; shrimp and prawn cocktails.
SALAD AND SALAD DRESSINGS	Tomato or cucumber salad; in French dressing. Freshly chopped fresh or green-dried basil, possibly reconstituted, may be added to fresh tomato or mixed green salad or to their dressing.
EGG AND CHEESE DISHES	Creamed eggs, cheese soufflés, and fondue.
SOUPS	Tomato, minestrone, pea and turtle soup.
FISH	Sole, shellfish, and mackerel. With melted butter as a sauce or a seasoning for fish and shellfish.

	Basil, parsley, onion green, and summer savory may be added to the water in which fish is to be boiled or poached.
MEAT	All meats—sausages and stuffings. Finely chopped or shredded green-dried basil may be sprinkled onto fried tomato slices while they are still very hot as a garnish for pork chops.
POULTRY AND GAME	Poultry, rubbed on before cooking —in chicken and rabbit stews; with game.
VEGETABLES, RICE, AND PASTA	All tomato dishes; with mushrooms and fungi. Flavors insipid vegetables; also spaghetti and rice.
SAUCES, DIPS, AND ACCOMPANIMENTS	Basil sauce, basil butter. Finely chopped fresh or green-dried basil and parsley may be added to any herb butter.
SANDWICHES	Tomato sandwiches.

Bay leaves (Laurus nobilis)

Bay leaves come from the handsome laurel, which, in ancient times, was a symbol of glory for poets and heroes—hence the Poet Laureate. Nowadays its glorifies the flavor of many dishes. It is the only one of its genus which was and is used in cookery. The volatile oil of the sweet bay provides an aromatic, slightly bitter, but important flavor, and stimulates the appetite.

The shiny leathery leaves are typical of this evergreen, aromatic, shrub-like tree, which may reach a height of about 30 feet and is usually pyramid shaped. The dark green leaves are a pale yellowish green on the underside, and the flowers are greenish yellow, growing in small umbels.

The bay tree needs some protection, and for this reason grows well in the shade of other trees. It cannot withstand long periods of severe frost. However, if the leaves go brown because of frost it is wise to keep the tree or shrub until well into the following summer, as it may grow green leaves again. Small trees can be successfully grown in tubs in moderately rich soil and in a sunny position and taken indoors during winter, or into a sunny greenhouse. The leaves may

in any case be picked all the year round, though it is quite easy and
better to dry them; then the flavor becomes stronger.

They should be dried in the dark, not in the sun, in thin layers,
and must retain the exact color and not become brown. They should
be pressed under a board and packed into hard, dark, uncrushable
containers, not bags, as otherwise volatile oil exudes all the time.

Bay leaves are an important part of the bouquet garni necessary
for roasting fowls and in stuffings; shredded, they are an important
part of the green-dried bouquet for poultry and game, and the bouquet for fish; marinades for poultry and game, especially venison,
which has the reputation of being tough, should consist of oil, wine,
and herbs, to which shredded bay leaves or half a bay leaf has been
added. They should always be added to court bouillon or to stock
in which fish has been boiled. A bay leaf alone gives a new taste to
the old-fashioned vegetable soup. It gives a subtle flavor when boiled
with vegetables, such as artichokes, aubergine (eggplants), etc., even
potatoes; and it improves tomato juice and tomato soup. Two leaves
may be added to the water for boiling ham and tongues.

The bouquet garni, however, is most often used and for so many
dishes. This should contain 2 sprigs of parsley, 2 of chervil, 1 of
marjoram, 1 of thyme, and ½ a bay leaf. While the proportion of
bay leaf to other herbs seems small, it should be remembered that
it is a strong herb, that it becomes stronger when shredded, and for
all purposes it should be used CAUTIOUSLY. Experience must be allowed
to be the guide.

Chilled Salmon   Sauerkraut Spareribs
  (page 211)   (page 228)
Chicken in Vegetable Soup
  (page 205)

Day-to-day dishes for which bay leaves are traditionally used:

APPETIZERS	In aspics; also seafood, and tomato juice—dried and shredded.
SALADS AND SALAD DRESSINGS	French dressing for green or vegetable salads.
SOUPS	Beef, lamb, mutton stock; chicken soup—dried and shredded. One whole leaf or shredded equivalent may be added to bouquet garni.
FISH	Most fish and shellfish; court bouillon for poaching.

MEAT

Beef, lamb, tripe, or veal stews. Corned beef; all smoked meat, such as ham and tongue, for boiling; pickled meat; marinades for meat. As part of bouquets for beef, lamb, or mutton stock; in court bouillon for poaching. One or two leaves may be put in bottom of roasting pan.

POULTRY AND GAME

Chicken fricassee and stews. For all roasted birds, one or two leaves may be put in the roasting pan. Chicken pies. All poultry stuffings (dried and shredded). Almost any game. All marinades for game, particularly for venison.

VEGETABLES,
    RICE, AND PASTA

Spaghetti dishes and almost all their sauces. In the water for boiling potatoes and carrots. Artichokes, beets, eggplant. Pilaffs.

SAUCES

Meat, tomato, and wine sauces.

SWEETS AND DESSERTS

Custards and creams.

Celery leaves (Apium graveolens)

Celery leaves are a seasoning of such worldwide reputation that they are a necessary addition to the herb and spice shelf. They are actually a by-product of growing celery or celeriac as a vegetable, but the season during which celery leaves are available is very short. Only when the plants are ready to be harvested can the leaves be used, and it is therefore a great help that celery leaves are also available green-dried. They are wanted in all recipes where celery flavor is called for; and most soups, sauces, and stews are much better for a liberal addition of celery leaves.

The celery plant was originally a medicinal plant and is rich in various vitamins and mineral salts, and also has many active principles. Celery also has an effect on the whole glandular system, stimulates the digestion, and is good for gout and rheumatism. All parts of the plant are edible—the leaves, stalks and roots, either raw or cooked. The leaves are as tasty and aromatic as the stalks, and even the seeds have the same nutty flavor. Their sharp pungency has, at

the same time, an almost sweet flavor. They are an excellent seasoning for diabetics and for anyone on a salt-reduced diet.

If celery leaves are dried it is most important to retain the color
and the specific flavor. To soups, sauces, stews, clear broth, and stuffings, celery leaves may be added at the last moment. They should
not cook more than three minutes with any of these dishes. The
stalks of celery and the roots of the celeriac are also used chopped
and grated raw in many salads, and when cooked give a basic flavor
to any good strong soup. Enough celery leaves should be used to
provide a celery flavor.

Cold Cucumber Soup   Macaroni and Shrimp Salad
   (pages 199–200)   (pages 174–75)
Celery Sticks with Cream
   Cheese (pages 164–65)

Day-to-day dishes for which celery leaves are traditionally used:

APPETIZERS	Cheese, fish, meats, shellfish, and all canapés. Add one teaspoon chopped celery leaves to ingredients. Use leaves and stalks as garnish.
SALADS AND SALAD DRESSINGS	Blend chopped celery leaves with all fruit and vegetable salads before adding dressing. As a garnish.
EGG AND CHEESE DISHES	Add chopped or green-dried celery leaves to creamed, deviled, and stuffed eggs, and omelettes. Blend chopped celery leaves with soft cheeses.
SOUPS, STEWS, AND CASSEROLES	Cream, fish and shellfish chowders, meat and vegetable dishes. Stews of fish, meats, shellfish, especially clam or oyster. Add one-fourth cup chopped celery leaves to milk when preparing fish, shellfish, or game stews.
FISH	Court bouillon. Stuffed fish. As a garnish.
MEAT	All meat dishes. Place celery leaves in pot with ingredients; may be removed before serving. Stuffings.

POULTRY AND GAME	All game ragouts. All stuffings.
VEGETABLES	Carrots, onions, peas, tomatoes, green peppers, and other sweet vegetables.
SAUCES	Brown and cream sauce for meat and vegetables.
SANDWICHES	Canned and chopped meats, fish, shellfish, and tomato.

Chervil (Anthriscus cerefolium)

The aroma of chervil is as fragrant and as delicate as the appearance of this lovely biennial. It is a most useful herb for the cook because of its very special subtle flavor, which needs repeated tasting to be appreciated. It is slightly sweetish and has a pleasant aromatic scent and taste, difficult to describe. As it is not dominant, it may be used in large quantities; at the same time it improves the flavor of any other herb with which it is combined. It has therefore always been an important part of fines herbes, a mixture called for in so many dishes.

The Romans used this herb a great deal. Today it is widely used in France, where it often takes the place of parsley. On the continent the delicious chervil soup is extensively made, and many famous sauces are based on this herb.

Chervil, similar also in appearance to parsley, is more delicate and fern-like, and the leaves are a lighter shade of green. It grows to the height of one to one and a half feet, with small white flowers growing in umbels; in many cases it will remain smaller and become bushy. A hardy biennial, it grows best when sown in late summer, in well-drained light soil, for harvesting in the spring, and it is one of the first herbs to be used after the winter has gone. A weed-free sunny spot is liked by chervil during winter, but it prefers half shade in the summer. It is a mild-flavored herb and is used rather in the quantity of a vegetable, for instance, for soup; it should, therefore, be grown in greater quantities than other herbs. Sown in flat boxes it will grow inside or on the window-sill. The contents of half a box to a box may be used for a soup.

It has always been known that chervil has blood-cleansing qualities and in years gone by was used in particular for Lenten dishes to help the spring cleaning of the body. With its refreshing flavor, it has been greatly welcomed after the winter as the first fresh, green, yet spicy addition to whet the appetite. It was also taken to increase perspiration, and the leaves finely chopped and warmed were applied to bruises and painful joints.

Chervil improves every dish to which it is added and can flavor all foods for which parsley is used. Béarnaise sauce requires chervil, and it should be put in vinaigrette and wine sauces. It will benefit all salads, particularly in spring. While its flavor is most noticeable when added to food which need not be cooked, it is at its best in chervil soup; for this and the equally good chervil sauce it must be used GENEROUSLY.

Chervil Soup   Chervil Sauce
  (page 200)   (page 260)
Baked Potatoes with   Chervil Soufflé
  Chervil   (pages 188–89)
  (page 254)

Day-to-day dishes for which chervil is traditionally used:

APPETIZERS	Vegetable cocktails; crab; canapés.
SALADS AND SALAD DRESSINGS	Raw vegetable salads; green, potato, and cucumber salads.
EGG AND CHEESE DISHES	Cream cheese; chervil omelette; any other egg dish.
SOUPS	Chervil soup, spinach soup, sorrel soup, and green or spring soup.
VEGETABLES	Boiled or buttered vegetables; spinach, tomatoes, and peas before serving.
SAUCES	Melted chervil butter on steaks and fish. Béarnaise sauce, green sauce, and all sauces for poultry.

Chives (Allium schoenoprasum)

The smallest of the onion family, chives, the "Infant Onion," has the mildest flavor of them all. Widely known today, it has been used for centuries in many parts of the world, its history going back to the days of the ancient Chinese in 3000 B.C. It is an excellent herb for flavoring, even for those who dislike onion taste, and it avoids the slight digestive disturbances which are sometimes caused by onions. Chives also have a stimulating effect on the appetite and are important in invalid cookery.

A hardy perennial, chives have slender grass-like leaves growing from small white flat bulbs which are close together in clusters. The small, round mauve flowerhead grows from the main stem, but this is usually nipped off because the plants are grown only for their "grass." They are easy to grow if the soil is not too poor, and require little attention. They are important for the gardener, because chives will be available for use early in the year before other onions are ready. Indoors they will flourish in pots in good rich soil.

Chives is really one of the most indispensable herbs for our daily use. Its delicate savor is a great improvement to salads, raw vegetables, cheese, and omelettes. Soups, thick or clear, potatoes, pancakes, and sauces would never be the same without chives. It is also the main ingredient of the famous Frankfurter green sauce, excellent with new potatoes, boiled beef, or cold meat. Chive butter—chopped chives mixed with butter—makes an excellent accompaniment for grilled meat or fish. Finally, the little flat bulbs may be pickled like small onions. Only with delicate vegetables must chives be used with care; in most dishes it may be used GENEROUSLY.

Frankfurter Green Sauce   Vichyssoise
  (pages 265–66)   (page 199)
Chive Potato Cakes   Sausage Salad
  (pages 252–53)   (page 175)

Day-to-day dishes for which chives are traditionally used:

APPETIZERS	Nearly any *hors d'oeuvres*.
SALADS AND SALAD DRESSINGS	Green, mixed-vegetable, potato, or cucumber salad; shellfish salad.
EGG AND CHEESE DISHES	Cottage and cream cheese; omelettes; pancakes; stuffed eggs.
SOUPS, STEWS, AND CASSEROLES	Asparagus, bean, or potato soup; clear consommé; vichyssoise; stews and casseroles where mild onion flavor is required.
VEGETABLES, RICE	As a garnish over potatoes, carrots, and other vegetables; add to plain rice just before serving.
SAUCES, DIPS, AND ACCOMPANIMENTS	White and tomato sauces—add before serving; herb butters.

Dill (Anethum graveolens)

Dill cannot be compared with or substituted for by any other herb:

it stands alone. Such is the nature of this herb that, once tasted, its fascinating flavor is demanded again and again. It is sharply aromatic and yet slightly sweetish, with a fragrance peculiarly its own. Its popularity stretches from America to Russia.

In Scandinavia dill is as popular as parsley and is used not only for most of the fish dishes and vegetables but also for decoration. Poland, Czechoslovakia, Germany—in fact, the whole of Central Europe is passionately interested in the traditional dill flavor. It is most used for pickling cucumbers, probably with the intention of making them more easily digestible. At the same time, bland vegetables are greatly improved by dill flavor.

Apart from its flavor, it has digestive and sedative qualities. Its name arises from the Norse word *dilla* (to lull), and its digestive power is illustrated by its traditional use in babies' bottles of water. It may be that, as a solution to digestive uneasiness, in the baby as well as in the adult, it leads to quieting the baby and makes it sleep. Dill seeds, called "Meeting House" seeds, were taken at church in the early morning to prevent people from feeling hungry.

Dill is an annual which can grow to about three feet, with a hollow stem and finely cut thread-like leaves. These are similar to fennel but are set more widely apart and are bluish-green in color. At the top of the main stem grows the flower umbel, consisting of tiny yellow flowers, which appears from June to August. These flowerheads, when already starting to develop seeds, are used for pickling cucumbers. The root structure is weak, so transplanting is not usually successful. It should not be grown near fennel, as cross pollination takes place and the resulting plants are neither dill nor fennel.

Dill is grown from seed. While it needs no special requirements as to soil, it will be found that it is, however, a tender fragile plant which has difficulties in withstanding adverse conditions. With favorable soil and good weather conditions dill grows like a weed, but if dill becomes dry in light soil during a drought or has to stand stagnant humidity, it may not grow at all. A well-drained soil and a sunny spot give dill the best chance, and if kept well watered it will produce a mass of foliage.

Dill can be planted in pots or boxes indoors, as it is a quick-growing plant, but it will never reach the height of outdoor dill. Leaves may be picked from the indoor plant when needed.

The difference between dill herb and dill seed lies in the degree of pungency, and there are occasions where the seed is better because of its sharper flavor. Where a salt-free diet must be followed, the seed, whole or ground, is a valuable replacement. In the kitchen, dill seed is used as a flavoring for soups, lamb stew, and grilled or boiled fish. It also adds spiciness to rice dishes.

The most frequent use for the dill herb is with fish, salads, and delicate vegetables, and in particular for pickling cucumbers. Fresh leaves, finely chopped or green-dried, mixed with cream cheese, make an unusual spread. For many dishes dill may be used generously, but it is an herb which improves rather than dominates the flavor of food. For this reason it should be used WISELY, sometimes GENEROUSLY.

Dill Potatoes   Avocado-Dill Dressing
  (page 253)   (pages 181–82)
Dill Meatcakes
  (page 223)

Day-to-day dishes for which dill is traditionally used:

APPETIZERS	Fish spreads; canapés.
SALADS AND SALAD DRESSINGS	Green, cucumber, potato, and tomato salads; sour cream on cucumbers; pickled cucumbers; in dressing (seeds); avocado pears.
EGG AND CHEESE DISHES	Egg sandwiches; cottage or cream cheese; pancakes; omelettes.
SOUPS	Bean, pea, tomato, chicken, fish soups.
FISH	Halibut, mackerel, salmon, sea trout; in fact with most fish recipes.
MEAT	Grilled steaks, chops, boiled meats; seeds in meat pies, lamb stews.
POULTRY	Roast chicken, turkey, or duck; seeds in fricassees.
VEGETABLES	String beans, peas, tomatoes; mashed potatoes, and parsnips; seeds with cabbage, beets, cauliflower; potatoes.
SAUCES	All fish sauces; on its own as dill sauce.
SANDWICHES	Cucumber sandwiches, in place of salt and pepper.

The Elder (Sambucus nigra)

The elder tree is the most useful plant. All parts were used in former times: the hollow stem, the leaves, the flowers, and the fruit. We are mainly concerned here with the flowers, which have versatile uses; they are usually white and can be detected by their sweet heavy scent in June and July. The dried flowers contain a volatile oil and a number of other important constituents which explain their manifold uses for culinary, medicinal, and cosmetic purposes.

The elder grows to a considerable height. It has large, dark green leaves; the flowers hang in umbel-like clusters and have to be picked carefully. The outer flowers open first, and there is difficulty in harvesting, as all the flowers must be out, but not finished. The flowerheads must be carefully handled, not bruised, and should be spread out, without touching each other and their heads down, on fine nylon net over a frame for drying. If all this care is taken they will retain their color. The little fruits, which ripen in September or October when they become shiny violet, are excellent for sauces and juices, and have a reputation of being very helpful against autumn and winter colds.

The fresh flowers may be used for one of the best summer desserts—elder-flower fritters—made from fresh elder flowers picked from the hedgerows. The flowers also make an excellent refreshing summer drink, very popular with children. They add a pleasant distinctive sweet flavor to milk dishes, jellies, jams, gooseberry and apple tart. They may be tied in a muslin bag, boiled or baked with milk or cooked with jam, and removed before serving. The dried flowers make a delightfully flavored tisane, strongly reminiscent of muscatel. It promotes perspiration in the case of colds and is a pleasant alternative to aspirin, particularly if mixed with equal parts of lime flowers and chamomile, most effective if taken hot in bed. This tisane is also sleep inducing. It has the effect of stimulating the glandular system.

Indian or China tea may be flavored by adding one part dried elder flower to two parts of tea.

Elder-flower water or tea has been used for eye or skin lotions, and it is good for washing and as a bath addition.

The elderberries may be added to jam or made into a juice. They have the reputation of cleansing the bloodstream. Juice made of elderberries is good for chills, sciatica, and neuralgia. Wherever they grow, both flowers and berries are found in large quantities and may be used LAVISHLY.

Elder-Flower Fritters   Elder-Flower Drinks
  (page 283)   (page 41)
Elder-Flower Milk   Elderberry Sauces
  (page 305)   (pages 272–73)

Day-to-day dishes for which the elder is traditionally used:

SAUCES   Elderberry sauce.

SWEETS AND DESSERTS   Elder-flower fritters; apple dishes;
                               milk dishes; jams and jellies.

DRINKS   Elder-flower milk; on its own as a
                               tea; added to Indian or China tea;
                               as a refreshing summer drink.

HEALTH VALUE   Elder-flower tea in case of colds.

COSMETIC SUGGESTIONS   Elder-flower water for eye and skin
                               lotions. Elder flowers (dried) for
                               washing and as a bath addition;
                               also as addition to facial steam
                               bath, face packs, and face cream.

Fennel (Foeniculum vulgare)

Fennel is one of the earliest known herbs. Its close association
with fish is most likely due to its reputation that for many generations it has helped in the digestion of oily fish such as mackerels,
eels, and salmon, and to the fact that it also grows wild round the
coast of Britain. Fishermen used fennel for flavoring fish and avoiding
any digestive difficulties it might cause. It also had the reputation
among the Greeks of making fat people lean. Apart from digestive
qualities, it is an excellent herb for the eyes; and its cosmetic effect
on the skin has also been known throughout the ages.

Fennel is a tall, graceful perennial of bushy growth, with strong
shiny stems and leaves divided into feathery segments. The flowers,
appearing in June, are light yellow and arranged in umbels. As a
garden herb it will grow on almost any soil, but thrives best in a
sunny well-drained position. Cut down to approximately four inches
fennel will do well in a pot, even in the smoky atmosphere of a
town.

The various constituents, apart from the fatty oils which are
contained in fennel, give it an anti-spasmodic, anti-inflammatory
calming effect. It also stimulates the appetite and is given to babies.
Its main effect is considered to be on the eyes, and compresses steeped
in fennel tea are suggested for inflamed eyelids and watering eyes, as

well as for strengthening the eyes and improving the sight. Fennel was used for its anti-flatulent effect, and it also satisfied the cravings of hunger on fast days during Lent. The reputation for reducing overweight could probably be attributed to the wish for slimming. The cosmetic properties, which are recommended against wrinkles, suggest facial packs.

There are many suggestions and recipes for using fennel which come from various countries. One elegant and subtle way is to use fennel with bass or other similar fish. It is centered round the idea of grilling bass on a bed of fennel, then pouring brandy over it; it is set alight and served burning, impregnated with the noble flavor of burnt fennel.

The feathery leaves, with their very slight aniseed flavor, added to salads, soups, and sauces make these delicious. Also, with soft cheeses, in pickling cucumbers, and with cabbage, fennel finds its place. Though it has a hidden tang, it may be used lavishly when familiar, but at first it is one to be used WISELY.

Fennel Sauce
 (pages 260–61)
Bass, Mullet, or Mackerel
  Flambé au Fenouil
 (page 212)

Mimosa Eggs
 (pages 190–91)
Fish Soup
 (page 206)

Day-to-day dishes for which fennel is traditionally used:

APPETIZERS	Slimming cocktails; spreads for canapés, mackerel, crab, snails.
SALADS AND SALAD DRESSINGS	Salads and salad dressings, especially cucumber, potato, green salads.
SOUPS AND STEWS	Most soups; stock; fish stews; add to water or stock for fish.
FISH	Oily fish like mackerel, eel, and salmon. Fish garnish (bass on burnt fennel, etc.); in fishcakes and fish casseroles.
VEGETABLES	Most vegetables, mixed with other herbs: beans, cabbage, cauliflower, tomatoes; young peas instead of mint.
SAUCES	Fennel sauce with fish.
HERB TEAS	Seeds in fennel tea and in seed tea. Reputed to have slimming qualities.

Face packs for wrinkles. Fennel tea
                                      excellent for the eyes.

Lemon Balm (Melissa officinalis)

The sweet lemon-scented lemon balm, or melissa—to give it its Greek
name—is an old and highly valued medicinal, as well as culinary,
herb. Wholesome and refreshing teas were made from the leaves,
which, while preserving good health, were also delicious to drink.
The relaxing effect of this anti-spasmodic tea suggests its use as an
early cup of tea or as an after-dinner drink, a custom which has been
accepted by an increasing number of people. It was believed to bring
long life; for example, Llewellyn, a Prince of Glamorgan, who took
melissa tea morning and evening, lived to be 108. At the same time, it
adds a refreshing lemon flavor to many other drinks and dishes, particularly to sweets.

Lemon balm is a shrubby perennial growing from two to three feet
high. It has light green, heart-shaped leaves which are wrinkled and
deeply veined, give off a strong lemony scent, and have a very distinct
flavor. The little flowers are creamy white and grow in tiny loose
bundles in the axils of the upper leaves.

Lemon balm can be grown from seed or by dividing the roots
in spring or autumn. It is extremely easy to grow anywhere, though
it prefers fairly rich moist soil in a sunny sheltered position. In fact,
it often spreads like a weed and people do not know what to do with
it. It grows well indoors or in a windowbox, again with rich soil and
plenty of moisture. It is one of the first herbs to appear in early spring.

The health-giving properties of lemon balm are many: it has a calming effect on the nervous system which helps relaxation and dispels
overtiredness and incipient headaches and migraine. It also stimulates
the heart.

A few lemon-balm leaves added to China tea make a refreshing
drink. In the summer it adds its cool fragrant flavor to fruit juices,
particularly fresh orange juice, wine cups, and iced teas; on its own
as melissa tea it is excellent and has all the refreshing, medicinal
effects described above. Freshly chopped or green-dried, the leaves
may be used in salads, sauces, egg, and milk dishes. It is also good
with chicken and fish dishes, where its delicate lemon taste adds a
distinctive flavor. It is one of the sugar-saving herbs and, together
with sweet cicely, adds a sweet lemon flavor to all sweet dishes. It
may be used LAVISHLY.

Melissa Tea   Peach Tart
  (page 46)   (page 276)
Orange Chiffon   Flavored Salzburger Nockerl
  (page 277)   (pages 281–82)

Day-to-day dishes for which lemon balm is traditionally used:

APPETIZERS	Tomato juice. Shrimp and prawn cocktails.
SALADS AND SALAD DRESSINGS	Tomato or cucumber salads; French dressing. Freshly chopped or green-dried lemon balm (possibly reconstituted) may be added to fresh tomato or mixed-green salad or to their dressings.
SOUPS, STEWS	Asparagus and vegetable soups (add just before serving). Add to stews.
FISH	Fish baked or boiled.
MEAT	Lamb—rub with chopped leaves before roasting.
POULTRY AND GAME	Chicken—rub on before roasting. Stuffings for poultry and game.
VEGETABLES	Mushrooms.
SAUCES	Herb sauces; fish sauces; cream sauces; in marinades.
SWEETS AND DESSERTS	Fruit salads; jellies and custards.
PARTY IDEAS WITH HERBS, INCLUDING DRINKS	Fruit drinks, lemonade, wine cups, sherbet, and cooling drinks.
HERB TEAS	Melissa tea, hot.

Lovage (Levisticum officinalis)

Lovage is almost an herb garden in itself. In shape of leaves and flavor it resembles celery but is much larger and much stronger; it can replace celery leaves, however, when they are not in season. Its flavor is reminiscent of Maggi, the famous yeast extract. Indeed, it is known on the continent as the "Maggi herb," and is widely used in soups, stews, and casseroles.

Lovage is a giant-sized perennial herb which grows six to seven feet high. From the straight hollow stem grow dark-green shiny leaves, themselves stalked; they are divided into narrow ridge-like segments. Towards the top of the stem the leaves diminish, and the stalks end in the flowerheads which are clusters of greenish-yellow flowers. The seeds are brown when ripe, resembling those of caraway, and they have as strong an aromatic smell and flavor as the plant itself.

There are few requirements for growing lovage. It prefers rich, moist soil where the roots can go deep; heavy clay soils are less suitable. Propagation can be done by sowing seed, though germination is slow; by buying plants; or by dividing roots in spring. It flowers from June to August. Though it dies down in the winter, lovage can withstand quite severe weather and can remain in the sa. ground for a number of years.

The reputation lovage has for deodorizing both internally and externally is well known in Europe. It stimulates the digestive organs and has a diuretic action through its cleansing properties. Lovage was also used as a "bath herb," a refreshing cleanser of the skin.

The unique flavor of lovage will give character to vegetable, meat, and fish dishes, and it is most excellent when used in soup. Its strong yeast-like flavor gives the impression that a complete soup extract has been added; as it replaces meat and bones in a soup or casserole it should be used in sufficient quantity to give strength to such dishes. It is a little spicier than other herbs and, until it becomes familiar to the herb cook, it should be used ECONOMICALLY.

Lovage Soup	Ham-Lovage Spread
(page 201)	(page 166)
Farmer's Omelette	Lovage Cream Sauce
(page 193)	(page 261)

Day-to-day dishes for which lovage is traditionally used:

APPETIZERS	Lovage biscuits; ham spread.
SALADS AND SALAD DRESSINGS	Tossed green salads; all raw salads. Mayonnaise; kohlrabi; and sauerkraut.
EGG DISHES	Omelettes.
SOUPS, STEWS	Any mixed-vegetable soup, lovage soup, clear stock; meat stews; fish chowders.
POULTRY AND GAME	Birds—rub on before roasting.
VEGETABLES	All vegetables; leaves and stems cooked as a vegetable.
SAUCES, ACCOMPANIMENTS	Lovage cream sauce; fish sauce; meat gravies.

Fragrant tisane—more like a broth —may be taken with salt rather than with sugar. Lovage cocktail.

Marigold (Calendula officinalis)

Marigold—a flower which can be found in most gardens—is easy to grow. Only the florets of marigold are used for culinary and cosmetic purposes, though they have also had the reputation of having medicinal value in former times. The flower petals may be used in salads, omelettes, rice and buns, and as a substitute for the expensive and rare saffron. They color and flavor dishes; the coloring substance, which is similar to that in carrots, has an excellent subtle flavoring quality itself.

Marigold is an annual, growing to a height of 20 inches, and the simple, boldly colored flowers, in many shades from light yellow to orange red, are a pleasant addition to any garden. They grow in any kind of soil, and like a position in full sun. They can be sown straight onto the site in March or April. If the dead flower heads are picked, they will bloom continuously until November.

The petals may be used either fresh or dried. They have to be pulled away from the flower center for drying. If they are dried in thin layers in a low temperature they will retain the beautiful yellow or orange color. Marigold petals impart a very delicate flavor and a strong color. A small addition of crushed petals, as well as chopped leaves, gives a delightful tang to salads. The dried petals in buns, bread puddings, or any baked sweets make an interesting change. When marigold is used in place of saffron with rice, it provides the look of saffron rice, but a slightly different subtle flavor. Marigold in omelettes and savory rice makes these dishes much more attractive.

For buns and cakes marigold petals may be soaked in a muslin bag in a small cup of hot milk; then the milk can be used for baking after it has cooled. Marigold petals have been used externally in oils and ointments, and in the treatment of wounds, old scars, or other skin troubles. They may be used in quantity, particularly for coloring; indeed at all times they should be used LAVISHLY.

Marigold Rice
(page 256)

Poultry Pilaff
(pages 237–38)

Day-to-day dishes for which marigold is traditionally used:

SALADS AND SALAD DRESSINGS	All salads and salad dressings.
EGG DISHES	Omelettes.
FISH	Fish stews and stock in which fish is cooked—half teaspoon crushed petals.
MEAT	Roast beef.
POULTRY AND GAME	Venison or any game stew; chicken broth.
SWEETS AND DESSERTS	Bread pudding. Marigold buns and cakes.
COSMETIC SUGGESTIONS	Soaked in oil or used in ointments for the skin; for scars, particularly old ones. For tired feet.

Marjoram, Sweet (Origanum majorana)

Marjoram has a strong, sweet, yet spicy flavor and is essentially a meat herb. It combines well with made-up dishes such as sausages and meat loaf, adding a very special flavor to them. It is often used together with thyme, to which it is considered a twin. Marjoram has been a popular herb throughout its long history; this was mainly due to the fact that marjoram contains preserving and disinfectant qualities, which—before the days of refrigeration—made it invaluable in the kitchen.

There are several varieties of marjoram; the most important for cooking is sweet knotted marjoram. Pot marjoram (Origanum onites) is a perennial and stays with us throughout the winter, but has not as good a flavor as sweet marjoram. Wild marjoram (Origanum vulgare) is a spicier plant, particularly so when grown in hotter climates such as Spain or Mexico; it is known as oregano.

Sweet marjoram is a half-hardy annual—it cannot withstand frost. The bushy plant grows about eight inches high with very small greyish-green leaves. The knotty flower growth appears at the top of the tough, woody stem, and these green knots eventually become pale mauve. The flowers bloom from June to September and have a strong aromatic scent. Marjoram should be cut when the knots are about to break open.

Marjoram seed should be sown in a frame in March, and in May planted out in the warmest, most sheltered spot available. The plants need a medium-rich, moist soil. In the window box it needs rich soil and a sunny sill.

For medicinal purposes marjoram was rarely used, though the volatile oil it contains is a good external application for sprains and bruises; also the freshly expressed juice from the leaves, sniffed up the nostrils, is helpful for headaches and insomnia. The crushed dried leaves were used as a snuff.

Strong meats are all improved by being rubbed with marjoram before roasting. It makes any potato dish more interesting and may be used with most vegetables, above all with legumes. Its characteristic flavor comes out best when used for stuffings or forcemeat of any kind. However, it is a strong herb and can easily overpower other flavors; those new to this herb should use it JUDICIOUSLY.

Boned Stuffed Chicken
    (page 241)

Goulash
    (page 221)

Marjoram Potato Pie
    (page 253)

Marjoram Liver Dumplings
    (pages 231–32)

Day-to-day dishes for which marjoram is traditionally used:

APPETIZERS	Cream cheese; stuffed mushrooms.
SALADS AND SALAD DRESSINGS	French dressing (very little); chicken salad.
EGG AND CHEESE DISHES	Scrambled egg; cheese dishes.
SOUPS AND STEWS	Small sprig or quarter teaspoon green-dried in soups and stews.
FISH	Seafood and salt fish.
MEAT	Beef, pork, lamb, and veal—add before roasting; sausages, meat loaf, liver dumplings, rissoles; stuffings and forcemeat.
POULTRY AND GAME	Rabbit; rubbed inside and out for poultry; poultry stuffings.
VEGETABLES	Carrots, peas, marrows, and mushrooms (sparingly); lentils and all legumes; potato dishes: stuffed vegetables.
SWEETS AND DESSERTS	Milk puddings (sparingly).

The Mints: Spearmint (Mentha viridis *or* M. spicata)
        Bowles Mint (Mentha rotundifolia—Bowles variety)
        Peppermint (Mentha piperita)

The distinctive and fragrant flavors of mints play an important part in the preparation of many foods and drinks. There are three main varieties used in cooking: spearmint, bowles mint, and peppermint. Spearmint is the one most commonly used, but bowles mint, though stronger, can be used equally well for the same flavoring purposes and is considered best for mint sauce. Ideally the two should be mixed. Peppermint is used mainly as a beverage—peppermint tea—and in sweets, but there are many dishes where its extra spiciness may be used with advantage.

Spearmint grows about one foot high with a straight stem and long, narrow leaves. The flowers grow in pinkish clusters at the top of the stem. Bowles mint has large round woolly leaves of a lighter green and grows much taller. Peppermint grows about two feet high, and the leaves are a distinctive reddish-green color with a strong aroma. As the mints are hybrids and have various strains in their ancestry they cannot be sown. Either plants have to be bought or root divisions or cuttings taken. They grow well in moist rich soils in a warm, sheltered position, and the strong roots spread rapidly; they have to be restricted not to encroach on other plants. Spearmint can be grown successfully in a four-inch pot on a windowsill, where the height should be kept to about six inches.

Mint is most commonly used for mint sauce, but it also improves peas and beans, carrots, beets, boiled potatoes, and spinach. It combines well in fruit salad and other fruit dishes, also in cooling drinks. The famous mint julep is not only refreshing but is also a "pick-me-up." Peppermint is best known as a health-giving tea, refreshing and settling digestive upsets at the same time, but, as a culinary herb, it adds a delicious flavor to roast meats and vegetables, also to jellies and jams. The mints enhance both sweet and savory dishes and may be used GENEROUSLY, with the exception of peppermint, which has to be used CAREFULLY.

Mint Sauce with Lemon   Mint Julep
    (page 261)   (pages 302–3)
Mint Syrup   Peppermint Tea and Milk
    (page 304)   (page 46)

Day-to-day dishes for which mint is traditionally used:

	Mint	*Peppermint*
APPETIZERS	Fruit juices	Fruit and vegetable cocktails.
SALADS AND SALAD DRESSINGS	Vegetable salads.	Potato salad.
CHEESE DISHES	Cream cheese and processed cheeses.	
SOUPS, STEWS	Pea soup, lamb stew.	Lentil soup.
FISH	Baked, boiled, or grilled fish.	Eels.
MEAT	Roast beef and lamb.	Roast beef and lamb.
POULTRY	Chicken, rubbed on before roasting.	
VEGETABLES	Carrots, peas, all beans, spinach, cabbage, new potatoes.	Carrots, potatoes, peas, cabbage, cauliflower.
SAUCES	Meat marinades; herb sauces; mint sauce.	
SWEETS AND DESSERTS	Stewed fruit, ice cream, jellies, custards; mint syrup; pears, melon, apple sauce.	Jams and jellies.
DRINKS	Fruit and wine punch; chocolate; iced drinks; mint julep; tea.	Hot and iced tea, fruit cups, chocolate drinks.

Nasturtium (Tropaeolum majus *or* minus)

Here is a tasty and health-giving herb which was hardly ever considered an herb at all. Its leaves, petals, and seeds have been used in the East and in Europe for centuries. As it is so simple to grow this attractive flowering plant in every garden, it seems worthwhile to discuss its properties, some of which were only discovered recently. The peppery pungency of the leaves makes nasturtium an excellent substitute for pepper, and, as there are many people these days who like their food spicy, but should not take too much pepper or salt, nasturtium may become a necessity to them. In addition it is considered a valuable antibioticum—a kind of herbal penicillin—and is used as such in German-speaking countries. It is possible that these antibiotic qualities are connected with the unusually high content of vitamin C in nasturtium leaves. They have, therefore, become a food which is both attractive and protective and healthy at the same time. Research has shown that the highest vitamin C content was found in the leaves before flowering in July.

The custom of eating petals and using them for tea and salads came from the Orient. The flowers do not dry well and have to be used while fresh, but the leaves may be dried and used all the year round as garnishes for food and chopped up for canapes.

The plant likes a sandy, moderately rich soil but will grow everywhere; it is usually a strong-growing annual climber with orange flowers, but the more recently developed dwarf variety is a non-climber. The colors are usually attractive, and a more colorful border with a background of a hedge or shrubs can hardly be imagined. The leaves are kidney shaped and the flowers grow in many shades from yellow-orange to brownish-red. The best varieties are those of compact habit, while trailers may be left to cover walls and boundaries. All seeds can be sown where the plants are to bloom. Nasturtium also helps to provide an aid against pests, because it sometimes attracts aphids to itself, keeping roses, soft fruit, etc., free from them. If nasturtiums are grown in an herb garden among other herbs they are often not visited by pests at all. Nasturtium will grow well if sown in a window box and will not only be an attraction in every window, but provide vitamin C for apartment dwellers.

Nasturtium leaves have to be used cautiously because of their strong peppery flavor. In sandwich spreads they provide and retain a spicy flavor. In cream cheese, for instance, two teaspoons to a quarter pound cheese are excellent, but they must not be allowed to stand mixed with the cream cheese for a long time, as nasturtium will turn the cheese bitter. Mixed shortly before serving, they are an excellent addition, as they are for tossed, dressed, or undressed salads and between slices of bread and butter. Both young leaves and flowers are delicious in salads; and the seeds, pickled when young and green, are a substitute for capers. When the young leaves are finely chopped they are not only the best substitute for pepper, but in the case of a need for vitamin C to prevent infections, or as an antibiotic to combat any existing infection, ways and means will have to be invented in which chopped nasturtium leaves can be used. However, it is not advisable that more than one-third to two-thirds of an ounce should be eaten at one time—or one ounce per day should be distributed over several meals. Most of this may be eaten on bread and butter. Use this herb WITH CAUTION.

In the case of flu symptoms, such as sore throats, difficulty in swallowing, pains in joints, and general aches and headaches, it has been observed that the finely chopped green leaves of nasturtium produce a noticeable reduction of symptoms and—if used over longer periods—the symptoms may disappear altogether.

Nasturtium Dressing   Nasturtium Canapés and Sand-
   (page 93)   wiches
                                    (pages 166–67 and 287)

Day-to-day dishes for which nasturtium is traditionally used:

APPETIZERS	Canapés; spreads.
SALADS AND SALAD DRESSINGS	Leaf and flower in green salads; pickled seeds as mock capers; vegetable salads.
CHEESE DISHES	Cream cheese (pages 166–67)
SAUCES	Pickled seeds in nasturtium sauce.
SANDWICHES	Young leaves chopped between bread and butter.
HEALTH VALUE	High vitamin C content. Antibiotic against colds and other infections.

Onion Green (Allium fistulosum)

The grass-like leaves of the Welsh onion are often called "onion green." While they are stronger than chives, which belong to the same family, they are yet milder than onion. They are a most useful flavoring, not only for those who dislike a strong onion flavor, but even in conjunction with onions, for they add something more to a dish which onion alone does not give.

Welsh onion is a hardy perennial and multiplies rapidly through division of roots. They grow on right through the winter so that the leaves (or "grass") are available all the year round. They are, therefore, very useful. While onion greens form the bulk and the basis of onion flavor in cooking, chives with their more distinguished flavor are preferable in uncooked dishes, like salads, cream cheese, and even omelettes.

The main qualities of onion green come out best, however, when using it as a basic flavor for preparing vegetables, soups, stews, casseroles, and fillings. At the very start, after chopped onions are sautéed, onion green and then parsley should be added and sautéed before the vegetables or other ingredients are included. This adds a special punch and a wider range of onion flavor, as well as strength, to such dishes.

A vegetable filling of ravioli should have onion green as a basis to which bread and spinach can be added (page 259).

Onion green may also be used for most dishes for which chives are used; it is excellent in cream-cheese and egg mixtures to be used as spreads. In all cases onion green may be used freely ACCORDING TO TASTE.

Savory Onion-Green Tart   Vegetable-Filled Ravioli
  (page 249)   (page 259)
Savory Bread Mixture
  (pages 297–98)

Day-to-day dishes for which onion green is traditionally used:

APPETIZERS	Nearly any *hors d'oeuvres.*
SALADS AND SALAD DRESSINGS	Green, mixed-vegetable, potato, cucumber, shellfish salads.
EGG AND CHEESE DISHES	Cottage and cream cheese; omelettes; pancakes; stuffed eggs.
SOUPS, STEWS, AND CASSEROLES	Mixed-vegetable soup, minestrone, asparagus, bean, or potato soup; clear consommé; vichyssoise; stews and casseroles.
VEGETABLES, RICE	Garnish over potatoes, carrots, and other vegetables; plain rice (add just before serving); bread or meat filling; forcemeat.
SAUCES, DIPS, AND ACCOMPANIMENTS	White and tomato sauces (add before serving); herb butters.

Parsley (curly) (Petroselinum crispum)

Parsley will go with every dish and cannot be surpassed for its versatility in the kitchen. Also, any dish takes on a party look when garnished with parsley. Its fresh green appearance and fragrant aroma delight the eye and stimulate the appetite. It is, in fact, the main herb in the kitchen, and cooking in general can hardly be imagined without parsley.

Parsley is a hardy biennial; and the variety most used is curly parsley. The bright green leaves are deeply divided and curled over; it grows about two feet high. The delicate greenish-white flower clusters appear during the second year. Parsley is not difficult to grow, but it is slow in germinating. The soil needs to be rich and well worked so that the roots can grow deep. Parsley likes a shady position. It is advisable to sow parsley every year to ensure a good crop. It grows successfully in pots or boxes indoors and outdoors on the windowsill.

Parsley has always been in demand from ancient times, when it was considered a family medicine and all parts of the plant were used. It has been used as a diuretic tonic tea and as a help for rheumatism. It has many health-giving properties due to its vitamins and minerals; its content of vitamin C, particularly, makes it an important daily addition to our food.

Parsley emphasizes the flavor of foods without itself adding a strong accent. It even masks the odor of strong vegetables such as onions and carrots. It flavors soups and sauces, salads, and egg dishes; while there are special dishes like parsley stuffing and parsley butter for which it is used in quantity. One delicious specialty is fried fresh parsley, which is a delicate garnish for fish. Parsley combines well with every other herb and is the basis for most herb mixtures, but whether together or on its own it is an excellent flavoring and may always be used GENEROUSLY.

Persillade   Lincolnshire Stuffed Chine
   (page 264)   (pages 226–27)
Parsleyed Chicken
   (page 242)

Parsley may be used with every dish; no list of special uses is therefore added here.

Rosemary (Rosmarinus officinalis)

Perhaps the most fragrant herb of all, rosemary, has a pungent resinous taste which imparts a subtle flavor to foods both sweet and savory. At the same time it is excellent medicinally, helping a weak digestion and neuralgic pains, and stimulating the circulation and other functions. For these it is taken as a tea and in wine or liqueur. Externally, oil of rosemary is used as a liniment in cases of gout or for sprains and bruises. Water in which rosemary has been boiled is excellent for the skin and, when used in hair washes, is said to stimulate hair growth.

An evergreen shrub, rosemary grows to about five feet. It has succulent leaves green on top and greyish beneath, spiky, which curve slightly, resembling pine needles. The little blue flowers grow in clusters and the whole plant gives off a delicate spicy aroma. It grows best in a light, sandy, dryish soil, requiring a sheltered position. The herb needs more protection in winter than any other herb, and, unless it is given this against walls or hedges, it should be grown in pots or tubs and taken indoors during the cold season. Rosemary can be raised from seed or by division of roots or layering. Indoors, it grows most successfully in an enriched loamy soil, but needs to be kept well watered and restricted in size.

Rosemary has a character very much its own, with its history going back hundreds of years. There are more legends and customs attached to it than to any other herb. One such is the belief that rosemary grew to the height of Our Lord while He was on earth and after His death remained the same height, only growing in breadth.

With its fresh, exciting flavor rosemary can equally well be used for savory dishes as for jams, jellies, and biscuits; it adds subtlety to fruit salads and cider or claret cup. A few sprigs added to roasting meats, especially lamb, also to poultry, game, and fish, give a delicious taste. It is, however, a strong herb and should at first be used ECONOMICALLY.

Beef Casserole with Rosemary   Rosemary Biscuits
   (pages 221–22)   (page 285)
Rosemary Sauce   Rosemary Walnuts
   (page 263)   (page 168)

Day-to-day dishes for which rosemary is traditionally used:

APPETIZERS	Fruit and vegetable cocktails.
EGG AND CHEESE DISHES	Omelettes, pancakes, scrambled eggs, cream cheese.
SOUPS	Meat, chicken, pea, spinach soups; minestrone.
FISH	Strong-flavored fish like eel, halibut.
MEAT	Beef, lamb, pork, and veal, roasted.
POULTRY AND GAME	Roast poultry and venison; stuffings for rabbit, partridge.

VEGETABLES, RICE	Beans, peas, cauliflower; dumplings; risotto; baked potatoes.
SWEETS AND DESSERTS	Apple jellies, jams; rosemary sugar; fruit salads.
DRINKS	Summer fruit cups—wines and cider cups.
COSMETIC SUGGESTIONS	Rosemary water or tea for skin and hair.

Sage (Salvia officinalis)

In spite of its wide use and popularity sage has lost part of its excellent reputation and its value in the eye of the discriminate user. This may be due to two reasons: firstly, it has been overused so often, and, secondly, if it is badly dried or packed it can spoil dishes with its poor flavor. Only if sage has been carefully dried, stored, and packed, and used with discretion, can one begin to understand the tremendous appreciation which the Chinese and Arabs, the Greeks, the Romans and the Saxons felt for sage. While other herbs may simply lose some of their aroma or qualities if badly dried or handled, sage seems to pick up a musty flavor not originally its own.

Sage is a sub-shrub about two feet high with slender greyish-green leaves, pebbly to the touch; the flowers are spikes of a light purple color. It will grow almost anywhere, though it will do best, like all herbs, on well-drained soil and grows most luxuriantly in a warm, sunny position. Sage can be increased by division or cuttings and should be renewed every three or four years, for the plants grow woody. They should be planted well apart; otherwise they tend to turn yellow. All sages are good honey plants.

Several old proverbs, Arabian to Old English, testify to the belief that "sage ensures long life," and sage tea was considered not only a popular drink before tea became well known, but a health-giving one, particularly during spring.

Apart from sage-and-onion stuffing and its use with rich meats such as pork and duck, there are many more ways in which sage can show its particular qualities (with liver, fish, legumes, game, and cottage or cream cheese; in herb butter, for omelettes, in fritters, pancakes, bean dishes, etc.). Whole leaves, fresh or green-dried, can be wrapped round lamb, veal, and eels for unusual dishes. Sage also gives a surprisingly delicious flavor to summer fruit drinks and cups. But, at all times, sage must be of first-class quality, and as it has a pungent flavor it must be used WITH DISCRETION.

Country-Style Pork   Sage Sauce
  (page 226)   (page 262)
Fresh Eel in Sage Leaves   Sage Fritters
  (page 219)   (page 197)

Day-to-day dishes for which sage is traditionally used:

EGG AND CHEESE DISHES	Cream cheese, herb cheese, soft cheese spreads, fritters, pancakes, omelettes.
SOUPS, STEWS, AND CASSEROLES	Cream, meat, vegetable soups; fish chowders; beef, lamb, veal stews and casseroles.
FISH	Court bouillon or water for boiling fish (with other herbs); eels and all fat fish when broiling or grilling.
MEAT	Beef, lamb, mutton, and especially pork and veal, when roasted; stuffings (with other herbs). Meat loaf and puddings; sausage and liver.
POULTRY AND GAME	Chicken, goose, turkey, for rubbing and in stuffing (also with other herbs) sparingly. Hare, rabbit, venison, for rubbing before roasting (also with other herbs).
VEGETABLES	Spinach, beets, onions, eggplants, legumes.
SAUCES	With butter sauces for vegetables. In meat gravies.
SANDWICHES AND SNACKS	Sage butter, sage toast, sage jelly.
DRINKS	Sage tea, sage in "cups," and apple juice, etc.

Salad Burnet (Sanguisorba minor)

Salad burnet is easy to grow and will stay with us throughout the winter. It provides fresh green foliage all the year round and is therefore suggested to those who grow their own herbs. It has been used since time immemorial.

The leaves have a nutty flavor and a slight taste of cucumber. They are suitable in salads—therefore the name salad burnet—and enhance all winter salads. The herb may also be used with other herbs for soups or all dishes requiring mixed herbs. Like borage it is an excellent herb for flavoring drinks.

The decorative plant grows to a height of twelve to fifteen inches. The leaves are pinnate with serrate leaflets, and the flowers grow in small round heads, first green and then becoming reddish. The plant flowers from June to the end of August and is pollinated by wind. When the first flower shoots appear the first cut may be made. The rosette of leaves is a most attractive little bush of greenery during winter in an otherwise dormant herb garden. It even pokes its head through a light fall of snow.

Salad burnet has no special requirements, but likes chalky soil. It should be sown in April, and if it is allowed to go to seed it will self-sow. Its broad leaves are always tender and are therefore such a help throughout the winter, and will brighten up in spring. Salad burnet can be cut again and again; therefore only a few plants are needed. A few seeds will grow in a flowerpot for those who have no garden, providing green leaves during the winter.

Salad burnet provides a taste of cucumber for salad mixtures, herb soups, and sauces, and particularly for claret cups and cocktails. It has a similar reputation to borage and may be used as a tonic. Its delicate foliage is an attractive decoration and adds to the appearance of iced drinks, as well as to their flavor. All salads with French dressing or mayonnaise, as well as asparagus, celery, bean, and mushroom soups, benefit by it. The herb should be placed in the soup at the beginning of cooking. Altogether it may be used GEN-EROUSLY.

Burnet Cocktail   Burnet-Mint Fish Sauce
   (page 301)   (page 269)
Burnet Vinegar
   (page 183)

Day-to-day dishes for which salad burnet is traditionally used:

SALADS AND SALAD DRESSINGS   Fresh young tips in vegetable salads;
                                  such as in lettuce or mixed-green
                                  salads; chopped in French dress-
                                  ing or in mayonnaise. Herb vine-
                                  gars.

SOUPS   Mushroom, celery, asparagus, and
                                      bean soups.

DRINKS   Herb teas; iced drinks; claret cup.

Sorrel (Rumex acetosa *and* Rumex scutatus)

Sorrel's contribution to cookery is contained in the slight acidity
of its herbage. The best member of the family is French sorrel because of this slightly acid taste, which cannot be obtained by any
other means. French sorrel soup, made of the leaves, is one of the
most excellent soups and is famous in France. The slightly sour
flavor stimulates the appetite and is a culinary virtue in itself. It can
also be used as a slightly sour seasoning. Care has to be taken that
not too much of sorrel is used, and not too often, because part of the
plant contains oxalic acid which may be damaging to health if taken
in excess; but as a seasoning it can be invaluable with vegetables or
any dish which is insipid in itself and for which pepper alone is not
the answer.

The Greek and Roman doctors used sorrel leaves for medicinal
purposes as a diuretic plant, and it has, at times, been recommended
for kidney stones. Sorrel is considered to have blood-cleansing and
blood-improving qualities, in a similar way to spinach, which improves the hemoglobin content of the blood; and sorrel is said to
contain vitamin C and, most likely, iron.

The broad-leafed French sorrel is one of the most frequently cultivated varieties of the sorrels. The leaves are oblong, slightly arrow
shaped at the base and succulent. It is a slender perennial plant about
two feet high with spikes of reddish-green flowers from May to July.
It grows abundantly and can be easily cultivated. Sorrel can best be
propagated by division of the roots in spring or autumn; these should
be planted approximately 15 feet apart. It grows best in light, rich
soil and full sun, but can also be grown in the shade; if a sheltered
position is available it will do well in it. The flowering plants should
be cut back to prevent their going to seed and leaves becoming tough.
At the end of March, sorrel can be sown like spinach in rows. Four
months after the plants have started to grow they can be cut. Sorrel
leaves can also be dried successfully in the same way as other herbs,
but color and flavor must be preserved.

Sorrel, and particularly French sorrel, is excellent if combined
with other leaves or herbs, as it is sometimes too bitter alone. In a
salad sorrel combines well with lettuce and herbs; sorrel soup with
some lettuce added is much improved. For instance, if there is a

surplus of lettuce in a garden, lettuce may be cooked and made into a vegetable like spinach by adding sufficient sorrel to make it tasty and valuable. When cooked early in spring as greens, with lettuce and spinach added, sorrel provides a very good vegetable dish. The leaves also feature in a cream soup.

It is an excellent herb with which to experiment and to find out in which of your favorite dishes it will make a difference to the flavor, particularly if used CAREFULLY.

Sorrel Soup
  (pages 200–1)

Potato Salad with Sorrel
  (page 87)

Spinach Purée with Sorrel
  (pages 250–1)

Sorrel Turnovers
  (page 285)

Day-to-day dishes for which sorrel is traditionally used:

SALADS AND SALAD DRESSINGS	Tossed green salads (a pinch)
EGG DISHES	Omelettes; soufflés.
SOUPS	Sorrel soup; sorrel and lettuce soup.
VEGETABLES	Spinach, cabbage, and lettuce; or young leaves on their own.
PASTRY	Sorrel turnovers.

Summer Savory (Satureia hortensia)

Summer savory is a favorite in Europe and in America. It is widely used for all bean dishes. Underlining the flavor of beans rather than adding a new one, it has a piquant pleasant taste, strong and slightly peppery; it may be used almost as a spice. It can replace both salt and pepper and is a great help to those on a salt-free diet.

A bushy delicate annual, summer savory grows about one foot high with sparse dark-green leaves along the stems; the whole plant looks purplish. The pink flowers grow five together in the axils of the leaves and bloom from July to September. It is best to grow from seeds sown in a sunny position. If sown in May or June the herb will be ready for broad, French, runner, and haricot beans. Summer savory can be sown in pots indoors. Its fresh leaves are available throughout the winter.

There is a high content of volatile oil in summer savory which is of medicinal value and, in the sixteenth century, was infused as a tea for indigestion. This attribute is noticeable when summer savory is added to dishes usually difficult to digest such as cucumber salad, lentils, all the beans, pork, and sausages.

Nowadays beans are available all the year round either fresh, frozen, or canned, and green-dried summer savory can be bought to go with them. No other dish benefits as much from the addition of summer savory as frozen beans. Any bean flavor lost is recaptured by this addition, and the flavor becomes almost that of fresh beans. Besides its excellence with all bean dishes it gives flavor to meat stuffings and vegetables such as cabbage and brussels sprouts. However, it is a pungent herb and until one is familiar with its strength it should be used CAREFULLY.

Chicken with Summer   Bean Salad
  Savory   (page 178)
  (pages 242–43)
Broad Beans Sauté
  (page 252)

Day-to-day dishes for which summer savory is traditionally used:

APPETIZERS	Vegetable cocktails; cocktail biscuits and rolls.
SALADS AND SALAD DRESSINGS	Raw vegetable salads; bean and tomato salads; pickling cucumbers.
EGG DISHES	Omelettes, pancakes, and soufflés.
SOUPS, STEWS	Clear broth; bean, lentil, and pea soups; stews.
FISH	Baked or boiled fish.
MEAT	All roast meats; smoked pork and ham.
POULTRY AND GAME	Stuffings for chicken, duck, and turkey; venison and rabbit stew.
VEGETABLES	Broad, French, runner, haricot beans; cabbage, peas, lentils, stuffing marrow, and potatoes.
SAUCES	Savory butter; tomato and fish sauces. Horseradish sauce and cream.

Sweet Cicely (Myrrhis odorata)

Sweet cicely, unknown to most people for its uses, is an herb with special qualities in cooking as well as ease of growing. It has a sweetish flavor faintly reminiscent of anise and provides numerous uses as a fragrant herb and as a sugar saver. It has also a great attraction in the garden because of its beauty as a plant, its charming name, and the profusion in which it grows wild as well as cultivated. It is one of the herbs which gives us the longest use during the year, as it appears in our gardens in early spring and is one of the last to go in fall. It is therefore a good fresh standby almost all the year round; an ever-increasing perennial.

It has been known through the ages among the English north-country folk as a useful herb plant. "It is so harmless you cannot use it amiss."

Sweet cicely improves all "bouquets" or mixtures of herbs; it deserves a place in salad dressings, slimming cocktails, herb butter, and delicate soups, and enhances all root vegetables. It tempts children to eat salads or drink juices, particularly when they are not well. It improves sweets, creams, trifles, and fruit salads, and is delicious with whipped cream and fruit, to which it adds a fresh aromatic flavor.

It has been found most useful as a pleasant way of reducing acidity in tart fruit and in this way helps to save sugar. This is experienced with rhubarb, unripe gooseberries, red or black currants, plums, etc. The large fresh leaves and stalks, or two to four teaspoons dried sweet cicely, perhaps with some lemon balm, added to the boiling water in which fruit is stewed add a delightful flavor and help to save almost half of the sugar. This is not only a great help for diabetics but also for the many people who are now trying to cut down on sugar, partly for reasons of slimming, partly because sugar has fallen into disfavor for various health reasons, and partly to help children whose sugar intake is usually beyond what is good for their health or their teeth.

As sweet cicely is one of the herbs which flavors Chartreuse and therefore suggests many experiments with all kinds of drinks and all kinds of sweets, it has already inspired new sweets which may go down in culinary history. It is certainly one of the herbs you cannot go wrong with, unless its anise flavor is disliked, but this is so slight that it is hardly noticed when used in cooking. Sweet cicely may, in fact, be used as it grows: LAVISHLY.

Hard Sauce
  (pages 271–72)
Plum Salad
  (page 280)

Elderberry Sauce *or* Soup
  (pages 272–73)
Orange-Apple Milk Drink
  (page 305)
Fruit Cocktail
  (page 161)

Day-to-day dishes for which sweet cicely is traditionally used:

SALADS AND SALAD DRESSINGS	Mixed with other herbs on green salads; avocado dressing.
VEGETABLES	Cabbage and root vegetables.
SAUCES AND ACCOMPANIMENTS	Sweet sauces; Herb butter.
SWEETS AND DESSERTS	Fruit salads; rhubarb and other tart fruits. Creams, custards, and trifles, and with whipped cream.
DRINKS	Milk drinks, fruit drinks, and fruit cups.

Tarragon (Artemisia dracunculus)

Tarragon is lord of all culinary herbs. The *haute cuisine* of France considers it of supreme importance and bases famous sauces, such as béarnaise, hollandaise, or mousseline on tarragon. Though a strong aromatic herb, it has an unusual flavor which is sweet and slightly bitter at the same time. But for all its delicate fragrance it has a hidden tang which only comes out if too much tarragon is used. Tarragon has certainly the most outstanding and distinguished reputation as an herb in sophisticated cookery, but has not been used for medicinal purposes.

There are two varieties of tarragon, the French or true tarragon and the Russian, which has a less interesting flavor; both are perennial. French tarragon has smoother, shinier, and darker leaves, widely spaced on the stems, which also carry clusters of whitish woolly flowers. It can never be propagated by seed; plants or cuttings have to be obtained. Russian tarragon is said to improve in flavor if grown in the same place for some time; in fact, however, it is never as excellent as the French tarragon.

For growing, the plants need a dry sunny position in light, well-drained, fairly poor soil. The soil should be richer for indoor growing. It should be kept a compact bushy plant; also care must be taken to ensure sufficient drainage—tarragon does not like to have its feet in water.

Chopped tarragon leaves enhance a French dressing, and they may be sprinkled on green salads. It is an important ingredient of "fines herbes," the herb mixture used in omelettes, in marinades for meat, and in stuffings for fish and poultry—in fact it is good in all "bouquets." It is excellent on steaks and grilled fish.

Delicate vegetables, such as asparagus and artichokes, are delicious when accompanied by melted butter with chopped tarragon; the herb is also used in fillings for avocado pear. If using good fresh or green-dried French tarragon it may be used GENEROUSLY; otherwise JUDI-CIOUSLY—beware of hidden tang!

Tarragon Butter   Chicken with Tarragon
   (page 275)   (page 240)

Sauce Béarnaise   Tarragon Eggs
   (page 264)   (page 191)

Day-to-day dishes for which tarragon is traditionally used:

APPETIZERS	Tomato cocktails, fish cocktails.
SALADS AND SALAD DRESSINGS	French dressing; green, asparagus, bean, chicken salad; tarragon vinegar.
EGG DISHES	Omelettes and scrambled eggs.
SOUPS	Clear broth; chicken, mushroom, tomato, and turtle soups; fish chowders.
FISH	All fish and shellfish when baked or boiled.
MEAT	Steaks, veal, sweetbreads, liver.
POULTRY AND GAME	Stuffings; chicken, duck, hare, and rabbit.
VEGETABLES	Spinach, zucchini; sauerkraut, salsify, celeriac, asparagus, artichokes.
SAUCES AND ACCOMPANIMENTS	Herb butter. Marinade for meat. béarnaise, hollandaise, mousseline, and mayonnaise sauces. "Fines herbes." Yorkshire pudding.

Thyme (Thymus vulgaris)

Thyme is stronger and more "outspoken" in flavor than any other herb; it is clove-like and pungent and should be used with discretion, as it can easily overpower more delicate herbs if too much is used. With tarragon it holds an important place in French cooking. Lemon thyme (Thymus citriodorus), another culinary variety, is not so versatile as garden thyme but can give a most delicious tang and exciting flavor to sweet dishes and drinks.

It was once the emblem of courage, and soup made of thyme and beer was considered a cure for shyness! Thyme helps in the digestion of fatty food and stimulates the appetite; it also has strong anti-septic qualities in its volatile oil, thymol. Today the disinfectant and digestive properties of thyme are of great value in sausages and made-up meat and fish dishes. Thyme tea is excellent for coughs and colds, when sweetened with honey. Oil of thyme, distilled from the plant, is used for liniments and in toothpastes and mouth washes.

Garden thyme is a low perennial evergreen bush and grows about 12 inches high. It has pale mauve flowers which bloom throughout June, and the leaves are very small. Lemon thyme is a creeper, grow-ing only about six inches high, and is most suitable for rock gardens. The golden leaves have a sharp, aromatic, slightly lemony scent.

Thyme flourishes best on chalky but fertile soil; the plants seed themselves and very quickly spread. For indoor growing the plants need to be well trimmed back; when they have recovered from this, they may be transplanted into pots and gradually adapted to indoors.

Thyme helps in the digestion of foods and is the herb to use with fat meats such as mutton or pork and with rich fish such as eels and all shellfish. Thyme is a necessary part of a bouquet garni. Such a strong aromatic herb goes a long way, so it should be used with GREAT CARE.

Thyme Jelly
  (page 274)

Cheese Logs
  (pages 294–95)

Five-Herb Cheese
  (page 198)

Cheese-Herb Bread
  (page 291)

Day-to-day dishes for which thyme is traditionally used:

APPETIZERS	Raw vegetable juice; tomato juice; fish and seafood cocktails; crabs, mussels.
SALADS AND SALAD DRESSINGS	All raw salads (very small amount).
EGG AND CHEESE DISHES	Pancakes; cream cheese; cheese sauce for eggs.
SOUPS, STEWS	Thick soups (bean, minestrone, split-pea soup); jugged hare, rab-bit stew; other stews.

FISH	Lean and fat baked and boiled fish, eel.
MEAT	Beef, lamb, mutton, fat pork, and veal—rub lightly before roasting. Sausages.
POULTRY AND GAME	Stuffings; over chicken, turkey; pies, ragout.
VEGETABLES	Beans, beets, carrots, potatoes, and mushrooms and other fungi.
SAUCES	Tomato sauce; herb sauce.
SWEETS AND DESSERTS	Lemon thyme in custards and fruit salads and other sweets.

PART THREE

COOKERY RECIPES

SOME RECIPES such as CHERVIL SOUP, FENNEL SAUCE, ROSEMARY BIS-
CUITS, TARRAGON CHICKEN, etc., are based on one main herb; many
other recipes, old and new, are collected from this and other countries for various types of dishes, traditionally flavored with many
herbs. The recipes marked (B) are suggestions for a limited budget.

Cooking Temperatures

The cooking temperatures in this book are all given in degrees
Fahrenheit.

Oven Temperatures F.°	Description
225 to 250	Cool
250 to 275	Very slow
275 to 300	Slow
300 to 350	Very moderate
375	Moderate
400	Moderately hot
425 to 450	Hot
475 to 500	Very hot

Basic Methods of Cooking

Casserole—Cooking slowly in a covered container in the oven or
on top of the stove.

Deep Frying—Cooking in fat, two or more inches deep, at 370 to
375° F.

Grilling—Browning quickly without fat or with a very small amount
of fat under direct heat. Synonymous with *broiling*.

Sauté—Browning quickly in a small amount of fat in a skillet or frying pan.

Braising—Food is first sautéed, then cooked in liquid in a container with a tight-fitting lid. The word "stewing" has much the same meaning. It is often advisable to shake the pan frequently to avoid burning.

Simmering—Cooking in liquid below the boiling point; liquid should only bubble gently.

Boiling—Literally, this means that the liquid should bubble or plop vigorously; in fact, most "boiled" foods actually simmer.

Chapter 1

*F*ruit and *V*egetable
*C*ocktails, *A*ppetizers, and *D*ips

Fruit and Vegetable Cocktails

For figure watchers and those who like the clean taste of fruit and
vegetables before a meal.

(*a*) Fruit Cocktail

Ingredients:

Juice of 1 orange
Juice of ½ grapefruit
1 teaspoon lemon juice

½ teaspoon fresh chopped or green-
dried sweet cicely
Honey to taste

Mix ingredients well together.

Leave to stand (covered) for 15 minutes at least. Use honey for
sweetening unless preferred unsweetened.

These quantities will provide a seven-ounce "meal" for the slimming day or several small cocktail glasses for a party. If one teaspoon
nut butter *or* creamed almond emulsified with drops of water is
aded to the juice, a more nourishing "juice meal" results.

(*b*) Peach Cocktail

Ingredients (per person):

2 fully ripe, chilled peaches, peeled
and pitted
1 egg
½ teaspoon fresh chopped or green-
dried sweet cicely

½ teaspoon fresh chopped or green-
dried lemon balm
1 tablespoon orange juice
¼ cup milk
1 teaspoon honey

Combine peach with egg, orange juice, and milk, and add herbs.
Whirl in a blender or electric mixer until smooth.

(c) Rosemary Cocktail

Ingredients:

Juice of ½ lemon as base   Piece of celery
3 carrots   ½ teaspoon fresh chopped or green-
1 tomato   dried rosemary
Leaf of spinach *or* lettuce

Method:

1. Squeeze lemon.
2. Peel and put pieces of carrots into juice extractor.
3. Pass tomato through sieve or juice extractor.
4. Put celery and spinach or lettuce leaves into juice extractor.
5. Add rosemary and allow to stand for 10 minutes.
6. Strain, as rosemary should be removed before its flavor becomes too strong.

Note: When no juice extractor is available, root vegetables or such hard vegetables as celery can be grated, their leaves chopped, and all squeezed through muslin.

(d) Vegetable Cocktail

Use similar vegetables as for rosemary cocktail, passed through juice extractor, and flavored with such herbs as:

Parsley   Lemon Balm
Chervil   Tarragon
Fennel   Dill, etc.,

and leave standing for a longer period.

Serve strained or with the herbs (finely chopped fresh, or green-dried reconstituted) floating.

All vegetable cocktails improved in flavor by topping with a little cream before serving.

(e) Tomato Cocktail

Ingredients:

1 ripe chopped tomato   ¼ teaspoon fresh chopped or green-
1 teaspoon lemon juice per glass   dried basil (according to taste)
½ teaspoon fresh chopped or green-
    dried lemon balm

Method:

1. Force tomato through a sieve or whip in blender with remaining ingredients.
2. Add the lemon juice and herbs.
3. Allow the herbs to permeate the cocktail by leaving to stand before serving.
4. Strain if preferred.

(*f*) Tomato Cocktail for the Family

Ingredients:

1 pint plain tomato juice
Pinch salt
Pinch sugar
1 lemon
½ teaspoon each fresh chopped or

green-dried basil, thyme, marjoram, summer savory, and tarragon
1 teaspoon fresh chopped or green-dried chives

Method:

1. Add herbs, salt, and sugar to tomato juice and allow to steep at room temperature for one hour, stirring occasionally.
2. Add juice of one lemon, put into refrigerator, and leave until ready to serve, preferably four to six hours.
3. Strain before serving.

Eggplant Caviar

An excellent mixture—may be used as an appetizer on toast, on crunchy biscuits, on whole-grain bread and butter; as a spread, for buffet parties and receptions; and as a dip with potato chips.

Ingredients:

1 large, whole, undamaged eggplant
Oil
1 teaspoon lemon juice (approx.)
Salt
Paprika
1 teaspoon finely chopped onions

2 teaspoons fresh chopped or green-dried parsley
1 teaspoon fresh chopped or green-dried chervil
½ teaspoon fresh chopped or green-dried tarragon (if green-dried, reconstitute in lemon juice)

Method:
1. Wash or wipe whole eggplant.
2. Bake in its skin in the oven and turn frequently to get it evenly baked.
3. After 30 to 45 minutes (according to size); when it is soft it may be removed from the oven.
4. In order to retain the light color, peel carefully with a wooden, horn, or plastic fruit knife, removing first all burned or dark bits of the peel.
5. Then quickly mash the flesh with a wooden spoon (or in an electric blender)—it should retain light green color.
6. Add oil, approximately half of the quantity of the mashed eggplant, and mix well; add lemon juice according to taste—taking into account lemon juice already used for reconstituting the herbs; and add salt and paprika.
7. Add onions and herbs.
8. Will keep in the refrigerator for a few days, but should always be served chilled.

Avocado Appetizers

Highly recommended—to be used as an *hors d'oeuvre* on savory biscuits, as a dip with potato chips, on whole-grain and French bread, etc.

Ingredients:

½ avocado pear
1 small tomato, very finely diced
1 teaspoon onion, finely chopped
1 teaspoon each fresh chopped or green-dried basil and chervil

2 mixed teaspoons oil and lemon juice
Pinch of salt

Method:
1. Mash avocado well.
2. Add salt, oil, and lemon.
3. Add tomato and onion.
4. Add basil and chervil.

Celery Sticks with Cheese

Clean celery sticks and choose long and flat ones. Leave on some leaves. Pass cream cheese through sieve; add top of the milk until smooth and fluffy. The mixture should remain thick. Add freshly chopped or green-dried celery leaves according to taste or until mixture looks fairly green.

Either serve as a dip with celery sticks or arrange small heaps of cream cheese on the lower white base of the celery stick.

Celery sticks may be served in the same way with roquefort. For this purpose mash cheese with a fork and mix well with butter until a smooth but thick mixture is obtained. Add celery leaves according to taste and serve small heaps on celery sticks.

Cheese and Horseradish Paste

This paste may be served on celery sticks as an appetizer, on bread and canapés, or, if thinned a little with extra cream, as a dip.

Ingredients:

4 oz. cream cheese
2 oz. butter
1-1½ heaped tablespoons finely grated horseradish (varies according to taste and whether horseradish is very hot)
1 tablespoon lemon juice
2 level tablespoons fresh chopped or green-dried tarragon
Pinch of sugar and salt
1 teaspoon double cream

Method:
1. Cream butter.
2. Pass cheese through a sieve and blend with butter.
3. Add tarragon, sugar, salt, and lemon juice.
4. Add horseradish.
5. Add double cream.
6. Mix all well to a firm paste.

Pâté made with Chicken Liver

A delicate paste for the not-so-health-conscious but more gourmet-minded of your guests.

Ingredients:

½ lb. chicken livers
2 tablespoons cream cheese
½ teaspoon fresh chopped or green-dried marjoram
1 tablespoon fresh chopped or green-dried chives
Pinch of fresh chopped or green-dried rosemary (crushed)
¼ lb. butter
1 tablespoon brandy, sherry, or wine
Salt
Paprika } According to taste
Nutmeg

Method:

1. Cook livers slowly in covered pan with tablespoon of butter—DO NOT BROWN.
2. Remove pan from the heat, take out liver and pass it through a sieve or mash in liquidizer.
3. Add the wine to the liquid left in the pan; stir well.
4. Mix the remaining butter, cream cheese, herbs, and seasoning with the liquid from the pan to a smooth consistency.
5. Add sieved liver and whisk well.
6. Put into covered dish and keep cool until needed.
7. Serve on thin dry toast or crisp wheat wafers.

Note: Becomes better when kept for a day or two in the refrigerator.

Ham-Lovage Spread (*makes ⅔ cup*)

Served on small biscuits, whole-grain bread, or rye wafers as an appetizer.

Ingredients:

½ lb. minced cooked ham
6 oz. butter
Pinch of paprika

2 tablespoons fresh chopped or green-dried lovage (if green-dried, reconstitute in lemon juice)

Method:

1. Blend ham with butter and lovage.
2. Add paprika.
3. Mix well.
4. Use on canapés or as sandwich spread.

Note: The spread may be made from lovage seed or any other herb seeds, such as dill seed, celery seed, or poppy seed.

Herb Canapés

There are many recipes elsewhere in the book which are suitable for canapés, especially on pages 104 and 287. Here follow three herb canapés in particular:

Nasturtium

Blend quarter pound cream cheese with two teaspoons chopped tender leaves and stems of nasturtium. Decorate with nasturtium flowers.

This spread should be eaten at once, as it becomes bitter if left standing for any length of time.

Rosemary

To quarter pound finely chopped walnuts, add two ounces finely chopped green olives and two teaspoons crushed fresh or green-dried rosemary.

Tarragon

Place asparagus tips on bite-size pieces of buttered whole-grain bread. Sprinkle liberally with fresh chopped or green-dried tarragon, reconstituted in lemon juice.

Garnish with dabs of mayonnaise to which a little tarragon has been added.

Bachelor Toast with Herbs (*serves 4*)

Substantial starter or TV snack.

Ingredients:

1 clove garlic, minced or crushed   4 slices French bread
2 tablespoons butter   Grated Cheddar cheese
½ teaspoon each fresh chopped or
    green-dried marjoram and chives

Method:

1. Mix crushed garlic with butter.
2. Add herbs.
3. Spread garlic butter on French-bread slices and sprinkle heavily with grated cheese.
4. Place in hot over (400°) until bread assumes a rich yellow-brown color and the cheese has melted and mingled into the bread with the butter.

Shrimp Toast (*serves 6–8*)

A delicately flavored *hors d'oeuvre* or snack.

Ingredients:

8 oz. shrimp
4 oz. fat raw pork
2 tablespoons onion, minced
1 tablespoon cornflour
1 egg, beaten
¼ teaspoon oil
1 teaspoon sugar
1 teaspoon salt
2 tablespoons fresh chopped or green-dried parsley

½ teaspoon fresh chopped or green-dried fennel
1 teaspoon fresh chopped or green-dried dill
½ teaspoon fresh chopped or green-dried marjoram
6 slices stale bread
Oil for cooking

Method:

1. Finely mince together shrimp, pork, and onion.
2. Mix cornflour, egg, and oil together, and add to shrimp mixture.
3. Add sugar, salt, and herbs, blending well.
4. Spread mixture on bread slices.
5. Heat oil in heavy frying pan and slide in bread slices, shrimp-side down.
6. Fry until the bread is a golden brown; it takes about 10 to 15 minutes.

Rosemary Walnuts

Serve as an unusual appetizer—also excellent for sherry and other wine parties.

Ingredients:

1 tablespoon melted butter
1 teaspoon crumbled rosemary
½ teaspoon salt

¼ teaspoon paprika
1 cup walnut halves

Method:

1. Mix together the melted butter, rosemary, salt, and paprika with the walnuts.
2. Pour into a shallow pan, spreading nuts in a single layer.
3. Roast until richly brown in a moderate oven (350°), shaking occasionally, for about 10 to 15 minutes.
4. Serve hot, as an appetizer. May be reheated.

Various Dips

Everyone likes an occasional snack, but it is extremely difficult for the figure watchers to find something which will not add to their calorie intake. The following snacks may be offered as *hors d'oeuvres* or may be served when the family watches a TV show. They are particularly good for the weight-conscious teenager, who will appreciate them when coming home from school.

Raw Fruit and Vegetables with Various Dips

Arrange a variety of raw vegetables, such as tomato slices, cucumber sticks, sliced raw turnips, cauliflower rosettes, green-pepper strips, carrot sticks, celery strips, suitably cut chicory, etc.

Wrap apple slices or small celery or cucumber sticks with narrow bands of boiled ham, salami, or other luncheon meat. Secure with cocktail sticks and serve on a flat tray.

Top carrot, cucumber, or celery sticks with ripe olives, securing with cocktail sticks, and serve in a bowl of crushed ice.

All these are intended to be used for dunking in special dips.

(*a*) Herb and Yogurt Dip

Ingredients:

2 cups sour cream *or* yogurt
1 teaspoon caraway seeds
2 teaspoons minced onion
2 teaspoons fresh chopped or green-dried onion green *or* chives

Salt
½ teaspoon fresh chopped or green-dried summer savory
A dash of fresh chopped or green-dried thyme

Method:
Blend sour cream or yogurt with all the other ingredients, allow to permeate, and then chill for several hours.

(*b*) Herb Mix Dip

Ingredients:

1 cup yogurt *or* sour cream
½ teaspoon fresh chopped or green-dried lovage

1 teaspoon each fresh chopped or green-dried rosemary, thyme, parsley, dill, tarragon, sage, and basil

Method:
Mix ingredients well together and season with a little salt and a little paprika.

(c) Rainbow Cheese Bowl

Ingredients:

½ lb. cottage cheese
1 teaspoon salt
1 tablespoon fresh chopped or green-dried chives
or 1 teaspoon fresh chopped or green-dried summer savory *or* nasturtium

½ cup coarsely grated carrot
½ cup sliced radishes
½ cup sliced spring onions
or ¼ cup chopped onions and fresh chopped or green-dried onion green

Method:

1. Mix cheese with salt and herbs and add a vegetable to each part, thus making three different flavors and colors (carrot, radish, onion).
2. Spoon into shallow bowl in three segments.
3. Separate segments with long sticks of any large vegetable, celery, for example.
4. Decorate each segment with the appropriate vegetable.

Note: Alternate apple wedges of red and green apples may be arranged around the bowl of these various cheese dips, but a variety of apple should be chosen which will not turn brown quickly.

For other dips, use:

Horseradish-Cheese Spread (page 111)
Tomato-Cottage Cheese Spread (page 104)

Red Radish Spread (page 104)
Carrot-Cheese Spread (page 105)

Dip for Shellfish

Something tasty and different for the imaginative party giver.

Ingredients:

¼ cup chopped onions
1 tablespoon butter
1 tablespoon bread crumbs
½ apple, grated
1 teaspoon lemon juice
3 tablespoons fresh horseradish (grated), or the equivalent of dried horseradish, according to taste

1 tablespoon fresh chopped or green-dried parsley
A pinch each of fresh chopped or green-dried marjoram, thyme, basil
Salt }
Paprika } according to taste
1 cup mayonnaise
½ cup curd (pot cheese) or cottage cheese

Use also Tarragon, Chervil, Celery leaves, Lovage, Rosemary, Summer savory; see PART Two for proportions.

Method:
1. Sauté onions in butter until golden.
2. Add bread crumbs and sauté until golden.
3. Remove from heat and allow to cool.
4. Add grated apple, lemon juice, the horseradish, the herbs, and seasoning.
5. Mix well with curd and mayonnaise.

Avocado Pear with Horseradish Cream

An elegant starter to a dinner or luncheon.

Cut ripe avocado pears into halves; if the avocados are large, cut into quarters. Remove stones and fill with the following mixture:

Horseradish cream:
(Quantities given are only approximate according to taste and strength of the horseradish available.)

½ horseradish stick, grated
Fresh bread crumbs
1 tablespoon butter
1 dessertspoon yogurt
1 teaspoon lemon (approx.)
Pinch of salt
Pinch of sugar

1 teaspoon fresh chopped or green-dried chervil
½ teaspoon each fresh chopped or green-dried tarragon and dill
1 apple
3–4 tablespoons double cream

Method:
1. Peel and grate horseradish.
2. Grate bread (clean grater by making more bread crumbs from stale bread).
3. Melt butter, add horseradish and bread crumbs, and fry until golden brown.
4. Take away from heat and grate apple into the mixture.
5. Add yogurt, lemon juice, salt, sugar, and herbs.
6. Put aside to cool (uncovered if horseradish is very hot; otherwise cover).
7. Allow to permeate until cold; then chill in refrigerator.
8. Whisk double cream to stiff consistency and chill in refrigerator.
9. Gently fold cream into the mixture, shortly before serving.
10. Arrange generously on halves or quarters of avocado pears.

Serve with lettuce leaves or curly endive, radishes, quartered tomatoes, etc.

Stuffed Tomatoes with Basil (*serves 3*)

An attractive and substantial *hors d'oeuvre*.

Ingredients:

3 large fully ripe tomatoes
2 oz. (¼ cup) cottage cheese
1 slice of processed cheese
1 teaspoon sunflower oil
Lemon juice

1 tablespoon fresh or chopped green-dried chives
½ teaspoon fresh chopped or green-dried basil, or according to taste
Paprika

Method:

1. Cut lids off tomatoes.
2. Scrape out insides.
3. Pass contents through a sieve.
4. Mix well with all other ingredients.
5. Fill tomatoes with this mixture.
6. Put lids back and serve.

Herb and Orange *Hors d'œuvre*

Equally good at the beginning or end of the meal.

Ingredients:

4 tablespoons double cream
Grated rind of ½ orange
Juice of whole orange
1 teaspoon each fresh chopped dandelion and spinach

1 teaspoon each fresh chopped or green-dried parsley and lemon balm
Lettuce leaves

Method:

1. Whip double cream until stiff.
2. Add grated orange peel and the juice, mixing carefully.
3. Mix dandelion, spinach, parsley, and lemon balm together.
4. Add herbs to the orange mixture and serve on lettuce leaves.

Pineapple-Yogurt Appetizer

A healthy and attractive way to begin a meal.

Ingredients: (per person)

2 tablespoons yogurt
Sweet cicely

Finely diced or crushed pineapple

Method:
1. Put yogurt in sherbet dish.
2. Add layer of pineapple and sprinkle with sweet cicely.
3. Repeat layers. Use yogurt for top layer; garnish with pineapple.
4. Serve chilled.

Cucumber-Herb Rings

A cool, nourishing beginning to a meal on a hot summer's day.

Ingredients:

1 cucumber
4 oz. cream cheese
1 teaspoon mayonnaise
A few drops of lemon juice

Paprika
1 tablespoon each, fresh chopped or green-dried parsley, chives, and dill

Method:
1. Cut cucumber into several pieces and take out the center.
2. Mix all other ingredients together.
3. Fill the cucumber with the cheese mixture and put in refrigerator until required.
4. Before serving, cut into thick slices; sprinkle the cucumber parts with salt and the whole slice side with paprika.
5. Serve on lettuce leaves.

Chapter 2

Salads and Salad Dressings

SALADS SHOULD BE made in good time before a meal—though not too long before—so that herbs, dressing, and the salad foods can have at least half an hour to permeate; after that the salad may be placed in the refrigerator, where this process will go on, but to a lesser degree. However, too long a period in the refrigerator will reduce the flavor of the uncooked parts of a salad, although dressings may be kept for several days. The ingredients should be carefully washed, roots scrubbed and peeled, then drained well in a salad basket.

If a salad is to be served in a salad bowl, much depends on arranging it so that the colors and the shapes do not get mixed, but are arranged, as in a garden, in separate beds, perhaps surrounded by green leaves such as lettuce and watercress. If salads are served individually, as is suggested in some of these recipes, the salad is arranged on top of a layer of leaves, perhaps garnished with egg, tomato, or olives. In this case the ingredients of the salad should be well mixed with the dressing in the salad bowl and then be arranged on plates.

The salad bowl should be a wooden one, except for fish salads or salads flavored with anchovy—these must be made in a glass or china bowl; otherwise the fish flavor will remain in the wood. The best way to serve all salads—other than fish—is in a wooden bowl, preferably a shallow one for those salads arranged in strips. Wooden servers should be used.

Macaroni and Shrimp Salad (*serves 8*)

An unusual and very tasty salad.

Ingredients:

4 cups elbow macaroni
Water
Salt
1 lb. cooked shrimps cut in pieces *or* small whole shrimps
1 cup fresh chopped *or* ¼ cup green-dried onion green

1 cup fresh chopped *or* ½ cup green-dried celery leaves
6 chopped hard-boiled eggs
Enough mayonnaise to bind (about 1 pint) (see page 82)
Lettuce

Method:
1. Cook macaroni in salted water until just tender.
2. Drain, rinse, and cool.
3. Combine with cooked shrimps.
4. Add onion green, celery leaves, hard-boiled eggs.
5. Bind with mayonnaise.
6. Add more salt for seasoning, if necessary.
7. Serve cold on beds of lettuce.

Sausage Salad (*serves 6*)

A concentrated salad—add diced potatoes if liked.

Ingredients:

6 frankfurters
3½ oz. Gruyère cheese, diced
Good quantity of fresh chopped
   or green-dried chives
1 tablespoon lemon juice

2 tablespoons oil
1 teaspoon fresh chopped or green-
   dried mint
Salt

Method:
1. Cut frankfurters into thin slices.
2. Mix frankfurters, cheese cubes, and chives.
3. Stir well together the lemon juice, oil, mint, and salt.
4. Add this mixture to sausages, cheese, and chives.
5. Allow to permeate half an hour before serving.
6. Serve on salad leaves.

Niçoise Salad (cooked salad) (*serves 4*)

For buffets and cold meals.

Ingredients:

5 boiled potatoes
4 tomatoes
Radishes
Olives
Gherkins
3 hard-boiled eggs
3 tablespoons oil
2 tablespoons lemon juice
Salt

1 tablespoon green-dried bouquet
   for salad
or 1 teaspoon each fresh chopped or
   green-dried chives and chervil
1½ teaspoons fresh chopped or
   green-dried parsley
½ teaspoon fresh chopped or green-
   dried basil
Cabbage lettuce leaves

Method:
1. Slice vegetables and eggs.
2. Prepare salad dressing with the herbs.
3. Mix dressing with vegetables and eggs.
4. Add lettuce leaves to the salad shortly before serving.

Raw Carrot and Horseradish Salad (*serves* 6)

May be served as *hors d'oeuvre,* but is best as accompaniment to cold meat.

Ingredients:

½ lb. grated carrots
1 tablespoon grated horseradish
1 tablespoon lemon juice
4 tablespoons top of the milk or single cream
1 tablespoon oil
1 tablespoon yogurt

1 tablespoon fresh chopped or green-dried salad burnet
or 1 tablespoon green-dried bouquet for salad
Pinch of sugar
Salt according to taste

Method:

1. Mix carrots and horseradish, immediately after grating, with lemon.
2. Mix other liquid ingredients well.
3. Add herb, sugar, and salt, and stir.
4. Mix this with grated roots.

Potato Salad

A substantial salad, suitable for many occasions.

Ingredients:

2 lbs. potatoes (approx.)
1 cup (10 oz.) vegetable stock
3 tablespoons sunflower oil
2 tablespoons lemon juice
2 tablespoons cream
1 tablespoon chopped onion

1 tablespoon each fresh chopped or green-dried onion green and chives
Salt
Nutmeg

Method:

1. Boil potatoes and peel while they are still hot.
2. Slice potatoes and cover immediately with hot vegetable stock.
3. Leave to stand for some time.
4. Make a dressing of oil, lemon juice, herbs, and cream, and mix well together.
5. Mix with potatoes while still warm.
6. Add seasoning to taste.

Note: Decorate with watercress or gherkins. May be served and decorated with hard-boiled eggs or frankfurters.

Radish-Lettuce Salad (*serves 4-6*)

Serve with cold poultry.

Ingredients:

2 small heads of lettuce	1 tablespoon lemon juice
1 small head curly endive (use inner leaves only) *or* chicory	1 dash of paprika
1 sweet fennel (if available)	1 teaspoon finely chopped onion
½ cup thinly sliced radishes *or* grated large white radish	1 teaspoon each, fresh chopped or green-dried fennel, chervil, tarragon, and chives
2 tablespoons oil	¼ teaspoon fresh chopped or green-dried summer savory

Method:

1. Tear lettuce and endive leaves into bite-size pieces; place in a large salad bowl.
2. Trim the head of the fennel and thinly slice the heart.
3. Add, with radishes, to salad bowl.
4. Pour oil into a small bowl.
5. Add lemon juice and all the herbs, paprika, and onion, blend until smooth, and pour over salad.
6. Toss lightly with wooden salad spoon or fork until mixture is evenly coated.
7. Divide for four or six salad plates.

Salmon Salad (*serves 4*)

An easy but substantial salad for an outdoor meal.

Ingredients:

1 lb. cold boiled salmon	1 teaspoon each fresh chopped or green-dried parsley and summer savory
3 sliced hard-boiled egg yolks	
Salt to taste	
1 dessertspoon each fresh chopped or green-dried chervil and dill	1 tablespoon mayonnaise
	1 medium-sized crisp lettuce

Method:

1. Skin, bone, and flake salmon (or use canned salmon).
2. Place in a mixing bowl with the egg yolks, herbs, salt, and mayonnaise.
3. Toss ingredients lightly together with wooden salad servers.
4. Line four cold salad plates with washed and dried lettuce leaves.
5. Divide salad equally between plates.

Bean Salad (*serves 4*)

A very good salad with cold poultry.

Ingredients:

1 lb. string beans
2 tablespoons sunflower oil
1 tablespoon lemon juice
1 medium-sized onion
1 minced clove garlic
1 teaspoon each, fresh chopped or

green-dried parsley and summer savory
Some lettuce leaves
1 chopped hard-boiled egg
Grated Parmesan cheese to taste

Method:

1. String and slice beans.
2. Cook in boiling salted water until crisp but tender; drain and cool thoroughly.
3. Place in a wooden salad bowl.
4. Gradually beat the oil into the lemon juice.
5. Peel and slice onion thinly.
6. Stir the onion and garlic into the oil mixture.
7. Add herbs and salt and stir until thoroughly blended.
8. Pour dressing over the beans.
9. Mix slightly with wooden salad servers.
10. Cover and chill in refrigerator.
11. When ready to serve, garnish with egg and Parmesan cheese. May be served on plates with lettuce leaves.

Curly Endive Salad (*serves 6*)

A summer salad.

Ingredients:

1 peeled clove garlic
1 head curly endive
2 cups sliced cold boiled potatoes
4 hard-boiled eggs, in quarters
¼ cup sunflower oil

Juice of 2 lemons
½ teaspoon each fresh chopped or green-dried marjoram, salad burnet, chervil, and tarragon
Salt to taste

Method:

1. Halve garlic and rub inside of wooden salad bowl.
2. Tear the endive into bite-size pieces.
3. Place the endive, potatoes, and egg in the bowl.
4. Blend in the oil with the lemon juice and herbs.
5. Toss lightly with wooden salad servers.
6. Season to taste with salt and toss lightly again.
7. Divide equally between six salad plates and serve at once.

Eggplant Salad (*serves 6*)

Nourishing and refreshing—an excellent main dish.

Ingredients:

2 medium-sized eggplants
1 tablespoon lemon juice
½ teaspoon finely minced onion
1 cup shredded celery
½ cup chopped nuts
Salt to taste
1 teaspoon each fresh chopped or green-dried tarragon and chervil

½ teaspoon fresh chopped or green-dried summer savory
1½ tablespoons oil
1 dessertspoon lemon juice
Crisp lettuce leaves
6 quartered hard-boiled eggs
Spanish stuffed olives (optional)

Method:

1. Peel and cut eggplants into one-inch cubes; place in a saucepan.
2. Cover with boiling salted water and add lemon juice.
3. Cover and boil until tender; then drain, chill, and place in wooden salad bowl.
4. Add onion, celery, nuts, salt, and herbs.
5. Mix the oil with the lemon juice, and add to the salad bowl. Mix well.
6. Divide into six equal portions.
7. Serve on salad plates lined with lettuce leaves.
8. Garnish with eggs and olives.

Basic French Dressing (*makes ½ pint*)

Enough for four medium-sized salads.

Ingredients:

¾ cup olive *or* salad oil
¼ cup lemon juice
½ teaspoon salt
½ teaspoon castor sugar
¼ teaspoon each fresh chopped or green-dried tarragon, summer savory, and chervil

¼ teaspoon paprika
Freshly ground black pepper to taste
1 saltspoon dry mustard

Method:

1. Place all the ingredients in a glass jar with a tightly fitting screw top.
2. Shake until thoroughly blended, then chill.
3. Shake well each time before using.

Piquant French Dressing (*makes 8 oz.*)

Ingredients:

1 dessertspoon salt
¼ teaspoon castor sugar
1 saltspoon freshly ground black pepper
1 saltspoon paprika
½ teaspoon prepared mustard
2 teaspoons fresh chopped or green-dried tarragon

¼ teaspoon onion juice *or* minced onion
½ clove garlic, crushed
1 dessertspoon boiling water
¼ cup olive *or* salad oil
1¾ tablespoons lemon juice *or* wine vinegar

Method:

1. Mix the seasonings in a bowl with a small wooden spoon.
2. Add tarragon, onion, and garlic.
3. Stir in boiling water.
4. Gradually stir in the oil and lemon, or vinegar.
5. Beat till blended; then beat again before using.

Mayonnaise (see page 82)

Horseradish Mayonnaise

Ingredients:

2 tablespoons grated horseradish, or according to taste

1 cup mayonnaise (see page 82)

Method:

Simply blend ingredients well together.

Green Mayonnaise

To serve with lobster.

Ingredients:

2 tablespoons fresh chopped or green-dried parsley
1 tablespoon each fresh chopped or green-dried chives and tarragon

1 teaspoon each fresh chopped or green-dried chervil and dill
2 cups mayonnaise (see page 82)

Method:

Blend all ingredients well together; allow to stand an hour before serving.

Herb Salad Dressing (*makes 8 oz.*)

For any mixed salad to be served with cold lamb or duck.

Ingredients:

1 teaspoon each fresh chopped or green-dried mint and lemon balm
½ teaspoon each fresh chopped or green-dried marjoram and summer savory

2½ tablespoons oil
1 tablespoon lemon juice
1 clove garlic
1 lightly beaten egg
Salt and pepper to taste

Method:

1. Mix the herbs with the oil and the lemon juice in a small basin.
2. Chop or crush garlic finely and add with egg.
3. Stir, till blended, with a small wooden spoon.
4. Season to taste with salt and freshly ground black pepper.
5. Stir thoroughly before using with any salad.

Yogurt Dressing (*about ½ pint*)

A salad accompaniment, especially for a green salad.

Ingredients:

½ clove garlic
¼ cup finely chopped onion
¼ cup each fresh chopped or green-dried celery leaves and parsley
1 tablespoon fresh chopped or green-dried basil

½ teaspoon salt
1 teaspoon castor sugar
¾ tablespoon tomato puree
1 cup yogurt

Method:

1. Peel and finely mince the garlic.
2. Mix all ingredients, in order given, in a small basin.
3. Stir till smoothly blended.

Avocado-Dill Dressing

This light-green, speckled dressing, delightful to look at, is a delicious accompaniment to any delicate vegetable salad, goes well with fruit salads, and is excellent with asparagus.

Ingredients:

1 medium-sized avocado
Salt
1 tablespoon honey
⅓ cup sunflower *or* other good salad oil
4 tablespoons lemon juice
1 teaspoon each fresh chopped or

green-dried sweet cicely and lemon balm
2 teaspoons fresh chopped or green-dried dill
¼ cup water

Method:

1. Halve avocado, discarding the stone.
2. Scoop the flesh out of the skin and cut directly into blender.
3. Add salt, honey, salad oil, herbs, lemon juice directly to the blender; add the water; turn on blender and blend about two minutes, or until smooth.
4. Store the dressing in the refrigerator.

Note: This salad dressing is lower in calories than mayonnaise or even French dressing and looks very attractive served with salads, particularly for a buffet. Some additional water may have to be used to thin the dressing. It makes about two cups.

Remoulade Dressing (*makes 1⅓ cups*)

Almost a sauce, to go with salads, asparagus, vegetable fritters, and grilled meat.

Ingredients:

1 cup freshly made mayonnaise (see page 82)
¼ cup finely chopped gherkins
1 dessertspoon finely chopped capers (optional)

½ teaspoon prepared mustard
½ teaspoon each fresh chopped or green-dried chervil, parsley, and tarragon

Method:

1. Place mayonnaise in a small mixing bowl.
2. Stir in remaining ingredients in order given.
3. Blend till smooth.

Chiffonade Dressing (*about ¾ pint*)

A thin dressing for any mixed or tossed salad.

Ingredients:

1 cup sunflower oil
¼ cup lemon juice

½ teaspoon fresh chopped or green-dried summer savory

½ teaspoon salt
½ teaspoon castor sugar
1 teaspoon fresh chopped or green-dried basil

½ teaspoon paprika
½ teaspoon minced onion
¾ tablespoon diced green pepper
1 finely chopped hard-boiled egg

Method:
Mix all ingredients thoroughly together, in order given, in a mixing bowl or electric blender, until blended.

Herb Vinegars

The acid in salad dressings may be supplied either with lemon juice, yogurt, or vinegar, but the vinegar should be preferably wine or cider vinegar, and may often be a vehicle for herbs. One tablespoon of chervil, chives, mint, parsley, salad burnet may be added to the vinegar. Pour it into a porcelain jar; cover with a cheese cloth; allow to stand for two to three weeks, strain off into bottles, and cork tightly.

(*a*) Burnet Vinegar

Ingredients:
½ pint white wine vinegar
½ pint dry white wine
½ cup fresh chopped burnet leaves
or 1½ tablespoons green-dried leaves

½ chopped shallot
Lemon verbena leaves (optional)
or lemon thyme (optional)

Method:
1. Mix vinegar and wine in a deep enamel pan.
2. Add burnet leaves.
3. Add shallot and (if desired) a pinch of lemon verbena or lemon thyme.
4. Simmer the mixture for 30 minutes.
5. Strain through filter papers or a wet linen cloth.
6. Pour into sterilized bottles and cork them tightly.
7. When the vinegar has mellowed for two weeks, pour it into smaller bottles in which fresh sprigs of burnet have been placed.

(*b*) Tarragon Vinegar

Ingredients:
Fresh tarragon leaves *or* shoots
or 1 tablespoon green-dried tarragon

Rind of ½ lemon (without white pith)
2–3 whole cloves
White wine *or* cider vinegar

Method:

1. Fill a quart glass jar with fresh tarragon leaves or shoots, putting them in loosely, or with the green-dried tarragon.
2. Place rind and cloves in the jar and fill up with vinegar.
3. Screw cover down tightly; allow to stand in the sun for two weeks.
4. Strain, pressing liquid from the leaves.
5. Pass through filter paper, pour into small bottles, and cork tightly.

(*c*) Nasturtium Vinegar

Ingredients:

Nasturtium blossoms
1 shallot, peeled
⅓ clove garlic

½ red pepper, thinly sliced
Cider vinegar
1 teaspoon salt

Method:

1. Fill a quart bottling jar loosely with full-blown nasturtium blossoms.
2. Add shallot, garlic, and red pepper.
3. Fill jar to the top with cold cider vinegar.
4. Cover closely and stand for two months in a shady spot.
5. Dissolve salt in the vinegar; then strain and pass through filter paper.
6. Pour into small bottles and cork tightly.

To all these vinegars, one or two sprigs of the herb in question may be added.

Sweet Dressing for Fresh Fruit Salad (*makes ½ pint*)

Ingredients:

1 tablespoon lemon juice
½ cup thick cream
Pinch of salt
1 dessertspoon fresh chopped or green-dried sweet cicely
1 teaspoon fresh chopped or green-dried lemon balm

1 pinch fresh chopped or green-dried lemon thyme
A dash of ground ginger
1½ tablespoons sifted icing sugar
1 avocado pear

Method:

1. Place the lemon juice, cream, herbs, salt, ginger, and sugar in a bowl or an electric blender.

2. Peel and stone pear; then cut into fine dice.

3. Blend until smooth and fluffy, either with a wooden spoon or in blender.

4. Chill thoroughly.

Note: To make a fluffier dressing, fold in an additional half cup double cream, whipped till thick, just before serving.

Lemon-Cream Dressing (*makes* ½ *pint*)

Delightful accompaniment to any fruit salad.

Ingredients:

1 teaspoon lemon juice
2 egg yolks
1 teaspoon honey
1 teaspoon each fresh chopped or green-dried sweet cicely and lemon balm

1 pinch fresh chopped or green-dried lemon thyme
1 cup cream, *or* sour cream, *or* yogurt

Method:

1. Blend the lemon juice with the egg yolks.

2. Stir in honey, herbs, and cream.

3. Beat with a wooden spoon until smoothly blended.

4. Use with fruit salad.

Chapter 3

*E*gg and *C*heese *D*ishes, *S*avories, *S*nacks

Eggs in Casserole

Ingredients:

2 teaspoons lovage
Pinch of summer savory
½ cup of double cream
½ cup of sour cream
(*or* all double cream)
¾ cup soft sharp Cheddar cheese
6 beaten eggs
2 teaspoons fresh chopped or green-dried herbs consisting of bouquet for omelettes

or a mixture of
1 teaspoon fresh chopped or green-dried chervil
1 teaspoon fresh chopped or green-dried chives and parsley
1 pinch each of fresh chopped or green-dried lemon thyme and marjoram

Method:

1. Add lovage and summer savory to cream and allow to stand for a while.
2. Pour half the seasoned cream into a buttered shallow baking dish.
3. Crumble cheese into the mixture and dot with butter.
4. Add herbs to beaten eggs, and pour eggs carefully over the cream and cheese mixture.
5. Bake in a moderate oven (350°) 20 to 30 minutes, or until the eggs have formed a light crust but are still soft.
6. Pour the remaining cream carefully over the eggs, and return the dish to the oven and bake for a further 10 minutes, or until the eggs have golden-puffed crust but are not dry.

Note: Any left over could be diced and served in clear soup.

Cold Egg Ring with Green and Red Sauces

A most decorative dish, excellent for a cold lunch or buffet with mixed raw salad and hot herb-buttered French loaf (page 290).

Ingredients:

8 eggs

Green sauce

1 tablespoon each chives, parsley, tarragon, chervil (fresh chopped or green-dried)
½ lemon (juice only)
⅔ cup mayonnaise (page 82)
Salt

Red sauce

1 cup mayonnaise
1 dash paprika
1 small can (5 oz.) tomato puree
1–2 teaspoons fresh chopped or green-dried basil
Pinch of sugar
Salt

Method:

If green-dried herbs are used, reconstitute them in the lemon juice in a small bowl, and, if necessary, add a little water. There should be just enough liquid for the herbs to soak up until fully reconstituted—no liquid should remain.

1. Oil well a small ring mold or tin (approximately six and a half inches).
2. Break eggs carefully into it.
3. Place in larger pan filled with boiling water.
4. Bake in moderate oven (350°) for 15 minutes or until set. (No longer, as eggs should not become hard-cooked.)
5. Turn out onto a round plate (larger than the ring) when cold.

Green Sauce

6. Chop herbs finely or reconstitute in lemon juice.
7. Add lemon juice to herbs if fresh herbs are used.
8. Whirl in a blender with mayonnaise, or whirl herbs by themselves and then add to mayonnaise.
9. Add a little salt.

Red Sauce

10. Mix well together mayonnaise, paprika, tomato puree, basil, a pinch of sugar, and salt.
11. Coat egg ring with green sauce, allowing surplus to flow to the outside.
12. Fill center with red sauce.

Herb Omelette

Individual omelettes are easier to make than larger ones.

Ingredients (per person):

2 large eggs
1 teaspoon cold water
¼ teaspoon salt
Fresh ground pepper to taste
2 tablespoons butter

1 tablespoon green-dried bouquet for omelette
or
½ teaspoon fresh chopped or green-dried tarragon
½ teaspoon fresh chopped or green-dried chervil
1 teaspoon fresh chopped or green-dried chives
1 teaspoon fresh chopped or green-dried parsley

Method:
1. Beat eggs slightly with the cold water and salt.
2. Heat a 6-in. omelette pan; add the butter and tilt the pan so that butter covers the bottom.
3. Pour in eggs all at once.
4. Stir with a fork 2 or 3 times through the bottom and round the sides, shaking pan constantly.
5. When omelette is set but still moist on top, sprinkle the herbs over it.
6. Fold it in half and place on a hot plate.
7. Keep warm until the required numbers are done.

Chervil Soufflé

Excellent, light, yet substantial, dish.

Ingredients:

3 tablespoons butter
2 tablespoons finely milled dry bread crumbs
2 tablespoons cornflour
1 teaspoon fresh chopped or green-dried chives
1 teaspoon strong stock

1 cup milk
½ cup grated mild Cheddar cheese
4 eggs
2 tablespoons fresh chopped or green-dried chervil
Pinch of summer savory
Salt

Method:
1. Butter bottom and side of three-pint casserole, using one tablespoon butter (going up one inch at the side).

2. Melt remaining two tablespoons butter in a saucepan, and stir in the bread crumbs and the cornflour.
3. Mix chives, stock, and milk, and add to the butter mixture.
4. Add the cheese and stir until thick and smooth.
5. Separate eggs; beat yolks.
6. Pour hot sauce slowly over egg yolks; return to pan.
7. Cook over low heat, stirring constantly until sauce begins to bubble and is thickened again.
8. Stir in chervil and pinch of summer savory.
9. Add salt to egg whites and beat until stiff, but not dry.
10. Fold egg whites carefully into sauce.
11. Pour into casserole and bake for 30 minutes in oven (375°).
12. Soufflé should be browned and well done.
13. SERVE AT ONCE.

Lentils with Eggs

A new taste to add to the humble lentil.

Ingredients:

½ cup lentils	A sprig of mint or ½ teaspoon green-dried mint
1 onion	
2 eggs	½ teaspoon fresh chopped or green-dried marjoram
Oil	
Garlic	½ teaspoon fresh chopped or green-dried lovage

Method:
1. Fry the chopped onion, garlic, and lentils in oil for a few minutes.
2. Add a pint of water and the herbs, and boil for 30 minutes.
3. Let it cool.
4. Meanwhile, hard-boil two or more eggs.
5. Cut eggs in quarters and serve with the lentils, leaving pieces of eggs for decoration.
   Note: Serve hot or cold.

Herb Eggs

From the cold table to the big reception, from the family supper to the garden party—a most excellent dish.

Ingredients:

4 eggs   1 tablespoon oil
1 tablespoon lemon juice   1 oz. softened butter
1 tablespoon grated cheese   A little salt
2–3 tablespoons of a mixture of the following fresh chopped or green-dried herbs (see GUIDE, page 119, for proportions):

Parsley	Chives	Onion green
Lemon balm	Tarragon	Marjoram
	Thyme	

or 2–3 tablespoons bouquet for omelettes

Method:

1. Hard-boil eggs.
2. Shell and halve.
3. Remove yolks and mash well with a fork, or pass through a sieve.
4. Add lemon juice and oil to the mashed yolks and mix well until smooth.
5. Add the herbs; the mixture should look more green than yellow when finished.
6. Add salt and grated cheese and the softened butter to smooth.
7. Let the mixture stand for 10 minutes.
8. Pile mixture into halved whites and smooth domes with a knife.
9. Serve eggs on lettuce leaves on a flat dish decorated with parsley.

Mimosa Eggs

Ingredients:

4 hard-boiled eggs   *Sauce:*
1 small can tuna fish   A little tomato purée
Home-made mayonnaise   1 carton single cream
   (see page 82)   Castor sugar
Salt
A little paprika
4 lettuce leaves
Fresh chopped or green-dried fennel

Method:

1. Halve eggs and remove yolks.
2. Mash the tuna fish and mix with mayonnaise; season with salt and paprika.
3. Fill egg whites with the mixture.

4. Put a lettuce leaf on each plate and place half egg on it.

5. Grate the yolks over the eggs, and sprinkle the eggs with plenty of fennel.

6. Surround with tomato sauce made in the following way:

Sauce:

Add a little sugar and enough tomato puree to the cream to color it pink.

Tarragon Eggs

Ingredients:

5 eggs	1 tablespoon fresh chopped or
2 tablespoons vegetable oil	green-dried tarragon
1 tablespoon fresh chopped or green-dried parsley	Salt

Method:

1. Boil the eggs for eight minutes; shell and halve.

2. Remove the yolks and mash with a fork.

3. Blend in the yolks with the oil (slowly) and herbs.

4. Add salt to taste and blend well together.

5. Fill the whites with the mixture.

6. Serve on lettuce with quartered tomatoes.

Picnic Omelette (*serves 4-6*)

This omelette is a good (hearty) dish for a family meal, but may also be taken cold for fork supper in the garden or to a picnic.

Ingredients:

1 can (15½ oz.) butter beans	½ teaspoon fresh chopped or green-dried summer savory
1 onion, finely chopped	
Sunflower oil	Pinch of thyme
Salt	6 eggs
½ teaspoon fresh chopped or green-dried sage	Knob of butter
½ teaspoon fresh chopped or green-dried basil	

Method:

1. Rinse butter beans well in cold water and drain them well.
2. Sauté the beans with finely chopped onion in just enough oil to prevent the beans from sticking.
3. When they begin to take on color, add all the herbs and salt, if necessary.
5. Beat six eggs with two tablespoons cold water.
4. Heat enough butter in a large omelette pan to cover the bottom.
6. Pour two-thirds of the eggs into the pan.
7. When the eggs have just set, spread the bean mixture on them.
8. Pour over this the remaining eggs and set the pan under the broiler under a low heat, until the surface of the omelette is formed.
9. Cover the omelette and chill in the refrigerator.

Poor Knight Fritters

This savory snack is quick and easy.

Ingredients:

1 egg	2 slices of bread
Salt, according to taste	½ oz. fat or oil
1 teaspoon fresh chopped or green-dried basil	2 tomatoes
	2 rashers bacon
½ teaspoon fresh chopped or green-dried summer savory	

Method:

1. Beat the egg well, adding salt and herbs.
2. Cut three or four half-slices of bread and remove crust.
3. Coat with the egg.
4. Melt the fat in a heavy saucepan and when very hot lay the bread in the fat.
5. Turn almost immediately to set the egg on both sides.
6. Brown under grill.
7. Garnish with grilled tomato halves, sprinkled with basil or chopped grilled bacon, if liked.

Farmer's Omelette (*serves 4-6*)

A hearty omelette, as its name implies.

Ingredients:

1 small cabbage
2 boiled potatoes
either
1 cup grated cheese
1 oz. oil
or
5 oz. coarsely chopped bacon
1½ oz. melted bacon fat

1 tablespoon fresh chopped or green-dried lovage
1 teaspoon fresh chopped or green-dried basil and tarragon, mixed
1 pinch nutmeg
3 eggs beaten up with 3 tablespoons double cream
Oil for frying

Method:

1. Boil quickly one small cabbage in salted water.
2. Drain well and press out liquid.
3. Chop up finely.
4. Grate boiled potatoes and mix with cabbage.
5. Add to this grated cheese and oil, or bacon and melted bacon fat.
6. Add eggs beaten up with cream, basil, tarragon, nutmeg, and lovage.
7. Pour the well-beaten mixture into a frying pan and cook over low heat.
8. Turn omelette and fry well on both sides; turn over with the help of a lid.

Note: Farmer's omelette may be made either with cheese or bacon.

Cream-Cheese Custards (*serves 6*)

Light and delicious with any vegetable.

Ingredients:

½ lb. cream cheese
½ cup, half each, milk and cream
¼ cup sauterne wine
1 tablespoon fresh chopped or green-dried onion green
4 eggs
1 teaspoon fresh chopped or green-dried rosemary

½ teaspoon salt seasoned with paprika
1 teaspoon fresh chopped or green-dried tarragon
Butter
Fresh herb sprigs or watercress

Method:

1. Thoroughly blend cheese with cream and wine.
2. Add onion green, rosemary, and tarragon.
3. Beat eggs with seasoned salt and combine with cheese mixture.
4. Butter bottoms of six ramekins or custard cups and fill.
5. Set in a pan of hot water, half depth of custards.
6. Serve hot from ramekins.

    or

7. Let stand five minutes and turn out on serving dishes.
8. Garnish each with a sprig of herb or watercress.
9. Serve at a luncheon or as a savory dish for dinner.

Cheddar Ring with Brussels Sprouts (*serves* 6) (B)

Brussels sprouts are the natural accompaniment to this light but satisfying ring; any other vegetables, prepared in a similar way, may be used instead.

Ingredients:

¼ cup melted butter *or* margarine
1¾ cups hot milk
1 cup soft bread cubes
3 cups (about ¾ lb.) shredded mild or medium sharp Cheddar cheese
2 cups cooked rice
3 eggs, beaten
1 tablespoon chopped onion
1 teaspoon salt
3–4 cups hot cooked and flavored brussels sprouts

1 tablespoon fresh chopped or green-dried marigold
1 teaspoon fresh chopped or green-dried summer savory
1 teaspoon fresh chopped or green-dried basil
1 teaspoon fresh chopped or green-dried parsley
1 teaspoon fresh chopped or green-dried chives
or
4 teaspoons bouquet for omelettes

Method:

1. Combine butter, milk, bread, cheese, rice, eggs, onion, herbs, salt.
2. Mix thoroughly.
3. Pour into well-buttered three- to four-pint ring mold. Set in a pan of hot water and bake in a moderately hot oven (350°) for one hour or until surface is brown.
4. Loosen edges with a knife and turn out onto a warm, flat serving dish.
5. Fill center with hot brussels sprouts, cooked with onions, onion green, lovage, and parsley (page 251).

Cheese Soufflé

This is a delicate savory which could be served as an accompaniment to vegetables for lunch or dinner and is also a substantial protein-supplying dish for the family.

Allow one egg per person; therefore the ingredients are given per egg.

Ingredients (per egg):

1 oz. grated Cheddar *or* Gruyère cheese

½ oz. butter

2 tablespoons of cream; *or* top of the milk; *or* sour cream; *or* half yogurt and half cream

1 teaspoon fresh chopped or green-dried chives

or

1 teaspoon bouquet for omelette

½ tablespoon plain flour

Method:

1. Cream the butter well with a little salt and a pinch of paprika, and gradually add one yolk after the other, the grated cheese, the cream, and the flour, beating all the time. When well mixed, gently add the stiffly beaten whites of eggs.

2. Fill mixture into well-buttered dishes lined with bread crumbs and bake at a temperature of 350°. If baked in individual dishes, 20 minutes may be enough, but if baked in one dish, at least 30 to 40 minutes are necessary.

Note: If a soufflé of six eggs is used for a festive occasion, the flour may be omitted and eight tablespoons of full cream, well whipped, gently folded in before baking.

If 5 or 6 eggs are used, a teasp. of one or the other (up to 5-6 teasp.) of the following fresh chopped or green-dried herbs can be used:

Parsley	Lemon balm	Chives
Tarragon	Onion green	Marjoram
	Thyme	

(See GUIDE, page 119, for proportions)

or

5-6 teasp. of bouquet for omelette.

Bread-and-Cheese Pie (*serves 3-4*) (**B**)

A savory edition of the well-tried bread-and-butter pudding.

Ingredients:

5 slices fairly thin dry bread	A little butter
1 large tomato	6 oz. grated Cheddar cheese
1 large onion, cooked	½ pint milk
1 dessertspoon fresh chopped or green-dried celery leaves	2 eggs
	Salt and pepper

Method:

1. Lightly butter and cut bread into squares of approximately one inch; put half in greased pie pan.
2. Slice tomato and place layer over bread (need not be completely covered).
3. Slice onion and place layer over tomato and bread.
4. Place a layer of bread squares over onion.
5. Sprinkle over celery leaves.
6. Heat milk, beaten egg, and cheese until cheese has melted, stirring all the time.
7. Pour over contents of pie pan and leave to soak through.
8. Bake in a hot oven (400° F.) for about 20 minutes, until set and top is golden brown.

Cheese Popovers (*serves 6*)

Delicious served with Frankfurter green sauce *or* spring sauce (pages 265 and 266).

Ingredients:

½ cup grated Cheddar cheese	½ teaspoon fresh chopped or green-dried thyme
2 eggs	
½ pint milk	1 teaspoon fresh chopped or green-dried chives
4 oz. flour	
½ teaspoon salt	

Method:

1. Grease six ramekins.
2. Divide the grated Cheddar, placing it in the bottom of each dish.
3. Beat together well the eggs and the milk.
4. Mix flour, salt, and herbs.
5. Make a well in center of flour and gradually add milk mixture, stirring all the time.
6. When batter is smooth and free from lumps, pour into ramekins.
7. Bake in a hot oven (425° F.) for about 20 to 30 minutes, or until they are puffed and brown.

Cheese Savory (*serves 4*) (B)

This makes a good luncheon dish. A slice of tomato and a strip of crisp bacon may be placed on the cheese.

Ingredients:

1 tablespoon flour
1 tablespoon butter
¾ cup milk
Pinch of salt
¾ teaspoon fresh chopped or green-dried basil
¼ teaspoon fresh chopped or green-dried summer savory

2 tablespoons tomato sauce
6 oz. grated Cheddar cheese
1 cup cooked vegetables such as peas, string beans, or spinach
Paprika

Method:

1. Blend flour and butter in a saucepan over a low flame.
2. Smooth out with milk; add salt, herbs, tomato sauce.
3. Add cheese, and stir until it is melted and smooth.
4. Add the cup of vegetables and stir in well.
5. Serve on toast with a dash of paprika over each.

Sage Fritters

Ingredients:

Fresh whole or green-dried whole sage leaves
Batter (page 289)
Frankfurter green sauce (page 265);
or
  Spring sauce (page 266);
or
  Remoulade dressing (page 182);
or
  Tomato sauce (page 267)

Batter:
4 tablespoons flour
Salt
6 tablespoons water
1 yolk of egg
1 white of egg
(*Method,* page 289)

Method:

1. Use fresh sage leaves, one or two per fritter, according to size. (If green-dried sage leaves are used, they should be reconstituted in water and then drained on a sieve.)
2. Dip sage leaves into batter.
3. Deep fry fritters in vegetable oil or butter until golden brown.
4. Drain and serve dry accompanied by one of the four sauces.

Cheese Snack (B)

For a one-woman lunch (takes 10 minutes), or for Sunday supper around the fire.

Method:
1. Put one slice of cheese between two slices of bread which have been lightly buttered on both sides.
2. Sprinkle either chives or bouquet for omelettes on both inner-buttered sides facing the cheese, or chives on one side and bouquet for omelettes on the other.
3. Grill on both sides of sandwich until bread is golden brown and cheese is softened.

Five-Herb Cheese (*makes about 1 cup*)

For your cheeseboard—excellent for snacks.

Ingredients:

½ lb. Cheddar cheese, shredded	2 tablespoons whipped cream
1 dessertspoon each fresh chopped or green-dried parsley, chives, thyme, sage, and summer savory	4 tablespoons sherry

Method:
1. Blend well by hand (or with electric mixer) the cheese, herbs, cream, and sherry.
2. Refrigerate for several days, or use immediately.

Chapter 4

Soups

Vichyssoise (*serves 6*)

Traditionally a creamy cold soup, but equally good served hot in winter.

Ingredients:

6 leeks, finely chopped	1 pint milk
1 onion, finely chopped	⅛ teaspoon mace
2 oz. butter	¼ pint cream
1½ pints chicken stock	¼ cup chopped chives, fresh or
4 potatoes, peeled and sliced	green-dried
Salt	

Method:

1. Gently sauté the leeks and onion in butter.
2. Cover and cook, but do not brown.
3. Add the stock, potatoes, and salt.
4. Cook until all vegetables are tender.
5. Put the vegetables through a sieve.
6. Heat the milk with the mace.
7. Add to vegetable mixture.
8. Chill.
9. Beat for two minutes; add cream and beat again.
10. Serve very cold topped with a liberal amount of chopped chives.

   Note: If chives are green-dried, they should be reconstituted in a little stock before using.

Cold Cucumber Soup (*serves 6*)

The crunchy cucumber pieces make this an unusual soup for summer parties.

Ingredients:

2 cups milk

3 beaten eggs

2 tablespoons finely chopped fresh onion green

or 1 tablespoon green-dried onion green

or the same quantity of chives

1 tablespoon finely chopped fresh or green-dried celery leaves

1 cup sour cream

1 cup chicken broth

½ cup white table wine

1½ cups finely chopped peeled cucumber

½ teaspoon paprika

1 teaspoon salt

1 teaspoon fresh chopped or green-dried dill

Method:

1. Heat milk over direct heat in top part of double boiler.
2. Gradually stir in beaten eggs, onion green, and celery leaves.
3. Place over hot water, and cook, stirring, until mixture coats a spoon.
4. Remove from heat and cool.
5. Fold in sour cream.
6. Stir in broth, wine, cucumber, paprika, salt, and dill.
7. Chill thoroughly.

Chervil Soup (*serves 4*)

Best of all soups.

Ingredients:

2–3 tablespoons butter *or* oil

2 tablespoons flour

3 tablespoons fresh chopped or green-dried chervil

1 pint hot vegetable stock

Salt

1 tablespoon cream, fresh or sour

Method:

1. Sauté chervil in butter, or oil.
2. Add the flour and sauté again.
3. Smooth with a little cold water or stock.
4. Add the hot stock and salt.
5. Cook for 20 minutes.
6. Lastly, add the cream, shortly before serving.

Sorrel Soup (*serves 6–8*)

One of the most popular French soups.

Ingredients:

1 oz. butter *or* oil
1 lettuce (large)
2 tablespoons fresh chopped or green-dried sorrel, reconstituted
4 potatoes, quartered
1 onion *or* ½ leek, chopped

1 cup spinach *or* equivalent in lettuce
2 quarts boiling stock *or* water
1 tablespoon fresh chopped or green-dried chervil
(4 slices buttered toast, if liked)

Method:

1. Sauté onion or leek in hot butter or oil, without browning, in large saucepan.
2. Add sorrel, chopped lettuce, and spinach, and sauté.
3. Add potatoes and stock.
4. Simmer gently for 45 minutes.
5. Mash potatoes, or pass them through a coarse sieve.
6. Add chervil and simmer for five minutes.

   Note: For more substantial soup, serve over buttered toast.

Lovage Soup (*serves 4*)

A full-bodied nourishing soup.

Ingredients:

2 onions
½ oz. butter
½ oz. flour
1 pint stock
½ pint milk

Salt
2 tablespoons fresh chopped or green-dried lovage
1 tablespoon chopped parsley

Method:

1. Peel and slice onions.
2. Sauté onions in the butter until soft but not brown.
3. Add the lovage and sauté.
4. Add flour and cook for a further few minutes.
5. Add stock and salt. Stir until it comes to a boil.
6. Simmer for 20 minutes.
7. Add milk.
8. Put through a sieve or blender.
9. Heat again, and serve sprinkled with chopped parsley.

Herb Soup (*serves 6*)

A delicately flavored soup to be made all the year round.

Ingredients:

3 tablespoons flour

2 tablespoons butter *or* oil

2 pints stock

2 tablespoons cream

2½ tablespoons mixed fresh chopped or green-dried tarragon,

chervil, parsley, lovage, and basil (for proportions, see GUIDE, page 119)

or

2½ tablespoons herb bouquet for soups and stews

Method:

1. Sauté three tablespoons flour in butter or oil.
2. Add stock, and cook for 20 minutes.
3. Put herbs and cream into a large bowl.
4. Add thickened hot stock and mix well.
5. Allow to stand for half an hour.
6. Reheat and serve.

Note: This soup could also be made with chives only.

Herb Soup (2nd version)

This version is particularly suited to using green-dried herbs. It has the same ingredients as the above Herb Soup.

Method:

1. Sauté the flour in butter or oil.
2. Add all the herbs and sauté.
3. Smooth with stock and then add all the stock.
4. Cook for 20 minutes.
5. Add cream shortly before serving.

Green Soup (*serves 6*)

A substantial soup which also makes a good main course for lunch or supper.

Ingredients:

3 pints beef, ham, or strong vegetable stock

8 oz. minced raw spinach

4 oz. fresh chopped onion green *or* ½ oz. green-dried onion green (= 8 tablespoons)

4 oz. mixed greens (kale, brussels sprouts, or beet tops, etc.), chopped

1 teaspoon fresh or green-dried sorrel

Bouquet of parsley, celery leaves, and rosemary, *or* 1 teaspoon each of green-dried parsley and celery leaves

¼ teaspoon rosemary

1 tablespoon flour

5 tablespoons sour cream

2 tablespoons top of the milk

3 hard-boiled eggs

Method:

1. Bring the stock slowly to the boil.
2. Add the spinach, onion green, mixed vegetable greens, and the herbs tied together.
3. Simmer for one hour.
4. Remove pan from fire and take out the herbs, if in a bunch.
5. Mix flour with sour cream, gradually adding a little of the hot soup at the same time, until the mixture is fairly thin and smooth.
6. Add mixture to soup pan; return it to the fire and stir until it thickens slightly and just comes to a boil.
7. Serve with slices of hard-boiled egg in each soup bowl.

Thick Vegetable Soup (*serves 6–8*)

Ingredients:

1 tablespoon vegetable fat
1 tablespoon chopped onion
½ leek, shredded
½ celery, shredded
1 small carrot, diced
2–3 cabbage leaves, shredded
1–2 diced potatoes
Some spinach leaves
1 handful cooked beans
2 ripe tomatoes *or* 1 teaspoon tomato puree, diluted
4 pints water
1 teaspoon fresh chopped or green-dried chives

1 teaspoon fresh chopped or green-dried parsley
1 teaspoon fresh chopped or green-dried lovage
1 tablespoon of mixed summer savory, celery leaves, basil, onion green, marjoram (pinch), thyme (pinch), sorrel (pinch), rosemary (pinch)

or

2½ tablespoons bouquet for soups and stews

Method:

1. Melt fat and sauté onions in it.
2. Add all vegetables and sauté together.
3. Add tomatoes, or puree, and sauté again.
4. Then add water, herbs, and salt, and simmer for one hour.

Note: This soup can be made more substantial and thus becomes like the Italian minestrone, if the following ingredients are added:

5½ oz. noodles, spaghetti, *or* rice
1 tablespoon butter
2 tablespoons grated cheese (Parmesan or other)

Method:

5. Add noodles or rice and cook with the mixture for the last 15 minutes.

6. When cooked, put butter and grated cheese into a tureen or bowls and pour soup.

Thick Lentil Soup (*serves 6-8*)

Quite a good meal in itself, with or without smoked sausage or frankfurters.

Lentils are not only one of the most nourishing foods, but also are more easily digested than either beans or peas. They are an important substitute for meat, fish, or poultry. In spite of their reputation as "a poor man's meat," they have a delicious flavor, if properly cooked, particularly with herbs.

There are two kinds of lentils ordinarily available: the browny-green German lentils and the reddish-yellow small Egyptian lentils. The German lentils are "whole," while the Egyptian lentils are sold without a seed coat, looking more like split peas.

Ingredients:
½–1 lb. pink *or* green lentils (select, rinse, and soak overnight)
1 large onion, chopped
1 clove garlic, chopped
2 leeks, cut up in slices
1 stalk celery, cut up in small pieces
1 small carrot, small strips
2 small potatoes, in dices

2 teaspoons fresh chopped or green-dried lovage
¼ teaspoon fresh chopped or green-dried marjoram
1 tablespoon fresh chopped or green-dried parsley
} *or* 2 tablespoons bouquet for soups and stews, with a little extra marjoram

3 pints water *or* stock
1 oz. flour
1 oz. butter *or* dripping
½ pint stock *or* water
Salt
1 ring of smoked sausage or a round of thick, small, smoked sausages
or
1 pair of frankfurters per person

Method:
1. Sauté onions and garlic.
2. Add and sauté vegetables and herbs.
3. Add soaked lentils and their water.
4. Add diced potatoes and salt.
5. Boil until tender (1 hour or more) or cook for 15 minutes in the pressure cooker.
6. Melt the butter, add the flour and sauté.
7. Smooth with water or stock.
8. Allow to boil for 2-3 minutes.
9. Add to the lentil soup and allow to boil.
10. If sausage is served, add it now and allow to simmer for 10 minutes (or less if small sausages are used).

Chicken in Vegetable Soup

Ingredients:

1½ lb. bony chicken parts (such as wings and backs)
2 pints water
6 carrots, cut in halves
3 sprigs parsley *or* 1 tablespoon green-dried parsley
1 medium-sized onion, sliced
1 small stalk celery
1 bay leaf
¼ teaspoon fresh chopped or green-dried thyme

¼ teaspoon fresh chopped or green-dried marjoram
1 teaspoon fresh chopped or green-dried tarragon
1 teaspoon fresh chopped or green-dried summer savory
1½ teaspoon salt
Chopped chives

Method:
1. In a large saucepan put the chicken, water, carrots, parsley, onion, celery, bay leaf, thyme, marjoram, tarragon, summer savory, and salt.
2. Bring to a boil, cover, and simmer for two hours.
3. Strain and chill stock; when cold, discard fat layer.
4. Force carrots through a wire strainer and add to stock.

Chicken Vegetable Soup

This same soup can have its flavor heightened by the addition of minced chicken to the stock.

5. Put meat and skin from chicken through the mincer; add to stock.
6. Heat and serve, sprinkling each serving with chopped chives.

Court Bouillon—Stock in which to Boil Fish

Ingredients:

2 shallots
6 tiny onions
1 shredded carrot
1 bay leaf
Small strip of lemon rind
1 teaspoon fresh chopped or green-dried parsley
1 teaspoon fresh chopped or green-dried summer savory
1 tablespoon fresh chopped or green-dried lovage

1 teaspoon fresh chopped or green-dried thyme
1 teaspoon fresh chopped or green-dried basil
½ teaspoon salt
4 peppercorns
Equal quantities of water and dry white wine *or* cider to cover

Method:

1. Put all ingredients into a large saucepan.
2. Bring to the boil, cover, and allow to simmer for half an hour.
3. When tepid, put in prepared fish and simmer until cooked, about 15 minutes.

Note: If the fish is to be served cold, allow to cool in the court bouillon.

Fish Soup (*serves 4*)

An appetizing and unusual soup.

Ingredients:

2½ lbs. mixed boned fish
2 large onions
3 tomatoes
2 cloves garlic
½ cup corn oil
4 teaspoons fresh chopped or green-dried fennel

2 teaspoons fresh chopped or green-dried parsley
A pinch of marigold petals
1 bay leaf
Salt and pepper to taste
Bread
Butter

Method:

1. Pound garlic, chop onions, and tomatoes, and place in stew-pan with seasoning, herbs, and olive oil.
2. Set over heat and bring to simmering point.
3. Simmer for 5 minutes, add water, and bring back to simmering point and cook until all is tender.
4. For each person, fry a slice of bread in butter, lay in the bottom of a hot plate and strain soup over this.

Alternatively—serve the whole contents in a tureen; remove bay leaf.

Tomato Soup with Herbs (*serves 4*)

A delicate summer soup.

Ingredients:

1 teaspoon fresh chopped or green-dried basil

1 teaspoon fresh chopped or green-dried lovage

Fresh chopped or green-dried chives

2 lbs. ripe tomatoes

Salt

1 teaspoon sugar

2–3 tablespoons thin *or* sour cream

1 teaspoon lemon juice

Method:

1. Chop tomatoes finely; add salt, sugar, basil, and lovage.
2. Bring to a boil; then simmer slowly until tomatoes are pulpy.
3. Sieve.
4. Add lemon juice and cream and serve at once piping hot, garnished with chives.

A number of soups gain a special flavor and strength by the addition of herbs. In many cases this avoids using salt or seasonings for those who should not have them or who at least reduce the use of salt in cooking and eating. Apart from this purpose, the herbs often replace meat and bones; vegetable broth and yeast extracts may be used instead, as the herbs strengthen the soup.

Rice Soup (*serves 4–6*)

So good—and yet so simple to make.

Ingredients:

1½ oz. brown rice

1 tablespoon butter *or* oil

1 small onion, finely chopped

1 leek, finely chopped

Some celery *or* celeriac, finely chopped

1 small carrot, sliced

2–2½ pints stock

2 teaspoons parsley, fresh chopped or green-dried

2 teaspoons parsley, fresh chopped or green-dried

1 teaspoon fresh chopped or green-dried chervil

1 teaspoon fresh chopped or green-dried basil

1 teaspoon fresh chopped or green-dried lovage

Nut of butter

Method:

1. Rinse rice in a sieve under running warm water; allow to drain.
2. Sauté onion in butter or oil; add vegetables and sauté; add rice and sauté.

3. Add boiling stock and allow to cook until rice is tender.
4. Add all the herbs and leave to stand in warm place for 15 minutes.
5. Before serving add nut of butter.

Cauliflower Soup (*serves 6*)

Ingredients:

1 small cauliflower
1 bay leaf
1 teaspoon fresh chopped or green-dried chervil
1 tablespoon butter *or* oil
3 tablespoons flour
4 pints vegetable stock
Salt
1 tablespoon fresh chopped or green-dried parsley

1 teaspoon fresh chopped or green-dried basil
1 teaspoon fresh chopped or green-dried salad burnet (if available)
½ teaspoon fresh chopped or green-dried lemon balm
1 teaspoon lemon juice
Nut of butter
2 tablespoons cream

Method:

1. Cook cauliflower florets carefully in salted water with a bay leaf.
2. Cut uncooked stalks into small pieces.
3. Heat fat and sauté flour.
4. Add small pieces of stalk and sauté together.
5. Add stock, salt and herbs and cook for three-quarters of an hour.
6. Put all through a sieve.
7. Add cooked florets, lemon juice, cream, and butter shortly before serving.
8. Heat through but do not allow to boil again.

Semolina and Leek Soup (*serves 4–6*)

Ingredients:

1 oz. semolina
1 dessertspoon whole-grain flour
1 small onion, finely chopped
2 dessertspoons butter *or* oil
2 leeks, finely chopped
2–2½ pints stock
Salt
½ teaspoon fresh chopped or green-dried basil

½ teaspoon caraway
1 teaspoon fresh chopped or green-dried lovage
1 teaspoon fresh chopped or green-dried lemon balm
2 tablespoons cream (optional)

Method:
1. Sauté onion in butter or oil until golden.
2. Add leeks and sauté.
3. Add semolina and flour, and sauté.
4. Smooth with a little stock; then add remaining stock and allow to cook for about 20 minutes.
5. Add salt, caraway, and all the herbs.
6. Leave in a warm place for 15 minutes.
7. Add cream before serving.

Curly Kale Soup (*serves* 6)

Ingredients:

½ lb. curly kale
¾ lb. potatoes, peeled and diced
1 large onion, finely chopped
Some celery *or* celeriac, finely chopped
1 small carrot, sliced
1 teaspoon tomato puree
1 oz. butter *or* oil

2½–3 pints stock
½ teaspoon mixed fresh chopped or green-dried marjoram and sage
½ teaspoon fresh chopped or green-dried basil
1 teaspoon fresh chopped or green-dried lovage
Butter (size of a nut)

Method:
1. Strip curly kale off stalks and ribs; wash and drain.
2. Cook, covered, with a little addition of stock for five minutes; chop finely.
3. Sauté onion in butter or oil; add all other vegetables and sauté.
4. Add boiling stock; mix this with curly kale; allow to cook until tender.
5. Add the herbs and allow to stand in warm place for 15 minutes.
6. Add a nut of butter before serving.

Spring Soup

Ingredients:

1 tablespoon butter *or* oil
4 tablespoons flour
3½ pints water *or* stock
Salt
1 small onion, sliced
1 small carrot, sliced
1 teaspoon fresh chopped or green-dried celery leaves

1 teaspoon fresh chopped or green-dried lovage
Some young spinach leaves, young nettel, *and/or* dandelion, sorrel, and lovage leaves, chopped finely

Method:
1. Heat fat, add flour, and cook gently for a few minutes.
2. Add stock, salt, vegetables, chopped leaves, and herbs.
3. Simmer for a half-hour.
4. Add milk, heat through again, and serve.
5. Put cream into bowl, or divide into individual bowls, and pour soup over.

Chapter 5

*F*ish

Chilled Salmon (*serves 10–12*)

An attractive party dish.

Ingredients:

4 lbs. fresh salmon
1 pint milk
1 pint boiling water
1 tablespoon salt
2 bay leaves
1 cup mayonnaise
1 grated carrot

1 teaspoon bouquet for fish
or 1 teaspoon mixed fresh chopped
or green-dried dill, fennel, and
parsley
½ teaspoon fresh chopped or green-
dried basil
1 hard-boiled egg

Method:

1. Wrap salmon in cheesecloth to hold it together.
2. Place milk, boiling water, salt, bay leaves, herbs, in a saucepan large enough to hold the whole piece of salmon.
3. Boil for five minutes.
4. Add fish and cook gently for 35 minutes.
5. Allow fish to cool in water.
6. Remove and drain; remove skin.
7. Chill, covered, in the refrigerator.
8. Blend mayonnaise and spread over cold salmon on a serving platter.
9. Decorate with slices of hard-boiled eggs and grated carrots, and sprinkle with bouquet for fish; or with parsley, fennel, and dill, and the basil.

Bass, Mullet, or Mackerel Flambé au Fenouil (*serves 4*)

An exquisite dish well known in France—for a dinner party.

Ingredients:

2 bass at approx. 1 lb. each
Little salt
3 teaspoons fresh chopped or green-dried fennel leaves, *or* 4 table-spoons green-dried fennel
1 sprig fresh chopped sage, *or* 2 teaspoons green-dried sage
Large bunch of fennel (stalks and leaves), green-dried straight from the plant, *or* 2 handfuls of green-dried fennel from a jar
4 tablespoons oil
1 lemon, cut in slices
Parsley for garnish
1 glass brandy

Method:

1. Wash and prepare the fish, dry, and salt inside and out.
2. Fill the fish with the chopped fennel and sage.
3. Arrange a bed of green-dried fennel in the bottom of the broiling-pan.
4. Brush fish on both sides with oil and place on wire rack of broiling-pan above the fennel.
5. Broil fish, turning once, and brushing with oil from time to time.
6. Warm brandy.
7. When fish is done, remove fennel bed to flat fireproof serving dish.
8. Place fish on fennel bed and decorate with lemon and parsley.
9. Pour warmed brandy over and light it; serve while burning.

Spanish Halibut Casserole (*serves 4-6*)

Substantial, yet tasty, family dish.

Ingredients:

2 lbs. cooked halibut
1 medium-sized onion, finely chopped
¼ cup chopped green pepper
1 cup chopped celery
2 tablespoons sunflower oil *or* butter
1 can (10½ oz.) condensed tomato soup
1 soup can water
Salt

1 teaspoon curry powder
2 teaspoons lemon juice
1 tablespoon bouquet for fish
or
   1 teaspoon each fresh chopped or green-dried tarragon, basil, and celery
      leaves; ½ teaspoon each fresh chopped or green-dried marjoram and
      summer savory; ¼ teaspoon fresh chopped or green-dried thyme
¼ lb. shredded sharp Cheddar cheese
1 cup dried bread crumbs

Method:

1. Sauté onions, green pepper, and celery in oil until soft, but not
   brown.
2. Add tomato soup and the can of water.
3. Add all other ingredients but halibut, cheese, and bread crumbs.
4. Let this simmer for 15 minutes.
5. Flake halibut into a large bowl and add previous mixture, together
   with bread crumbs.
6. Blend well.
7. Place in greased casserole and bake in a medium oven (350° F.)
   for about 30 minutes, until heated through.
8. Add grated cheese topping and put casserole under the broiler
   until cheese is slightly browned.

Fillet of Sole Rolls with Egg Sauce (*serves 6*)

Ingredients:
6 fillets of sole, approx. same size
2 teaspoons butter
1 small onion, chopped
½ cup bread crumbs, soaked in
  milk and then squeezed
15 cooked shrimps (about ½ lb.),
  finely chopped
½ teaspoon each fresh chopped or
  green-dried parsley, dill, chervil
½ teaspoon fresh chopped or green-
  dried summer savory
1 hard-boiled egg, finely mashed
Salt
1 egg white, beaten stiff

Egg sauce ingredients:
2 tablespoons butter
2 tablespoons flour
½ teaspoon salt
½ cup stock
½ cup dry white wine
2 hard-boiled eggs
2 tablespoons double cream
1 teaspoon each fresh chopped or
  green-dried parsley and summer
  savory
1 teaspoon chopped capers

Method:

1. Melt butter in saucepan and sauté onion until cooked, but not brown.
2. Add squeezed bread crumbs, shrimps, herbs, mashed egg, and salt.
3. Cook gently for three minutes and remove from heat.
4. Add egg white and fold in.
5. Fill fillets with this mixture, roll, and fix with toothpicks.
6. Arrange in a greased shallow baking dish; cover with foil.
7. Bake in a moderate oven (350° F.) for 20 minutes, or just until sole flakes with a fork. DO NOT OVERCOOK.
8. Remove toothpicks and serve with egg sauce.

Egg Sauce
1. Melt the butter in saucepan.
2. Add the flour and salt, and stir until smooth.
3. Whip with a wire whisk.
4. Add the stock and the wine.
5. Simmer for five minutes.
6. Add hard-boiled eggs, finely chopped, and double cream.
7. Heat again but do not bring to the boil; then remove from heat.
8. Add parsley, summer savory, and capers.
9. Serve hot with sole rolls.

Scallops and Shrimps with Herbs (*serves 6*)

The delicate herbs cooked together with the shellfish make it an excellent dish.

Ingredients:

½ lb. scallops
3 tablespoons butter
½ teaspoon green-dried tarragon
1 teaspoon green-dried chervil or freshly chopped parsley
2 teaspoons chopped onion
¼ lb. shelled shrimps
1 tablespoon flour

½ cup, equal portions, milk and cream
¼ cup chicken broth *or* dry white table wine
Salt and pepper
Toasted buttered croutons

Method:

1. Melt butter slowly in a frying pan; stir in tarragon, chervil, and chopped onion.
2. Add scallops, and cook over medium-high heat for three to four minutes, stirring constantly.
3. Stir in shrimps.

4. Blend in flour, cream, milk, and chicken broth.
5. Cook, stirring constantly, until sauce is thickened; season to taste.
6. Divide into six scallop shells, or serve on a flat fireproof dish.
7. Top with bread crumbs and dots of butter, and brown under the broiler.
8. Serve with hot thin toast.

Halibut in Wine and Lemon (*serves 6*)

An elegant dish for a dinner party. The halibut steaks should be marinated in a mixture of lemon and wine to which is added a mixture of the following herbs (or those which are available):

1 tablespoon mixed of parsley, tarragon, chervil, dill
1 teaspoon mixed of basil, marjo-ram, thyme, summer savory: and a bay leaf, or the equivalent in shredded bay leaves

This marinade becomes the basis of the sauce served with the halibut.

Ingredients:

6 halibut steaks (about 2 lbs.)
1 egg
2 tablespoons lemon juice
1¼ cups dry white wine
Salt
A dash of paprika
4 tablespoons butter *or* margarine
1 tablespoon fresh chopped or green-dried parsley

Method:

1. Arrange fish steaks in a single layer close together in a shallow dish.
2. Beat together egg, lemon juice, one cup of the wine, salt, and all the herbs.
3. Pour mixture over the fish.
4. Cover lightly.
5. Allow to chill for one hour.
6. Lift fish from marinade and drain well.
7. Heat two tablespoons butter in a wide frying pan.
8. Add fish steaks and brown on both sides, until cooked.
9. Place fish on a heated platter in a warm place.
10. Melt the remaining two tablespoons of butter in the frying pan.
11. Add one cup marinade and one-quarter cup of wine.
12. Bring to rapid boil.
13. Pour some of the sauce over the fish.
14. Serve remaining sauce in a sauce boat at the table to add to each serving.
15. Sprinkle fish with chopped parsley and garnish with lemon slices.

Fish Steaks (*serves 4*) (**B**)

A succulent way to serve fish for the family.

Ingredients:

4 cod steaks
2 tablespoons oil
1 tablespoon butter
1 teaspoon fresh chopped or green-dried basil
½ teaspoon fresh chopped or green-dried thyme
2 teaspoons fresh chopped or green-dried parsley
1 teaspoon fresh chopped or green-dried celery leaves

Salt and pepper
1 clove garlic, finely chopped
or ¼ teaspoon concentrated garlic salt
2 pints stock
6 oz. rice, long grained
1 stalk celery, chopped
1 onion, sliced
A knob of butter
4 tomatoes, thickly sliced
Chopped parsley for garnish

Method:

1. Dust fish steaks with flour.
2. Brown quickly in hot oil and butter.
3. Place in a fireproof dish.
4. Sprinkle over herbs, seasoning, and garlic.
5. Add one-half cup stock and put in slow-to-moderate oven (350° F.) for 15 to 20 minutes.
6. Bring rest of stock to boil; add rice, celery, and onion.
7. Boil till just tender, about 15 minutes; drain.
8. Stir knob of butter into the rice.
9. Fry quickly the sliced tomatoes.
10. Arrange fish steaks on the rice, garnished with tomatoes and chopped parsley.
11. Serve very hot.

Blushing Cod (*serves 4*) (**B**)

A tasty yet satisfying way of serving everyday fish.

Ingredients:

2 lbs. cod on the bone
2–3 bay leaves
Salt
1 oz. butter
1 onion, finely sliced

1 clove garlic
1 lb. peeled tomatoes *or* 1 large tin tomatoes
2 teaspoons fresh chopped or green-dried basil

Method:

1. Place fish in saucepan with water to cover well; add bay leaves and salt.
2. Bring slowly to a boil, cover and simmer until cooked—about 20 minutes.
3. Melt butter in a saucepan and sauté gently onion and garlic; do not let them get brown.
4. Add the tomatoes, one-half teaspoon salt, and the basil; stir well, simmering gently.
5. Remove skin and bones from fish.
6. Add fish to tomato mixture; cover and leave on very low heat for five minutes.
7. Serve very hot surrounded by broccoli spears (when available).

Baked Halibut (*serves 4*)

A very good main dish; also makes a good barbecue meal.

Ingredients:

2 lbs. halibut, in one piece
¼ cup soy sauce
½ cup dry white wine
1 tablespoon lemon juice
1 clove garlic, minced
¼ cup salad oil

1 tablespoon fresh chopped or green-dried rosemary
3 tablespoons fresh chopped or green-dried parsley
½ lb. mushrooms, chopped
3 oz. butter

Method:

1. Mix together soy sauce, wine, lemon juice, garlic, and salad oil.
2. Pour this mixture over fish and marinate two to three hours.
3. Pour off marinade; save.
4. Rub fish with rosemary and parsley.
5. Place in baking pan and cover with foil.
6. Place in a hot oven (450° F.) for about 40 minutes, basting fish twice with its own juices.
7. Sauté mushrooms in butter; add marinade and heat through.
8. Pour over fish and serve.

Note: To barbecue fish, put small pieces of it on skewers, grill over low heat; cook till fish flakes when tested, about 15 minutes.

Fish Soufflé (*serves 6–8*) (B)

A light fish dish, good for supper.

Ingredients:

3 lbs. cod *or* haddock

2 tablespoons butter

2 tablespoons flour

1 pint milk

4 eggs, separated

Salt and pepper

1 tablespoon fresh chopped or green-dried fennel

1 teaspoon fresh chopped or green-dried tarragon

½ teaspoon fresh chopped or green-dried thyme

2 tablespoons fine bread crumbs

Method:

1. Place fish in steamer over boiling water and steam for 10 minutes.
2. Remove skin and bones, and flake fish.
3. Melt butter in a saucepan and stir in flour.
4. Cook a few minutes; then add milk.
5. Stir until smooth and cook for five minutes; remove from heat.
6. Beat egg yolks and add with fish to saucepan.
7. Season with salt, paprika, and herbs.
8. Beat egg whites until stiff; gradually fold into fish mixture.
9. Grease soufflé dish or casserole and sprinkle bottom with bread crumbs.
10. Pour in fish mixture and place in pan of boiling water.
11. Bake in moderate oven (350° F.) for 30 minutes.

Stuffed Haddock (*serves 4*)

Makes a substantial family meal.

Ingredients:

2½ lbs. haddock

3 tablespoons bacon fat

4 oz. mushrooms, chopped

A little flour

1½ cups court bouillon (fish stock, page 206)

Stuffing:

1 tablespoon chopped onion

1 oz. butter

6 tablespoons fresh bread crumbs

1 tablespoon fresh chopped or green-dried parsley

1 teaspoon fresh chopped or green-dried summer savory

Grated rind and juice of ½ lemon

1 egg, beaten

Salt and paprika

Method:

1. Wash and dry the fish.
2. Sauté the onions lightly in the butter until soft, but not brown.
3. Mix with bread crumbs, herbs, lemon rind, and juice.
4. Season with salt and paprika and bind with egg.

5. Stuff the haddock with this mixture and tie securely.
6. Heat the bacon fat in baking pan; put in fish and baste.
7. Cover with foil; then cook in a moderate oven (350° to 400° F.) for about 40 minutes, basting once or twice during cooking.
8. Remove fish onto a hot dish.
9. Leave a tablespoon of fat in pan; cook the mushrooms in this.
10. Add flour; cook for a few minutes; then add stock.
11. Serve the sauce with the fish.

Fresh Eel in Sage Leaves (*serves 4-6*)

A most delicate outcome of an unusual combination; eels and sage.

Ingredients:

2 medium-sized young fresh eels	Bacon slices
¼ cup lemon juice	Whole fresh or green-dried sage
½ cup vegetable oil	leaves
1 large finely chopped onion	

Approx. 1 tablespoon of a well-blended herb mixture of:

fresh chopped or green-dried parsley, tarragon, dill *or* fennel, pinches of basil, marjoram, thyme, sage, summer savory, bay leaves *or* 1 tablespoon bouquet for fish dishes } See GUIDE (page 119) for proportions

Method:

1. Skin eels and cut into pieces two to three inches long, according to thickness, and pour over them the following marinade:
   Mix well lemon juice, oil, onion, and herbs, and if there is not enough liquid to cover the pieces of eel in a bowl, add a little water or stock to the marinade.
2. Set aside to marinate for about one to two hours.
3. Wrap each piece of eel in a slice of bacon, and then cover with sage leaves and tie with thread.
   (If green-dried whole sage leaves are used for the wrapping, they should be reconstituted in water or marinade for about an hour.)
4. Place wrapped pieces of eel in a flat fireproof dish and pour the marinade over them.
5. Bake in the oven uncovered for at least half an hour.

Chapter 6

Meat

Braised Silverside (*serves 6*)

An unusual way to serve this succulent piece of beef.

Ingredients:

2 lbs. unsalted silverside
½ lb. pork rind
3 onions
3 shallots
1 clove garlic
1 teaspoon fresh chopped or green-dried thyme
1 tablespoon fresh chopped or green-dried parsley
1 teaspoon fresh chopped or green-dried tarragon
1 teaspoon fresh chopped or green-dried basil
¼ pint red wine
Salt and pepper
½ pint water
1 lb. carrots, sliced

Method:

1. Chop onions, shallots, and garlic.
2. Put them in a basin with beef, wine and a half pint water.
3. Add the herbs.
4. Leave the meat to marinate 8 to 12 hours, if possible.
5. Cut pork rind into pieces to cover bottom of large heavy saucepan.
6. Put everything, except the carrots, but including the marinade, into the pan. Season well with salt.
7. Bring to a boil with pan uncovered.
8. Lower heat to gentle simmering point and cover the pan tightly, first with aluminum foil and then with the lid pressed down.
9. Simmer for three hours or until tender, adding more wine or water if necessary.
10. After two hours, add sliced carrots.
11. Serve with the gravy from the pan.

Goulash (*serves 4*)

Egg noodles or risotto can accompany this goulash "with a difference."

Ingredients:

1 lb. chuck steak
1 large onion, sliced
2 or 3 tomatoes, chopped
1 tablespoon butter *or* bacon fat
1 clove garlic, chopped
3 potatoes, peeled and chopped
Salt
Paprika
½ teaspoon bay leaf, shredded

1 teaspoon fresh chopped or green-dried marjoram
1 cup red wine *or* water
1 green pepper chopped
2 oz. sour cream (optional)
Parsley, fresh chopped or green-dried

Method:

1. Cut meat into one-and-a-half-inch cubes.
2. Melt butter in saucepan and brown beef slowly.
3. Add onions and continue to cook until onions are tender.
4. Add seasoning, garlic, tomatoes, herbs, green pepper, and half the wine.
5. Cover and cook slowly (without boiling) for three hours.
6. Stir occasionally, adding more wine if necessary.
7. Add chopped potatoes and cook for a further 30 minutes.
8. Stir in sour cream and heat again.
9. Serve sprinkled with parsley.

Beef Casserole with Rosemary (*serves 4*)

Rosemary gives the beef casserole its exciting flavor.

Ingredients:

2 lbs. topside *or* silverside
Some bacon for larding
Salt
A little flour
Oil
2 oz. butter *or* oil
1 clove garlic, chopped

4 cloves
2 teaspoons fresh chopped or green-dried rosemary
1 teaspoon fresh chopped or green-dried sage
¾ pint red wine

Method:

1. The prepared and salted meat is larded; in case larding is too difficult the beef can be wrapped in slices of bacon which are tied round the meat.
2. Dust the meat with flour and pour oil in drops onto meat.
3. Put the butter in a very heavy saucepan or fireproof casserole.
4. Add garlic, rosemary, sage, and a few cloves.
5. Cover well and allow the meat to simmer gently for two hours in low oven (300 F.°).
6. Add stock or water from time to time.
7. Add wine after two hours.
8. Allow to stew gently for another hour.
9. Any gravy which is left should be passed through a sieve and poured back over the meat.

Beefsteak Pie (*serves 4*)

To make this dish go farther, add a few small peeled potatoes.

Ingredients:

2 lbs. chuck steak
1 tablespoon cooking oil *or* fat
¾ teaspoon salt
A pinch of pepper
2 cups boiling water
2 teaspoons fresh chopped basil *or* 1 teaspoon green-dried basil

2 teaspoons fresh chopped thyme *or* 1 teaspoon green-dried thyme
1 medium-sized onion, sliced
2 teaspoons flour
A pinch of nutmeg
½ lb. flaky pastry

Method:

1. Cut steak into squares.
2. Heat fat in fireproof casserole placed over medium heat.
3. Add meat and brown quickly on all sides to seal in juices.
4. Season with salt and pepper.
5. Add boiling water; cover and simmer 10 minutes.
6. Add basil, thyme, and onion, and simmer 10 minutes more, or until meat is almost tender.
7. Blend flour in cup with very little cold water; add enough hot liquid from casserole to make smooth, thin mixture.
8. Pour mixture into casserole, stirring well.
9. Sprinkle ingredients lightly with nutmeg.
10. Cover with pastry and bake in moderate oven (375° F.) for 30 minutes.

Dill Meatcakes (*serves 4*)

A good supper dish.

Ingredients:

1 lb. minced meat	3 eggs
1 large onion	Salt
2 oz. grated cheese	3–4 oz. cooked rice
2 teaspoons fresh chopped or green-dried dill	Oil for frying

Method:

1. Mix well together the rice, meat, seasoning, dill, cheese, and chopped onion.
2. Add yolks of two eggs and knead well.
3. Form mixture into round flat cakes.
4. Roll the cakes in egg, then flour.
5. Fry in oil.

Mutton Hot-Pot (*serves 6*) (**B**)

A simple-to-make, substantial family dish.

Ingredients:

2 lbs. breast of mutton or lamb	1 tablespoon fresh chopped or green-dried celery leaves
1 pint stock	1 tablespoon fresh chopped or green-dried parsley
4 onions, chopped	
A few bacon bones	
1 small cabbage, shredded	1 teaspoon fresh chopped or green-dried thyme
Salt and pepper	
¼ lb. mushrooms	1 bay leaf
6 carrots, sliced	6–8 potatoes

Method:

1. Trim the meat and cut it into pieces. To remove excess fat, it is advisable to par-simmer the meat in advance in the stock, cooking it for 20 to 30 minutes. Cool the meat in the stock and skim off excess fat. Transfer the meat to the casserole.
2. Slice the potatoes and mushrooms and cabbage.
3. Put the meat, bacon bones, vegetables, herbs, and seasonings into a casserole, topping it with a layer of potatoes.
4. Add the stock.
5. Cover and cook in a moderate oven (350° F.) for about two hours.
6. Remove lid for last 20 minutes to brown the potatoes.

Note: If it is found to be too fatty, cook the day before required; take off layer of fat and reheat.

Lamb-and-Pork-Roll Roast (*serves 6*)

An unusual combination for a Sunday lunch.

Ingredients:

1 small leg of lamb, boned
1 lb. pork tenderloin
Salt and pepper
1 teaspoon fresh chopped or green-dried marjoram

1 teaspoon fresh chopped or green-dried thyme

Method:

1. Rub the inside of lamb with the herbs.
2. Roll the lamb round the pork tenderloin.
3. Tie with string or use skewers.
4. Roast in a slow oven 300 to 325° F. for 30 to 35 minutes per pound.
5. When cooked remove lamb and make gravy from juices in the pan.
6. Serve at once.

Lamb Stew in Foil Packets (*serves 4*)

An elegant and tasty way of serving lamb chops.

Ingredients:

4 double lamb chops
4 potatoes, diced
4 carrots, sliced
4 onions, sliced in rings
1 teaspoon fresh chopped or green-dried celery leaves

1 teaspoon fresh chopped or green-dried rosemary
4 tablespoons sherry
Seasoning

Method:

1. Cut four large squares of heavy tinfoil.
2. Rub the lamb chops on both sides with the herbs.
3. Place one double chop on each square.
4. On top of each place an equal quantity of onion, potato, and carrot.
5. Season with salt and pepper.
6. Pour one tablespoon sherry over each portion.

7. Fold foil so it is sealed and put on baking sheet.
8. Bake in a slow oven (300° F.) for an hour and a half to two
   hours.

Sweetbreads New Style (*serves 3*)

A light supper dish served with toasted garlic bread and a green
salad.

Ingredients:

1 lb. sweetbreads (lamb or calf)	Salt and pepper
½ lb. mushrooms	¼ teaspoon fresh chopped or green-
3 oz. butter	dried marjoram
½ cup fresh chopped or 4 table-	½ lb. cooked peas
spoons green-dried chives	¾ pint lovage cream sauce (page
¼ cup fresh chopped or 2 table-	261)
spoons green-dried parsley	Grated Parmesan cheese

Method:
1. Blanch the sweetbreads in salted water for 30 minutes.
2. Drain, cover with fresh water, and simmer for 10 to 12 minutes.
3. When cooked, remove membranes and cut into pieces.
4. Cut up mushrooms and sauté in butter with chives and parsley.
5. Season with salt, pepper, and marjoram.
6. Add this mixture to sweetbreads and put in a greased oven-proof
   dish.
7. Add peas and sauce and mix thoroughly.
8. Sprinkle with Parmesan cheese.
9. Bake in moderate oven (350° F.) for 20 minutes.

Kidney Margot (*serves 2*)

For an unusual supper dish—not too heavy, but tasty and quickly
prepared.

Ingredients:

4 lambs' kidneys	1 tablespoon fresh chopped or
2 oz. butter	green-dried basil
4 oz. mushrooms	1 tablespoon sherry
4 oz. tomatoes	Salt and pepper
1½ gill of stock	
2 tablespoons fresh chopped or	
green-dried chives	

Method:

1. Skin kidneys and cut in two, lengthwise.
2. Melt butter in deep frying pan and brown kidneys quickly on both sides—about four minutes; remove.
3. Sauté sliced mushrooms and tomatoes with the chives and basil. Cook about five or six minutes.
4. Stir in stock and sherry.
5. When this boils, replace kidneys; add salt and a dash of pepper.
6. Cover pan and allow to simmer gently 15 to 20 minutes.
7. Remove lid and continue simmering for a further five minutes. Serve.

Country-Style Pork (*serves 8*)

A good dish for a cold day—elegant enough to serve for dinner.

Ingredients:

3½ lbs. chump end loin of pork, boned
6 sage leaves
2 lbs. pork sausage meat
¼ cup oil
1 dessertspoon fresh chopped or green-dried sage
1 dessertspoon fresh chopped or green-dried thyme
Salt and pepper
2 cloves of garlic, chopped

Method:

1. With a sharp knife insert the sage leaves in the pork a day before cooking.
2. Spread sausage meat inside pork, roll up, and tie up with string or skewers.
3. Place in a roasting pan.
4. Pour over oil; then sprinkle with sage and thyme.
5. Season well and put garlic on top.
6. Roast on middle shelf in a very hot oven 445° F. for 40 minutes.
7. Reduce heat to moderate 355° F. for a further two hours.

Lincolnshire Stuffed Chine (*serves 8–10*)

Useful for picnics or a sandwich lunch.

Ingredients:

3-lb. *green* bacon collar (not smoked)

Sufficient fresh chopped parsley to tightly fill a pint basin, or the green-dried equivalent (approximately 6 tablespoons or more), reconstituted in half lemon juice, half water

Method:

1. Cut bacon into ½-in. strips right up to, but not into, the rind.
2. Fill the cut strips as full as possible with parsley and tie joint tightly with string.
3. Put into a cloth such as muslin, and tie around again (cloth must completely cover bacon).
4. Boil for two and a half hours with lid on saucepan.
5. Take out when nearly cold, but do not unwrap.
6. Place weight on top and leave for some hours.
7. Take off cloth, but leave on rind.
8. Cut across top of bacon so that each slice has a half inch of bacon and its quota of parsley.
9. Serve with sprinkling of lemon juice.

Pork Chops Madeira (*serves 4*)

A rich-tasting party dish—so easy to prepare.

Ingredients:

4 pork chops
Pinch of salt
Dash of pepper
A little crushed garlic
1 tablespoon fresh chopped or green-dried parsley
1 tablespoon fresh chopped or green-dried onion green

1 teaspoon fresh chopped or green-dried marjoram
½ pint condensed mushroom soup
3 tablespoons water
2 tablespoons madeira

Method:

1. Thoroughly brown the pork chops in frying pan.
2. Season with salt, pepper, and garlic.
3. Combine rest of ingredients.
4. Pour over chops.
5. Simmer until tender (30 to 40 minutes), turning chops once.
6. Pour sauce from the pan over the chops.

Note: Serve with green-bean salad (page 178) and piquant French dressing with tarragon (see page 180).

Sauerkraut Spareribs (*serves 6*)

A rare but tasty combination; can also be served with toasted whole-meal bread and garlic butter or Herb Butter Loaf (page 290).

Ingredients:

2 lbs. spareribs	1 clove
4 cups water	2½ lbs. sauerkraut
1 teaspoon salt	1 cup white wine
3 bay leaves	1–2 teaspoons caraway seeds
1 onion, chopped	3 bay leaves
1 tablespoon fresh chopped or green-dried celery leaves	2 cups pork broth

Method:
1. Put spareribs in water with salt, three bay leaves, onion, and celery leaves.
2. Bring to boil and simmer until meat is tender (about one and a half hours).
3. Leave to cool; then skim off fat, remove spareribs from broth.
4. In a large saucepan put sauerkraut, wine, three other bay leaves, caraway, and one to two cups of the pork broth.
5. Place meat on top; cover and cook very slowly for an hour and a half.

Ham in a Crust (*serves 8*)

An ideal dish for unexpected guests, if there is a can of ham in the larder.

Ingredients:

2 cups short pastry mixture (see page 288)	⅓ cup milk
1 teaspoon dry mustard	3-lb. boneless cooked ham
3 teaspoons fresh chopped or green-dried basil	

Method:
1. Mix the mustard, basil, and pastry mixture together.
2. Add the milk and knead into a dough.
3. Roll out dough on lightly floured board to a large rectangle.
4. Put ham in center and fold long ends of pastry over ham, making them overlap each other.

5. Turn over and carefully tuck in other ends of pastry, making a parcel.
6. Brush all the pastry with milk and place on greased baking pan.
7. Bake in moderately low oven 325° F. for about 40 minutes until crust is golden brown.
8. Allow crust to cool slightly before cutting.

Veal Tarragon (*serves 6*)

One of the most excellent ways of serving veal.

Ingredients:

1½ lb. veal, thinly sliced	Salt and pepper
1 tablespoon butter	2 teaspoons fresh chopped or green-
Juice of lemon	dried tarragon

Method:
1. Pound veal slices very thin; cut into serving pieces.
2. Sauté in butter very quickly on both sides.
3. Add lemon juice, salt and pepper to taste, and tarragon.
4. Cook until tender, about seven to ten minutes.
   Note: Serve with peas or asparagus.

Veal Olives (*1–2 olives per person*)

For one of those dinners when you want to show your skill.

Ingredients:
　Fillet of veal, cut into thin slices
　Chopped fat bacon
　Chopped onion
　Fresh chopped or green-dried herbs mixed of:

Tarragon	Rosemary
Lovage	Chervil
Lemon balm	Mint
Summer savory	Marjoram
Thyme	Basil

For proportions see GUIDE (page 119)

or
　The equivalent quantity of bouquet for meat dishes
　1 cup sour cream
　½ teaspoon cornflour

Method:

1. Beat and salt slices of fillet of veal and spread out on a flat board.
2. Put some finely chopped fat bacon, onion, and parsley on each piece.
3. Sprinkle the whole surface generously with mixed herbs or bouquet for meat dishes.
4. Roll each piece and tie with thread.
5. Fry these olives in butter in a heavy pan until golden brown on both sides.
6. Mix sour cream with cornflour.
7. Add this to the meat; cover and simmer until tender.
8. Before serving add some top of the milk if the sauce is too salty.
9. Remove thread from olives and serve sauce separately.

Veal Casserole (*serves 4*)

A good family meal; also an easy party dish for a buffet which can be prepared well beforehand.

Ingredients:

1½ lbs. stewing veal
4 oz. mushrooms, chopped
4 oz. tomatoes, chopped
4 oz. button onions, chopped
¾ pint stock
A little salt and pepper
1 green pepper, medium size, chopped
1 tablespoon flour
1 oz. butter

1 tablespoon mixed fresh chopped or green-dried herbs; parsley, mint, tarragon, chervil, sage, marjoram, thyme, basil (for proportions see GUIDE, page 119)

or

1 tablespoon bouquet for meat dishes

Method:

1. Cut veal into small pieces and roll in a little seasoned flour.
2. Sauté meat in butter in deep frying pan and remove.
3. Sauté onions, mushrooms, tomatoes, and green pepper; then remove.
4. Add flour; cook gently for a few minutes; then add stock and herbs.
5. Put all in a casserole dish.
6. Cover closely and cook in a slow oven (300° F.) for three to four hours.

Liver Casserole (*serves 4*)

This quick-to-make liver dish goes well with creamed spinach and dill potatoes (page 253).

Ingredients:

1 lb. calves' liver, thinly sliced
2 oz. butter
1 medium onion, chopped
1 clove garlic, crushed
¼ lb. mushrooms, chopped
2 carrots, sliced
Salt and a dash of pepper
1 teaspoon fresh chopped or green-dried parsley

1 teaspoon fresh chopped or green-dried thyme
1 teaspoon fresh chopped or green-dried basil
1 bay leaf
1 dessertspoon cornflour
¼ cup water
¼ cup wine

Method:

1. Sauté the liver gently in butter with onion and garlic.
2. Place alternate layers of onion, garlic, liver, mushrooms, and carrots in a pie pan.
3. Sprinkle well with the herbs and seasoning.
4. Blend the wine and water with the cornflour and pour over the dish.
5. Top with a bay leaf and bake for 30 minutes in moderate oven (350° F.).

Marjoram Liver Dumplings (*serves 4*) (B)

Marjoram adds a special flavor to this traditional dish from German-speaking countries.

Ingredients:

½ lb. (in one piece) calves' or pigs' liver
2 tablespoons butter *or* 1 tablespoon suet
Grated rind of 1 lemon
1 cup flour (approx.)
¼ cup water

½ teaspoon fresh chopped or green-dried marjoram
¼ teaspoon salt
⅛ teaspoon white pepper
1 clove garlic, chopped (optional)

Method:

1. Dip liver in boiling water. Simmer for two minutes.
2. Remove from water.
3. Grate or mince liver, removing all fibers.
4. Blend liver, butter or suet, lemon rind, seasonings, and marjoram in large bowl.
5. Gradually add sufficient flour until mixture can be formed into small round dumplings, not too firm (less than one cup of flour is usually enough).
6. Cook dumplings in boiling bouillon, consommé, or chicken broth for 10 minutes. Serve broth and dumplings immediately.

Note: Or remove from broth after cooking; drain, top with melted butter and fried onions, and serve with any vegetables or sauerkraut.

Chapter 7

*P*oultry and *G*ame

Chicken Casserole (*serves 4–6*)

This casserole with its vegetable makes a complete meal.

Ingredients:

2¼-lb. chicken, jointed
3 oz. butter
½ lb. sliced mushrooms
3 oz. (⅔ cup) flour
2 teaspoons salt
A little paprika
1 teaspoon each fresh chopped or green-dried sage and lemon thyme

1 teaspoon poultry bouquet (optional)
1 lemon, cut in half
½ teaspoon ground ginger
1 lb. fresh green beans, sliced, *or* 1 large frozen packet, thawed
½ cup stock

Method:

1. Melt butter in frying pan and sauté mushrooms for 5 minutes; remove.
2. Mix flour, salt, paprika, and herbs together.
3. Rub chicken with cut lemon and coat lightly with flour mixture.
4. Melt remaining butter in pan and brown chicken well.
5. Remove to large casserole and sprinkle with ginger.
6. Coat beans with flour mixture and lightly brown in pan.
7. Mix beans with mushrooms and spoon over chicken.
8. Add the stock and bake, covered, in hot oven (400° F.) about 30 to 40 minutes.

Marjoram Chicken (*serves 6*)

This delicately flavored chicken makes an out-of-the-ordinary party dish.

Ingredients:

3-lb. chicken, jointed

3 tablespoons butter

⅛ cup oil

1 teaspoon salt

Paprika

½ clove garlic, finely chopped, *or*

    ¼ teaspoon garlic salt

1 teaspoon grated lemon peel

½ teaspoon fresh chopped or
green-dried summer savory

2 teaspoons fresh chopped or green-
dried marjoram

Method:

1. Melt butter in shallow baking pan.
2. Coat chicken pieces in the melted butter and arrange in a single layer in the pan.
3. Pour oil over the chicken.
4. Season with salt, paprika, and garlic.
5. Sprinkle over it the lemon peel, summer savory, and marjoram.
6. Cover with foil and bake in moderate oven (350° F.) for 15 minutes.
7. Turn chicken pieces over and bake 15 minutes longer.
8. Remove foil. Increase temperature to 400° F.
9. Bake 15 minutes more, turning chicken once again during that time.
10. The juices in the pan make an excellent gravy.

Herbed Turkey

This recipe, using foil, produces not only the most succulent but also the most tasty turkey.

Ingredients:

12- to 14-lb. turkey

Lemon juice

Butter for brushing bird

Salt

2–3 tablespoons (or more) bouquet
for poultry and game

or more of the same herbs as for
stuffing

    (to rub the bird inside and out)

¼ pint white wine

¼ pint giblet stock

Flour

Cream (if liked)

Stuffing:

8 oz. butter

8 oz. bread crumbs

Grated rind of 2 lemons

Juice of 1 lemon

2½ dessertspoons fresh chopped or
green-dried parsley

1 teaspoon each fresh chopped or
green-dried thyme, lemon thyme,
and marjoram

or 4 dessertspoons bouquet for poultry and game

Paprika

½ medium-sized onion, minced

1 clove garlic, crushed

3 large eggs

Method for stuffing:

1. Reconstitute the herbs in juice of one lemon.
2. Blend herbs well with grated rind, minced onion, and minced garlic.
3. Cream the butter and add eggs and herbs.
4. Add bread crumbs and mix well.

Method for turkey:

1. Rub the bird inside and out with a cut lemon, sprinkle and rub with salt.
2. Rub the bird inside with the herbs.
3. Brush the outside with softened butter and sprinkle with the herbs.
4. Stuff the body and crop of the bird.
5. Sew the openings together with white thread.
6. Weigh the prepared bird and allow 15 minutes per pound for birds up to 14 pounds, and 10 minutes per pound for large birds.
7. Wrap in buttered foil and seal well.
8. Lay the bird on its back on a rack in a baking tin.
9. Place in pre-heated oven (400-425° F.).
10. Half-way through cooking, turn the bird.
11. Thirty minutes before the end, remove the foil, turn the bird breast upwards for browning.
12. When cooked, pour off the juices into a saucepan.
13. Add the white wine and giblet stock to the juices and herbs.

Note: If the sauce should be thickened, sauté the flour in butter until golden; then smooth with cold water, and giblet stock, mix in the gravy from the pan, add the wine and bring to the boil. Add cream (if liked) before serving.

Rabbit Casserole

Ingredients:

1 large young jointed rabbit	Salt
1 rabbit liver	4–6 juniper berries
4 oz. bacon	1 bay leaf
Some small shallots	1 teaspoon each fresh chopped or
1 finely chopped onion	green-dried lemon balm, rose-
1 chopped garlic clove	mary, summer savory
Flour	½ teaspoon lemon peel
1 pint stock	½ bottle red wine

Method:
1. Melt bacon in heavy casserole.
2. Brown the joints on all sides.
3. Add the rabbit liver and the chopped onion and garlic.
4. When meat is well browned, sprinkle with flour, stir well, and add gradually one pint boiling water or stock.
5. Season with salt, juniper berries, and herbs.
6. Add lemon peel, and pour half of the red wine over it.
7. Cover and allow to simmer on low heat until the meat is quite tender.

Note: Serve with noodles or rice.

Herb Chicken (*serves 6–8*)

Very easy to make and yet a surprising success!

Ingredients:

4-lb. roasting chicken, jointed	¼ pint red wine
2 bay leaves	1 tablespoon oil
6 sprigs, or 1 teaspoon each, green-dried tarragon and thyme	1 oz. butter
	¼ pint stock
4 leaves fresh sage, *or* ½ teaspoon green-dried sage	Cream

Method:
1. Cover the herbs with the red wine and leave for one and a half hours.
2. Brown the chicken in the oil and butter in a deep pan.
3. Pour over the wine and add stock.
4. Cover and put into a fairly hot oven (400° F.), center shelf, for 30 to 40 minutes.
5. Lift bird onto a hot dish.
6. Strain wine sauce into another pan and reduce a little by boiling; then add a little cream.
7. Pour over the chicken.

Hasenpfeffer with Marinade (*serves 6*)

The marinade ensures that the hare is tender and tasty.

Ingredients:

2 small hares or rabbits, jointed	1 cup stock
Marinade (recipe follows)	1 teaspoon sugar
½ cup flour	2 tablespoons sour cream

½ teaspoon salt
1½ teaspoon fresh chopped or
    green-dried thyme
½ cup dripping

1 tablespoon cream
If sauce is too thick, add another
    ¼ cup of stock

Method:
1. Marinate the joints for two days.
2. Drain, saving marinade, and then dry the meat.
3. Coat pieces with flour mixed with salt and one teaspoon thyme.
4. Sauté in dripping.
5. Drain off fat.
6. Strain marinade and add the stock.
7. Pour over meat. Cover and simmer 45 minutes, or until tender.
8. Season, if necessary, and add the sugar.
9. Arrange joints on a dish.
10. Thicken the sauce with flour, if desired; add the remaining thyme; allow to boil and then add cream.

Marinade (may be used for other game—makes about three-quarters of a pint)

Ingredients:
1 cup red wine
3 tablespoons lemon juice
½ cup oil
1 small chopped onion
½ clove garlic
6 juniper berries
4 cloves
Salt

1 tablespoon poultry and game herb bouquet *or*
1 tablespoon mixed fresh chopped or green-dried parsley, tarragon, celery, thyme, marjoram, sage, basil, bay leaves, rosemary (see GUIDE, page 119, for proportions)

Method:
1. Mix all the above ingredients, cover well, and allow to stand overnight at room temperature.
2. Then marinate poultry, and especially game, in it for 24 hours.
3. Use for tenderizing and preserving and for basting.
4. If used in the cooking, the marinade should be strained.

Note: This may be strained and kept in the refrigerator for several weeks.

Poultry Pilaff (*serves 6*)

This dish originated in Eastern countries, such as Egypt and Turkey, and can be made of fish, poultry, and rice. This is a suggestion for pilaff made of chicken or any other fowl.

Ingredients:

1 young bird
2–3 pints stock
2 oz. almonds
3 onions
1 clove of garlic, crushed
3 tablespoons butter
3 oz. seedless raisins
1 cup rice
2 tablespoons marigold petals

1 teaspoon each fresh chopped or green-dried summer savory and tarragon
½ teaspoon fresh chopped or green-dried thyme
¼ teaspoon cinnamon
Paprika
Salt

Method:

1. Put the bird, trussed for boiling, into the stock and cook until half tender.
2. Blanch almonds.
3. Peel onions and cut into rings.
4. Sauté onions and garlic in butter, but do not brown them.
5. Sauté raisins and almonds lightly.
6. Wash and dry rice and sauté in the butter until golden; add herbs and sauté.
7. Put rice mixture into deep saucepan and add onions, raisins, and almonds.
8. Make a well in the center and put the bird into it.
9. Cover rice and bird with two and a half to three cups of stock and simmer slowly until the chicken and rice are cooked and the rice has absorbed the stock (25 minutes).
10. Place the chicken on a hot dish and arrange the rice around it.

Cherry-Garnished Duckling

An excellent party dish, well worth the trouble for a special occasion.

Ingredients:

3–4-lb. duck
3 oz. butter
1 carrot
1 onion
¾ pint stock
1 bay leaf
1 teaspoon each fresh chopped or green-dried celery leaves and marjoram
1 teaspoon fresh chopped or green-dried parsley

1 pinch of fresh chopped or green-dried thyme
or 1 teaspoon bouquet for poultry and game
¼ pint wine
Salt and pepper
1 teaspoon cornflour
2 tablespoons water

Garnish:
Strained juice of 1 orange
Pinch of grated orange peel
1½ oz. castor sugar
¼ pint port *or* less
10-oz. canned cherries, stoned

Stuffing:
Duck's liver
Flour
1 oz. butter
Bread crumbs
Salt and pepper
1 teaspoon fresh chopped or green-dried marjoram
1 egg

Method for stuffing:
1. Toss the duck's liver in seasoned flour.
2. Melt the butter in a pan and sauté the liver for three minutes.
3. Remove from pan and chop finely.
4. Mix with bread crumbs, salt, pepper, marjoram, and bind with the egg.

Method for duck:
1. Stuff the duck with this mixture and rub with one ounce butter.
2. Prepare and dice vegetables and sauté in remaining butter until brown.
3. Put vegetables into a casserole and place duck on top.
4. Sprinkle duck with marjoram and celery leaves and add stock and other herbs.
5. Cover with tight-fitting lid and cook on center shelf of moderate oven (355° F) for an hour and a half.
6. Remove duck from casserole and keep hot.
7. Strain liquid from casserole into a pan, adding wine; season if necessary.
8. Blend cornflour with water and add to wine mixture; return to heat and stir until thick.

Method for garnish:
1. Mix orange juice, orange peel, sugar, and port in a pan and heat gently until sugar is dissolved.
2. Add drained cherries and heat through.
3. Serve the duck surrounded by the garnish, and hand the wine sauce separately.

Chicken Pie (*serves 6*)

Another way of serving a satisfying yet tasty chicken dish.

Ingredients:

3-lb. boiling fowl
1½ pints stock
3 medium onions, sliced
1 carrot, sliced
Salt and paprika
1 tablespoon fresh chopped or
  green-dried celery leaves
1 tablespoon poultry and game
  mixture
or 1 teaspoon each fresh chopped

or green-dried lemon balm, tarragon, basil, rosemary
½ oz. semolina
Small wineglass white wine
1 oz. butter
1 egg yolk
1 teaspoon lemon juice
3 rashers bacon, cut in strips
1 lb. easy pastry (page 290)

Method:

1. Joint the chicken into small pieces. Put into pan with stock and vegetables.
2. Add seasoning and all herbs.
3. Simmer for one hour.
4. Add semolina, wine, and butter, and simmer for further 15 minutes.
5. Blend egg yolk and lemon juice with half pint of the hot broth.
6. Place chicken in pie pan; add strips of bacon.
7. Pour over thickened broth.
8. Cover with pastry.
9. Cook in the middle of the oven (400° F.) for one hour or until pastry is golden.

Chicken with Tarragon (*serves 4*) (B)

A simplified version of the traditional French dish.

Ingredients:

1 chicken
2 tablespoons fresh chopped or
  green-dried tarragon

A nut of butter
½ pint stock or water
Some cream (optional)

Method:

1. Rub chicken inside and out with one tablespoon tarragon.
2. Put chicken and giblets in a casserole with the butter and the stock or water, and cook until tender.
3. Take chicken out of casserole and add one tablespoon tarragon to the liquid.
4. Cook for 10 minutes, adding a little flour if the sauce is too liquid, or a little cream, if necessary.
5. Pass the sauce through a sieve, if liked; and season, if necessary.

Boned Stuffed Chicken (*serves 10–12*)

Although a lengthy recipe, it is well worth the trouble for a cold buffet or picnic.

Ingredients:
(to stuff a 2-lb. chicken.)

Stuffing No. 1
1 lb. sausage meat
2 slices chopped bacon
1 egg
1 clove garlic, finely chopped
1 glass of sherry
1 chicken liver, minced
1 tablespoon fresh chopped or green-dried marjoram
or 1 tablespoon bouquet for poultry and game

Stuffing No. 2
2 oz. sliced mushrooms
1 hard-boiled egg, sliced
2 frankfurters, sliced
Chopped meat off chicken bones
Chicken jelly
Chicken bones
¾ pint water
¼ oz. gelatin
½ teaspoon each fresh chopped or green-dried chives, lovage, and parsley
Parsley for garnish

Method:
1. Bone the chicken, or ask the butcher to do it for you.
2. Place the chicken, skin side down, to make an even layer of meat.
3. Combine all ingredients of Stuffing No. 1 into a thick mixture.
4. Spread half of Stuffing No. 1 on chicken.
5. Over this place a layer of the ingredients of Stuffing No. 2.
6. Cover with the remainder of Stuffing No. 1.
7. Form a smooth compact roll of chicken.
8. Sew skin together to hold in filling.
9. Oil top of the chicken roll; put into a roasting tin with plenty of fat.
10. Cover with foil and seal well.
11. Place on lowest shelf of the oven at 350° F. for an hour to an hour and a half.
12. Remove foil for the last 10 minutes to brown the top.
13. Place on a dish and leave to cool.

Method for jelly:
1. Boil the bones in the water with the herbs added.
2. Remove the bones, add gelatine, and stir until dissolved.
3. Pour into shallow bowl and leave to set.
4. Serve chicken cold with chopped chicken jelly around it, and garnish with parsley.

Parsleyed Chicken (*serves 4–8*)

An attractive and unusual way to serve chicken.

Ingredients:
2 small chickens
A large bunch of parsley, chopped
or 6 tablespoons green-dried parsley
3 tablespoons soft butter
¼ cup butter
2 cups chicken stock
Fresh or green-dried parsley for garnish

Sauce:
2 tablespoons butter
2 tablespoons flour
1 tablespoon fresh chopped or green-dried tarragon
½ cup cream
Salt

Method:
1. Wash and dry chickens.
2. Mix parsley with the soft butter.
3. Stuff each chicken with half of this mixture and fasten openings with skewers, or sew.
4. Truss, tying legs and wings close to the body.
5. Melt quarter cup butter in a large, heavy frying pan.
6. Add chickens and brown lightly on all sides.
7. Put chickens in a large casserole, pour over the brown butter, and add two cups of chicken stock.
8. Cook uncovered in a moderate oven (350° F.) for 30 minutes or until tender, basting four or five times.
9. Arrange on a dish and garnish with parsley.

Method for sauce:
1. In a small pan, melt butter for sauce and stir in flour.
2. Strain the chicken stock and stir in gradually.
3. Add tarragon and simmer for at least eight minutes.
4. Stir in cream and salt; then heat again for one minute.
5. Pour this sauce over the chicken, or serve it separately.

Chicken with Summer Savory (*serves 4*)

The sauce is the important part of this lunch and supper dish; it may also be served with other poultry and game.

Ingredients:
2 lbs. chicken pieces
1½ pints water

Sauce:
2 tablespoons butter *or* oil
4 mushrooms

1 carrot, chopped
1 clove garlic, crushed
1½ teaspoon salt
1 teaspoon each fresh chopped or green-dried parsley and celery leaves
2 teaspoons fresh chopped or green-dried summer savory

1 dessertspoon fresh chopped or green-dried summer savory
1 teaspoon each fresh chopped or green-dried lemon balm and parsley
or 1 tablespoon bouquet for poultry and game
2 oz. flour
½ glass white wine
2 tablespoons sour cream
1 tablespoon top of the milk

Method:

1. Put chicken pieces into a large saucepan with water, carrot, garlic, salt, and the herbs.
2. Bring to the boil and simmer gently until chicken is cooked.
3. Remove chicken, then bone it.
4. Strain the stock and save for the sauce.

Method for sauce:

1. Heat butter or oil; then sauté mushrooms and herbs.
2. Add flour and cook gently for a few minutes.
3. Smooth with a little cold water.
4. Add all chicken stock and wine.
5. Cook for 20 minutes, stirring until it thickens.
6. Add sour cream and top of the milk.
7. Put chicken pieces back and heat well (but do not boil).
8. Serve in a rice ring.

Braised Pheasant with Chestnuts (*serves 4*)

An excellent game bird, enhanced by herbs.

Ingredients:

1 pheasant
1 tablespoon mixed of fresh chopped or green-dried parsley, tarragon, lemon balm, basil, bay leaves, and rosemary (see GUIDE, page 119, for proportions)
or 1 tablespoon bouquet for poultry and game

2 tablespoons butter
1 medium onion, sliced
4 carrots, sliced
1 lb. peeled chestnuts
½ pint marinade (see page 237)
or ½ pint game stock
¼ pint cream

Method:

1. Prepare pheasant for the oven and rub well inside and out with the herbs.
2. Melt butter in a deep pan and brown bird on all sides.
3. Add the sliced onion, carrots, and peeled chestnuts.
4. Moisten well with marinade or stock.
5. Cover the pan and braise in a slow oven for an hour and a half to two hours.
6. Remove bird and chestnuts to a warm serving dish.
7. Strain the sauce, add the cream, and pour over pheasant.
   Note: May be served with marjoram jelly (see page 274).

Wrapped Partridge

The foil retains, and the herbs underline, the flavor of this tasty partridge.

Ingredients:
1 bird to 2 persons

For each bird:
1 piece celery
¼ teaspoon fresh chopped or green-dried sage leaves
1 tablespoon onion, finely chopped
1 teaspoon fresh chopped or green-dried basil
1 pinch each of fresh chopped or green-dried summer savory and thyme
1 slice toast
1 slice bacon
Parsley for garnish

Sauce:
¼ cup red wine
¼ cup stock
1 teaspoon lemon juice
3 oz. cooked mushrooms, sliced
Salt to taste
1 tablespoon cream

Method:

1. Cut celery piece to fit inside bird.
2. Put sage in channel of celery and place this inside the bird.
3. Cut foil large enough to wrap bird in.
4. Place onions and herbs in center of foil.
5. Place bird on top, with slice of bacon on breast.
6. Wrap tightly, put in roasting pan, and place in moderate oven (375° F.).

7. Bake for 20 to 25 minutes.

8. Remove bird from foil and brown it in the oven or under the grill for five minutes.

9. Meanwhile, in a saucepan, combine the juices from the foil with wine, stock, and lemon juice, and reduce slightly.

10. Add mushrooms and salt, if necessary.

11. Continue cooking sauce until it thickens, and then add cream.

12. Serve birds on slice of toast, covered with the sauce, and garnish with parsley and the bacon and celery, chopped.

Chapter 8

Vegetables, Potatoes, Rice, and Pasta

Tomato Casserole (B)

This is an economical yet very good dish for a family when tomatoes are not too expensive; it has to be started early in the day.

As the casserole should be made according to the size of the family, onions, tomatoes, and potatoes should be washed and sliced as required.

Ingredients:
Onions, tomatoes, and potatoes, cut into really thin slices
Grated cheese
Paprika
Rosemary
Onion green ⎱
Parsley and basil ⎰ Fresh chopped or green-dried
Parsley, fennel *or* dill, marjoram, thyme
Caraway (optional)
½ cup sour cream, *or* cream, *or* top of the milk

Method:
1. Place a layer of grated cheese at the bottom of the casserole and sprinkle with a little paprika and rosemary over each layer of cheese.
2. Add next a layer of onion slices, sprinkled with onion green.
3. A layer of sliced tomatoes, sprinkled generously with parsley and some basil.
4. Then a thick layer of thinly sliced potatoes, sprinkled with some parsley, fennel or dill, marjoram, thyme, and caraway.
5. Repeat these layers until casserole is filled. Last layers should be potatoes and cheese.
6. Pour over sour cream, or cream.
7. Cover with well-fitting lid, and place in oven at 350° F. for one hour at least (according to size of casserole). Then turn to

300° F. for about two hours. Remove lid and brown for a further 15 to 30 minutes before serving.

Note: Onions and potatoes must be tender.

Ratatouille—A Southern Vegetable Stew

Ingredients:

2 large onions
1 clove garlic, chopped
8 tablespoons oil
2 green peppers, carefully cleaned inside and diced
2 large eggplants, diced
Salt
1 tablespoon fresh chopped or green-dried parsley

1 tablespoon mixed fresh chopped or green-dried marjoram, basil, rosemary, lemon thyme, and tarragon
2 large zucchini, thickly sliced
6 tomatoes, peeled, and each cut into 8 sections

Method:

1. Sauté onions together with garlic in oil until transparent.
2. Add peppers and eggplants, herbs, and a little salt.
3. Cover and cook for 15 minutes.
4. Add zucchini and cook for a further 15 minutes.
5. Add tomatoes, and allow to cook for one hour.
6. If there is too much liquid, leave off cover for a short time before serving.

Haricot Beans with Tomatoes

An excellent winter vegetable dish which can be used as a main course.

Ingredients:

1 lb. haricot beans
½ stick celery, diced
½ carrot
¼ leek, sliced finely
1 or 2 juniper berries
4 shallots *or* 2 onions, finely chopped
2 cloves of garlic, crushed
1 tablespoon fresh chopped or green-dried onion green *or* chopped leek
2 oz. oil

1 lb. tomatoes, peeled and chopped
1 tablespoon mixed fresh chopped or green-dried lovage, basil, summer savory, thyme, tarragon, and rosemary (see GUIDE, page 119, for proportions)
Salt
4 tablespoons fresh chopped or green-dried chervil
or 2 tablespoons fresh chopped or green-dried parsley
1 oz. butter

Method:
1. Pour boiling water over the beans and soak overnight.
2. Simmer in slightly salted water together with the celery, carrot, leek, and juniper berries until soft (about two hours), or cook in pressure cooker.
3. Drain.
4. Sauté onions with garlic and onion green in the heated oil, and simmer gently until soft.
5. Add the tomatoes and the mixed herbs.
6. Add salt, and cook a little longer; then add this puree to the beans and heat well.
7. Heat chervil or parsley in melted butter and add just before serving.

Note: This dish can be made more nourishing by topping with grated cheese and buttered bread crumbs and browning in the oven, or by adding fried lean bacon or sliced sausages.

Herb-Fried Tomatoes

A tasty accompaniment to a main course.

Ingredients:

4 or 5 large firm tomatoes
Salt to taste
3 tablespoons mixed fresh chopped or green-dried basil, parsley, tarragon, thyme, and summer savory (see GUIDE, page 119, for proportions)
or 3 tablespoons bouquet for salads
6–8 tablespoons flour
4 tablespoons butter

Method:
1. Cut unpeeled tomatoes into half-inch-thick slices.
2. Season both sides with salt.
3. Cover both sides with herbs.
4. Dip each slice in flour.
5. Sauté tomato slices on both sides in butter until golden brown —about seven minutes.

Savory Stuffed Onions (*serves 6*)

A good self-contained dish for lunch or supper.

Ingredients:

6 large onions
1 cup cooked rice
¼ cup tomato sauce *or* puree
Pinch of fresh chopped or green-dried thyme and pinch of summer savory

2 tablespoons oil   Salt
¾ cup grated cheddar cheese
1 teaspoon fresh chopped or green-
dried basil

Method:

1. Peel onions and cut slice off stem end of each one.
2. Cook uncovered in salted water for 30 minutes or until tender but firm.
3. Drain and cool.
4. Remove centers of onions (these can be used for sauce or stuffing for another dish).
5. Mix together rice, sauce, oil, ½ cup grated cheese, herbs and seasoning to taste.
6. Fill onions with this mixture.
7. Sprinkle remaining cheese over the onions.
8. Arrange onions in greased casserole.
9. Bake in hot oven (425° F.) for 20 minutes.

Savory Onion-Green Tart

This quiche can be made from freshly chopped onion tops or green-dried onion green.

Ingredients:

3 cups thinly sliced green onion tops
or ¾ cup green-dried onion green
3 tablespoons butter or margarine
8-in. flat tin lined with pastry (see page 288)

3 eggs
¼ cup single cream
1 teaspoon salt
½ teaspoon fresh chopped or green-dried summer savory
Nutmeg

Method:

1. Sauté onion green tops in butter for five minutes (if green-dried onion green is used, reconstitute in a quarter cup water with a few drops of lemon juice and wait until the liquid has been soaked up and the onion green reconstituted—do not use more water than absolutely necessary).
2. Turn into pastry-lined tin.
3. Beat eggs until well blended and add to them the cream, salt, summer savory, and nutmeg.
4. Pour egg mixture over onions.
5. Bake in a very hot oven (425° F.) for 30 minutes or until custard is just set.

Note: Cut into wedges as a hot appetizer, or use cold for buffets and picnics.

Summer Squash or Zucchini

An easy to prepare, unusual vegetable dish—good enough for a special occasion.

Ingredients:

2 lbs. summer squash or zucchini
3 tablespoons oil
Salt
½ teaspoon each fresh chopped or
    green-dried rosemary and dill

1 tablespoon fresh chopped or
    green-dried parsley
Vegetable stock, if necessary
Grated cheese
Sour cream

Method:

1. Select small squash (four to six inches long) wash, and cut off both ends.
2. Halve and put on a shallow fireproof dish.
3. Pour oil over and sprinkle with herbs.
4. Bake in a moderate (350°) oven.
5. Add a little vegetable stock if too dry.
6. Sprinkle with grated cheese and dot with sour cream.
7. Allow to brown in the oven.

Spinach Recipes

(*a*) Spinach Purée

Ingredients:

2 lbs. spinach
1 tablespoon oil
1 onion, chopped
1 clove garlic, chopped
1 heaped tablespoon flour
1 cup (10 oz.) vegetable stock
Salt
Nutmeg
2 oz. raw spinach

1 teaspoon fresh chopped or green-dried peppermint leaves (if available)
1 tablespoon fresh chopped or green-dried parsley
1 teaspoon or more sorrel (if liked)
1 teaspoon nettles, dandelion (if liked)
2 tablespoons cream or milk

Method:

1. Pick over spinach and remove any thick stalks.
2. Place the washed spinach in a saucepan; cover and cook over low heat until the water collects.
3. Drain well.
4. Mince or chop spinach finely.
5. Sauté onion, garlic, and parsley in heated fat.
6. Add flour and sauté.

7. Add stock, smooth, and cook for 15 minutes.
8. Add spinach and seasoning.
9. Chop raw spinach or put through a liquidizer.
10. Add this and the herbs to the cooked spinach just before serving. Do not allow to boil again.
11. Add cream or milk.

(b) Spinach Pudding

Ingredients:

1½ oz. butter *or* margarine	1 onion, chopped
6 oz. bread (French loaf or whole-grain)	1 tablespoon fresh chopped or green-dried parsley
3 eggs, separated	Salt
1 soup plate of leftover spinach puree (see previous recipe)	Nutmeg

Method:

1. Cut the bread, take off crusts, and soak in water.
2. Meanwhile, sauté onions in heated fat until golden.
3. Cream the butter.
4. Add sautéed onions, parsley, yolks of eggs, and the spinach.
5. When the bread is soft, squeeze the water out and add to the mixture.
6. Mix well and add salt and nutmeg.
7. Beat the egg white stiffly and mix in lightly.
8. If the mixture becomes too moist, add some bread crumbs.
9. Fill a well-greased ring or angel-cake tin and bake in the oven at 375° F. for at least an hour.

Brussels Sprouts with Herbs

Herbs make this everyday vegetable surprisingly different and delicious.

Ingredients:

2 lbs. brussels sprouts	Pinch of grated nutmeg
1 medium onion	Salt
1 tablespoon each fresh chopped or green-dried onion green and parsley	½ pint stock
	2 tablespoons oil
2 teaspoons each fresh chopped or green-dried chives and lovage	

Method:
1. Chop onions finely.
2. Sauté until golden.
3. Sauté onion green and other herbs.
4. Add brussels sprouts and shake.
5. Add nutmeg and salt.
6. Then add stock.
7. Cover well.
8. Allow to simmer until tender, or cook in a pressure cooker for three to five minutes.
9. Serve in cheddar ring (page 194), or as an accompanying vegetable.

Note: Another version—use a little garlic, marjoram, lovage, and tarragon, and two tablespoons sour cream; bread crumbs sautéed in oil may be sprinkled over brussels sprouts before serving.

Broad Beans Sauté

Ingredients:

1½–2 lbs. broad beans
1 large onion, finely chopped
1 clove garlic, finely chopped
1 tablespoon oil
1 tablespoon fresh chopped or green-dried parsley
1 teaspoon fresh chopped or green-dried summer savory
½ teaspoon fresh chopped or green-dried lovage
½–1 pint stock
Salt
1 tablespoon sour cream (optional)
Nutmeg

Method:
1. Sauté onions and garlic in the heated oil until transparent.
2. Add all the herbs and sauté.
3. Add broad beans and sauté.
4. Add stock, amount depending on size of the beans and cooking time.
5. Add seasoning.
6. Cover well and cook until tender, or in the pressure cooker.
7. Add sour cream just before serving.

Chive Potato Cakes

Ingredients:

4 medium boiled potatoes
2 tablespoons butter *or* margarine
Salt
1 tablespoon green-dried chives reconstituted in 1 tablespoon warm milk
1 beaten egg

Method:
1. Mash potatoes while still hot.
2. Mix well with butter and salt.
3. Add chives.
4. When cool, add well-beaten egg.
5. Shape into flat cakes and fry in butter.

Dill Potatoes

Goes well with fried or other dishes when served without a sauce.

Ingredients:

2 lbs. potatoes
1 onion finely chopped
1½ oz. oil *or* butter
2 tablespoons flour
¼ pint stock

Salt
2 tablespoons fresh chopped or green-dried dill
6–8 tablespoons sour cream *or* milk

Method:
1. Boil potatoes, peel, and cut into fairly thin slices.
2. Sauté onion in the fat until golden.
3. Add flour and sauté.
4. Smooth with cold water, stirring well; then add stock, salt, potatoes, and bring to the boil.
5. Add the dill and allow to simmer.
6. Shortly before serving, add cream or milk, and reheat.
   Note: If liked, a little crushed garlic may be added to the onion.

Marjoram Potato Pie

Ingredients:

2 lbs. peeled boiled potatoes
Oil *or* butter
Salt
1 teaspoon fresh chopped or green-dried marjoram leaves

½ teaspoon each fresh chopped or green-dried parsley, tarragon, and celery leaves
¼ pint sour cream
¼ pint yogurt

Method:
1. Sauté diced potatoes in butter until golden.
2. Add herbs and sauté again.
3. Place in well-buttered casserole.
4. Pour over yogurt and cream.
5. Bake in oven (375° F.) about one hour, or until golden.

Baked Potatoes with Chervil Sauce

Ingredients:

4 large potatoes
1 cup sour cream
1 tablespoon chopped onion
1 tablespoon fresh chopped or
    green-dried chervil

½ teaspoon salt
½ teaspoon fresh chopped or green-
    dried summer savory

Method:

1. Scrub potatoes; brush skins with oil.
2. Bake in hot oven (400° F.) until done.
3. Combine sour cream with all other ingredients.
4. Split potatoes lengthwise and spoon on sauce.

Potato Recipes—Using Herbs

For ringing the changes and making attractive dishes when flavoring and serving the everlasting potato.

(*a*) Sauté Potatoes

Ingredients:

Old *or* new potatoes (if they are
    new, brush, wash, and dry them
    and use unpeeled; otherwise
    peel potatoes)
Onions, chopped

Butter *or* oil
Fresh chopped or green-dried
    parsley
Fresh chopped or green-dried
    marjoram

Method:

1. Cut potatoes and onions into slices.
2. Sauté onion in butter or oil.
3. Add a generous quantity of parsley.
4. Then add potatoes and a little marjoram and turn over several times.
5. Cover with lid until almost tender.
6. Remove lid and sauté until golden yellow.

(*b*) Potato Snow

Ingredients:

Boiled potatoes in their skins
Fresh chopped or green-dried
    parsley

Fresh chopped or green-dried
    chives
Butter

Method:
1. Peel potatoes while hot.
2. Immediately pass through a potato press onto a hot dish.
3. Sprinkle with parsley and chives.
4. Add a little fresh butter.

(c) Potato Croquettes

Ingredients:

1 lb. potatoes (not new ones) boiled, peeled, mashed, cooled
1 oz. butter *or* margarine
1 egg (small)
Salt
1 tablespoon fresh chopped or green-dried chives

1 teaspoon fresh chopped or green-dried marjoram
3–3½ oz. flour
Bread crumbs
Oil

Method:
1. Cream butter and egg.
2. Add salt and herbs.
3. Mix in potatoes and flour, working until smooth.
4. Shape small sausages to the thickness of a thumb, and roll in bread crumbs.
5. Deep fry in hot oil.

(d) Parsley Potatoes

Ingredients:

2 lbs. small potatoes cooked in their skins
1 oz. butter

3 tablespoons fresh chopped or green-dried parsley

Method:
1. Peel potatoes while hot.
2. Put immediately in frying pan with heated butter and finely chopped parsley.
3. Cover and toss well.
4. Serve on hot dish immediately.

(e) Sage Potatoes

Ingredients:

2 lbs. boiled potatoes, peeled and diced
Oil *or* butter
2 teaspoons fresh chopped or green-dried sage

½ teaspoon each fresh chopped or green-dried parsley and tarragon
4 oz. cream cheese
or 4 oz. curd mixed smooth with a little top of the milk

Method:

1. Sauté potatoes in oil or butter until golden.
2. Add herbs and sauté again.
3. Put into well-buttered casserole.
4. Pour over cheese and milk.
5. Bake in oven (350°) for about one hour or until golden.

Marigold Rice (*serves 4-6*)

An excellent accompanying dish; serve instead of potatoes.

Ingredients:

1 chopped onion	A little fresh chopped or green-dried rosemary
1 tablespoon oil	
½ lb. rice	2–3 teaspoons marigold petals
1 pint vegetable stock	Grated cheese
Salt	A little butter

Method:

1. Sauté onion in fat.
2. Add rice and sauté again.
3. Add vegetable stock, salt, and rosemary.
4. Cook until tender.
5. Add marigold petals, dissolving in hot stock first.
6. Sprinkle with grated cheese and dot with a little butter.

Rice Soufflé with Tomatoes and Vegetables

A satisfying yet tasty savory rice dish.

Ingredients:

1 onion, chopped	Marigold petals
1 tablespoon oil	1 tablespoon each fresh chopped or green-dried onion green and celery leaves
7 oz. rice (preferably whole)	
2 pints hot stock *or* water	
Salt	4–6 tomatoes, sliced

Fresh chopped or green-dried rosemary
½ cup carrots, diced (cooked)

Fresh chopped or green-dried basil
2 tablespoons grated cheese
½ oz. butter

Method:

1. Sauté onion in heated oil.
2. Sauté rice until transparent.
3. Add stock, salt, and rosemary.
4. Mix rice with carrots, marigold petals, onion green, and celery leaves.
5. Place alternate layers of rice mixture and tomatoes in a well-buttered fireproof dish.
6. Sprinkle basil over each layer of tomatoes.
7. Finish with grated cheese and dot with the butter.
8. Bake in a moderate oven (375°) for about 10 minutes.

Genoese Spaghetti

This is a way of cooking spaghetti or any pasta as it is done in Genoa with the Genoese basil paste (page 269). When using this for pasta, boil spaghetti, macaroni, noodles, etc., in salted water until cooked but still firm. Drain pasta well and rinse with cold water in a sieve or colander.

Ingredients:

1–2 tablespoons of *pesto alla Genovese*
2 tablespoons cooking water in which the pasta has been boiled

Finely grated Parmesan cheese
Pine kernels (optional)

Method:

1. Dilute pesto in the two tablespoons of cooking water in a heavy frying pan.
2. Turn pasta in it until covered with green specks.
3. Serve with additional finely grated Parmesan cheese in a separate bowl, if liked.
4. If a genuine Genoese flavor is wanted, sprinkle with a few whole pine kernels.

Spaghetti with Tomato-Meat Sauce (*serves 4-6*)

One of the most delicious ways of serving spaghetti.

Ingredients:

Spaghetti:
1 lb. spaghetti
1 cup olive oil
1 clove garlic, chopped
1 onion, finely chopped
1 teaspoon fresh chopped or green-dried basil
Salt and pepper to taste

Sauce:
3 oz. fat bacon, diced
¾ lb. minced steak
1 clove garlic, minced
1½ cups red wine
4 large tomatoes, peeled and diced
4 oz. mushrooms, sliced
1½ cups water
2 teaspoons fresh chopped or green-dried basil
1½ tablespoons finely chopped parsley
½ teaspoon fresh chopped or green-dried rosemary
Pinch of ground cinnamon
1 tablespoon sugar
5-oz. can condensed tomato puree
Salt and pepper to taste
Grated Parmesan cheese

Method:

Spaghetti:
1. Boil spaghetti for 20 minutes, drain, and dry quickly over heat.
2. While spaghetti is cooking, place olive oil, garlic, onion, and basil in a large heavy saucepan over medium heat, and heat the oil, but not to smoking temperature.
3. Toss the drained spaghetti in the oil, turning with two forks until it is thoroughly coated with the hot oil mixture.
4. Season to taste with salt and pepper.

Sauce:
1. Cut bacon into small pieces and cook in a heavy saucepan over a low flame until fat is melted out.
2. Discard pieces of bacon and add steak to hot fat and brown quickly.
3. Add garlic and cook until golden colored.
4. Add wine and allow to simmer for about 10 minutes.
5. Add all other ingredients and simmer for one hour, stirring frequently.
6. Pour sauce over hot spaghetti and serve with grated Parmesan cheese.

Ravioli (vegetable filled) (*makes about 30*)

Ingredients (pasta):

5 oz. flour	1 tablespoon oil
1 egg	1 tablespoon water
Salt	

Method:

1. Work into a smooth paste and allow to rest for 15 minutes.
2. Roll out as thinly as possible, making two large rounds.
3. Allow to dry on a clean dish towel.
4. Spread the filling over the whole surface or make little heaps at small distances. Brush between fillings with water.
5. Cover with the second half of the paste and press down.
6. Cut with a pastry wheel in squares or oblongs.
7. Allow to dry a little more on a pastry board.
8. Cook ravioli in small quantities in a saucepan full of salted boiling water.
9. Simmer until they come to the surface.
10. Take out with perforated ladle.

Note: They may be served in clear broth as a substantial soup or in layers sprinkled with grated cheese, topped with melted butter or with tomato sauce.

Filling:

For ravioli filling, halve the quantity of savory bread mixture (page 297). It may be used well-mixed with a larger quantity of onion green, approximately a half to three-quarters of a cup (reconstituted if green-dried) and some cooked sieved spinach.

Chapter 9

*S*auces and *A*ccompaniments

Herb Sauces

These sauces bring variety to very many different dishes.

(*a*) Chervil Sauce

Ingredients:

½ oz. butter *or* oil
1 small onion, finely chopped
½ oz. flour
2 tablespoons fresh chopped *or*
green-dried chervil

½ pint vegetable stock
Salt
1 dessertspoon cream, sweet *or* sour

Method:
1. Sauté the onion in the fat until golden.
2. Add the chervil and sauté again.
3. Add the flour and sauté again.
4. Smooth with a little cold water.
5. Add the hot vegetable stock and salt.
6. Cook for 20 minutes.
7. Add the cream before serving.

(*b*) Fennel Sauce

Adds succulence to boiled or baked fish.

Ingredients:

4 oz. butter
2 tablespoons fresh chopped *or*
green-dried fennel

A little salt

Method:
1. Wash the fresh fennel, or reconstitute the green-dried fennel in water.
2. Melt the butter.

3. Mix the fennel with the hot melted butter, add salt if necessary, and serve.

Note: For any fish dish, add one tablespoon fresh chopped or green-dried fennel to a basic white sauce (see Lovage Cream Sauce, which follows).

(c) Lovage Cream Sauce (*makes ½ pint*)

To serve with leftover vegetables, minced meats, or poultry.

Ingredients:

1 oz. butter	½ pint milk
1 tablespoon fresh chopped or green-dried lovage	Salt and pepper
1 oz. flour	¼ cup cream

Method:
1. Melt the butter.
2. Add the lovage and sauté for a few minutes.
3. Stir in the flour and sauté again.
4. Add the milk all at once and the seasoning, stirring until it boils.
5. Simmer for three to five minutes.
6. Add the cream, heat again if necessary, and serve.

Note: The same recipe may be used for nasturtium sauce.

(d) Mint Sauce with Lemon (*makes ¼ pint*)

Making the sauce with lemon gives the mint a better chance. Serve with roast lamb and salads.

Ingredients:

2 tablespoons fresh chopped or green-dried mint	2 tablespoons warm water
1 tablespoon castor sugar	¼ pint diluted lemon juice (3 lemons and 2 oz. water)

Method:
1. Mix together mint and castor sugar.
2. Pour a little hot water over this (if green-dried mint is used there should be enough water to be soaked up by the mint).
3. Add lemon juice.
4. Allow to stand for a short time; then taste for flavor and add either lemon or sugar according to taste.

Note: A half pint of white wine vinegar may be used instead of the diluted lemon juice, but taste first to see how well the mint goes with lemon juice.

(e) Parsley Sauce (*makes ½ pint*)

Ingredients:

2 handfuls fresh chopped parsley
or 3 tablespoons green-dried parsley
1 tablespoon butter
1 tablespoon flour

Pinch of summer savory *or* pepper
  (optional)
½ pint stock (fish, chicken, *or*
  vegetable, according to main
  dish)

Method:

1. Melt fat and sauté flour, cooking thoroughly.
2. Add the stock and season with pepper.
3. Bring to the boil and simmer for three to five minutes.
4. Remove from heat; add parsley and cream.
5. Serve at once; will discolor if left standing.

(f) Sage Sauce (*makes about ½ pint*)

The traditional sauce to serve with boiled or roast mutton.

Ingredients:

3 medium onions, chopped
¼ teaspoon salt
1 pint stock *or* water
1 oz. flour

1 oz. butter
¼ pint milk
4 tablespoons cream
2 teaspoons fresh chopped or green-
  dried sage

Method:

1. Cook the onions in the stock with salt for 15 to 20 minutes.
2. Drain, reserve stock, and pass onions through the mincer.
3. Heat butter in a pan, add flour, and cook for a minute.
4. Remove from heat; beat in milk, reserved stock, and two tablespoons cream.
5. Allow to thicken slowly.
6. Add onions and sage to sauce and reheat, adding more salt if
   necessary.
7. Add rest of cream, and serve spooned around the meat.

(g) Sorrel Sauce (*makes ½ pint*)

Serve with grilled meats, broccoli, or potato dishes.

Ingredients:

2 handfuls of freshly chopped
  sorrel
or 2 tablespoons green-dried sorrel
1 tablespoon oil

1 cup stock
2 tablespoons flour
½ cup milk
Pinch of sugar

Method:
1. Wash sorrel and chop finely.
2. Sauté in fat.
3. Add stock and allow to boil until tender.
4. Blend flour with milk.
5. Add to sorrel and allow to boil.
6. Season with salt and sugar.
7. Serve at once.

(*h*) Rosemary Sauce (*makes 1 pint*)

Adds a delicate flavor to fish or lamb, according to kind of stock used.

Ingredients:

1 oz. butter
1 small onion, finely chopped
1 dessertspoon fresh chopped or green-dried rosemary, crushed

1 oz. flour
¾ to 1 pint fish, meat, *or* vegetable stock
2 tablespoons sour cream

Method:
1. Sauté onion in heated butter until transparent.
2. Add rosemary and sauté.
3. Stir in flour; sauté again, and smooth with some cold water or stock.
4. Add stock.
5. Add sour cream shortly before serving.

Green Herb Sauce (*makes approx. 1 pint*)

Ingredients:

1 small onion, chopped
1 oz. butter *or* oil
1 oz. whole-grain flour
¾ pint stock
¼ pint milk
1 teaspoon lemon juice
2 tablespoons sour cream

2–3 tablespoons of the following mixed fresh chopped or green-dried herbs: parsley, lemon balm, tarragon, lovage, salad burnet, a pinch of marjoram and sage (see GUIDE, page 119, for proportions)

Method:
1. Sauté onion in one-third of the butter or oil until golden.
2. Add half of the chopped herbs and sauté; add flour and sauté.
3. Smooth with a little stock.
4. Add remaining stock and allow to simmer for some time. Add milk and the remaining herbs and lemon juice.
5. Melt the rest of the butter and add this with the cream shortly before serving.

Persillade

Serve with cold lamb and butter beans.

Ingredients:

1 hard-boiled egg
3 tablespoons French dressing (see page 82)

6 tablespoons fresh chopped or green-dried parsley (if green-dried, reconstitute in lemon juice)

Method:

1. Finely chop the hard-boiled egg.
2. Mix together with the French dressing and parsley.
3. Allow to permeate at least 30 minutes before serving.

Sauce Béarnaise

King among French sauces, yet not difficult to make; it is usually served with grilled steak.

Ingredients:

2 tablespoons white wine *or* white wine vinegar
1 teaspoon finely chopped onions *or* shallots
3 or 4 peppercorns
1½ teaspoons green-dried bay leaves or ¼ fresh bay leaf

1 teaspoon each fresh chopped or green-dried tarragon and chervil
2 egg yolks
¼ cup stock *and/or* good gravy*
1½ oz. butter
1 teaspoon each fresh chopped or green-dried tarragon and chervil

Method:

1. Boil vinegar with onions, peppercorns, bay leaf, tarragon, and chervil in a small saucepan until reduced to half.
2. Strain and put aside.
3. Mix the egg yolks with one tablespoon stock and put in top of double boiler when the water is boiling fast.
4. Stir well.
5. Add the butter when soft in small pieces, stirring constantly.
6. Stir until this mixture thickens, adding stock and gravy.
7. Lastly add the boiled onion mixture.
8. Before serving, add tarragon and chervil.

---

* The liquid needed may vary; therefore a little more stock or gravy, or both, may be added.

Sauce Hollandaise

Another traditional sauce; may be served with salmon, food fried in batter, cauliflower, scampi, and other fried fish dishes.

Ingredients:

3 tablespoons water	½ bay leaf
1 tablespoon lemon juice	1 clove
1 small onion	1 level tablespoon cornflour
1 sprig fresh chopped tarragon *or*	½ cup (5 oz.) vegetable stock
1 teaspoon green-dried tarragon	2 egg yolks
	2 oz. butter

Method:

1. Boil the water, lemon juice, onion, herbs, and clove together until half the liquid has evaporated; strain.
2. Blend cornflour with the vegetable stock; bring to the boil, stirring all the time.
3. Beat egg yolks with the first liquid in a double saucepan over boiling water until creamy.
4. Cook until the sauce thickens; remove from heat.
5. Add small pieces of butter gradually.
6. Add vegetable stock and cornflour very carefully, stirring all the time.
7. Keep hot over boiling water but do not allow to cook any more.

Note: The vegetable stock and cornflour may be omitted, in which case double the quantity of all the other ingredients.

Mousseline Sauce

Method.

1. Make Sauce Hollandaise (see previous recipe).
2. Add ¼ cup (2½ oz.) stiffly beaten double cream just before serving.

Frankfurter Green Sauce (*makes ½ pint*)

A famous traditional spring sauce to be served with boiled beef and new potatoes, with fish, or with boiled potatoes only.

Ingredients:

1 cup mayonnaise (see page 82)
1 hard-boiled egg, chopped
Chopped capers
Gherkins or cucumber, diced
2 tablespoons fresh chopped or green-dried chives

1 tablespoon of the following mixed fresh chopped or green-dried herbs: borage, sorrel, salad burnet (if available), parsley, dill, chervil
or more parsley and
1 tablespoon bouquet for salads

Method:

1. Add to mayonnaise the chopped hard-boiled egg and all other ingredients.
2. Mix lightly but well.

Egg Sauce with Chives

A similar type of sauce for similar types of dishes.

Ingredients:

2 tablespoons fresh chopped or green-dried chives
Juice of half a lemon
3 hard-boiled eggs

4 tablespoons oil
½ teaspoon salt
A pinch of sugar

Method:

1. Reconstitute chives with the juice of half a lemon.
2. Pass all the yolks through a sieve.
3. Chop finely whites of eggs.
4. Add oil slowly to yolks (a spoon at a time) and stir well.
5. Add salt and sugar.
6. Add fresh or reconstituted chives.
7. Add chopped whites and mix well.
   Note: Keep in refrigerator and mix again before serving.

Spring Sauce (*makes ¾ cup*)

The traditional "Seven Herb" sauce to accompany spring dishes, such as new potatoes, lamb, veal; also boiled beef and fish.

Ingredients:

3 hard-boiled eggs (1 egg per person)
1 tablespoon vegetable oil
1 tablespoon lemon juice

1 tablespoon of the following mixed fresh chopped or green-dried herbs:
    Parsley

½ teaspoon salt

⅓ cup double cream

or ⅓ cup sour cream and ⅓ cup yogurt

2 tablespoons fresh chopped or green-dried chives

Dill

Borage (optional)

Chervil

Sorrel (optional)

Salad burnet (optional)

or 1 tablespoon bouquet for salads

Method:

1. Peel hard-boiled eggs.
2. Mash yolks with a fork.
3. Chop whites finely.
4. Add oil to the yolks and stir well.
5. Add lemon juice and salt.
6. Add cream, yogurt, and all the herbs.
7. Mix well—should be of thick consistency.

Tomato Sauces

(*a*) The unobtrusive *vegetable* basis brings out the full flavor of the tomatoes.

Ingredients:

1 tablespoon vegetable fat

1 onion

1 clove of garlic

½ cup mixed carrots, celery, and leeks

½ lb. tomatoes (approx.)

1 tablespoon flour

½ tablespoon tomato puree

1 pint vegetable stock *or* water

¼ bay leaf

Pinch of fresh chopped or green-dried rosemary

1 teaspoon mixed fresh chopped or green-dried basil and thyme

A little hot butter

A pinch of sugar

Method:

1. Cut up vegetables.
2. Melt fat and sauté onions and garlic in it.
3. Add vegetables and sauté in the fat.
4. Cut up tomatoes and add.
5. Cook slowly in a covered pan until the liquid has been absorbed.
6. Sprinkle the flour over the vegetables.
7. Add puree, stock, and herbs and cook for half an hour.
8. Put through a sieve.
9. Add butter and sugar to improve the flavor.

(*b*) The *herbs* bring out the full flavor.

Ingredients:

1 tablespoon vegetable fat
1 onion, chopped
1 lb. ripe tomatoes
Salt
¼ bay leaf
A pinch of fresh chopped or green-dried rosemary

½ teaspoon fresh chopped or green-dried basil *or* thyme
1 teaspoon cornflour
¼ cup (2½ oz.) vegetable stock
2 tablespoons cream
Pinch of sugar, if desired

Method:

1. Melt fat and sauté onion in it.
2. Cut tomatoes in pieces and sauté with the onion.
3. Cover and cook until tender.
4. Put through a sieve.
5. Add herbs.
6. Mix cornflour with stock and cook for a few minutes with the tomato puree.
7. Add cream and sugar if liked.

(*c*) Simple, *natural*, and delicate in flavor.

Ingredients:

1 lb. tomatoes
Salt

½ teaspoon fresh chopped or green-dried basil
2 tablespoons cream or a little butter

Method:

1. Cut tomatoes in pieces; cook until tender with salt and herb.
2. Sieve.
3. Add cream or butter.

Horseradish Sauce

Ingredients:

1 hard-boiled egg
2 teaspoons oil
2 teaspoons lemon juice
Salt
Drops of onion juice

Drops of garlic juice
1 heaped tablespoon finely grated horseradish
Chopped white of eggs (if used with fish)

Method:

1. Mix the yolk with the oil and the lemon juice to a thick cream.
2. Add salt, a few drops of onion juice, and garlic.

3. Add the horseradish (more or less according to taste).
4. Add finely chopped egg whites.

Apple and Horseradish Sauce

Serve with boiled fish, together with melted butter.

Ingredients:

6 peeled apples, large   1 glass lemon juice
2 tablespoons sugar   Grated horseradish (according to
1 glass white wine   taste)

Method:

1. Grate the apples.
2. Add the sugar, the white wine, and the lemon juice.
3. Add grated horseradish.
4. Mix well until the mixture appears frothy.

Burnet-Mint Fish Sauce

This variation of a classic French sauce for grilled fish uses burnet
in place of fresh cucumber.

Ingredients:

½ cup burnet leaves   Salt
½ cup spearmint leaves   Pepper
½ lb. butter

Method:

1. Chop burnet and spearmint leaves.
2. Melt butter in a saucepan, add herbs, and simmer for 10 minutes.
3. Season the sauce to taste with salt and pepper.
4. Pour over grilled fillet of sole or plaice.

Pesto alla Genovese (Genoese Basil Paste)

This delicious pesto, or paste, originally from Genoa, is traditionally
used with all pasta: macaroni, spaghetti, noodles, etc. If a jar of
pesto is prepared and kept, it may be used for this and other dishes
such as pizza, canapes, etc., at various times. It is excellent as a spread
on toasted French bread (see Herb-Buttered French Loaf, page 290);
or a spoonful of the pesto will give minestrone its authentic flavor.

The Pesto Genovese can be made of fresh or green-dried basil if the suggestions for reconstituting are carefully followed.

Ingredients:

1 tablespoon nuts (cashew *or* pine kernels)

¾ cup chopped basil leaves without stems

or 4 tablespoons green-dried basil, reconstituted in 4 tablespoons water (boiled and cooled)

2 cloves of garlic

14 tablespoons Parmesan cheese, finely grated

10 tablespoons oil (sunflower, corn, *or* olive oil)

Salt according to taste

1½ oz. butter

Method:

1. Grind the nuts finely.
2. Chop basil finely without stems, or reconstitute green-dried basil in equal quantity of water until all water has disappeared.
3. Chop garlic finely.
4. Add Parmesan cheese.
5. Pound all the above ingredients in a mortar or blend in the blender on half speed.
6. Add oil, drop by drop, while slowly turning.
7. Add salt.
8. Add butter in small pieces slowly and continue stirring or blending until it becomes a firm paste.

Note: The pesto should be firmly pressed into a jar; if it is to be kept, a thin layer of melted butter should seal it. The boiled water for reconstituting green-dried basil will keep the paste longer, and so will the thin layer of butter on the top. It may be kept in the refrigerator.

Rose-Hip Puree and Sauce

Rose-hip puree is necessary in order to make rose-hip sauce. The following directions are given for preserving rose hips as puree, if preserved rose-hip puree is unavailable in glass jars imported from Switzerland or Scandinavia.

Preparing Fresh Rose Hips for Puree

Ingredients:

2½ lbs. rose hips

1 lb. castor sugar for 1 lb. mashed rose hips

Castor sugar for covering jars

1½ pints water

Method:
1. Pick only ripe rose hips, vivid red and slightly soft, after frost has touched them.
2. Select whole, undamaged hips.
3. Top and tail (using scissors if soft).
4. Wash quickly and drain in colander (not aluminum).
5. Put the hips into boiling water in stainless steel or undamaged enamel saucepan and bring again to the boil.
6. Simmer with the lid on until the hips are soft, about 15 minutes (do not over-boil or the color and flavor will be spoiled; but the hips must be soft enough to sieve).
7. Rub through a fine hair or stainless-steel sieve, using a wooden spoon, masher, or pestle.
8. Beat hips and sugar for about 20 minutes, using a wooden spoon or stainless-steel mixer.
9. Bring to boil; then cook gently for 10 minutes.
10. Fill well cleaned, dry, hot earthenware or glass jars.
11. Allow puree to cool.
12. Cover with waxed or greaseproof paper, soaked in alcohol.
13. Cover waxed paper with about half an inch of castor sugar.
14. Cover with cellophane to make jars airtight.

Note: This puree will keep for one year if carefully prepared and stored in a dark, cool, and airy place, but its vitamin content will decrease with keeping.

Rose-Hip Sauce

Ingredients:

2½ oz. rose-hip puree	Lemon juice, if liked
1 cup (½ pint) water, clear apple juice, *or* grape juice	1 teaspoon each fresh chopped or green-dried lemon balm and sweet cicely
2½ oz. sugar	

Method:
1. Bring puree, water, and sugar to the boil.
2. Add lemon juice and herbs.

Hard Sauce

A pleasant variation of a well-known sauce for serving with Christmas pudding and mince pies.

Ingredients:

2 oz. butter

2 oz. castor sugar

1 level teaspoon icing sugar

1 tablespoon rum

1 teaspoon fresh chopped or green-dried sweet cicely (if green-dried, reconstitute in 1 teaspoon rum)

Method:

1. Cream butter.
2. Add castor sugar and icing sugar to butter and blend well.
3. Add the rum and sweet cicely.

Note: This can equally well be made with brandy.

Elderberry Sauces

Pick over elderberries, wash carefully, strip off their stalks, drain well, and express the juice.

(*a*) Uncooked Sauce or Soup

Ingredients:

¾ pint freshly expressed elder-berry juice

1 large eating apple, grated

2 cartons or jars plain yogurt

1 oz. brown sugar *or* honey

2 teaspoons fresh chopped or green-dried sweet cicely

Juice and peel of 1 lemon

Method:

1. Grate the apple.
2. Beat well elderberry juice with yogurt and apple, and mix immediately with lemon juice.
3. Sweeten with brown sugar or honey and add sweet cicely.
4. Flavor with some lemon rind.
5. Use as a sauce with a pudding.

Note: Use it as a breakfast dish with cereal flakes, as a cold sweet with ice cream for a later summer menu, or as a cold sweet soup.

(*b*) Cooked Elderberry Sauce

Elderberry sauce may also be cooked and served hot or cold in the following way.

Ingredients:

½ lb. elderberries

1 large apple

1½ pints water

¾ oz. cornflour

½ pint apple juice

Peel of a lemon

1 teaspoon lemon juice

2 teaspoons fresh chopped or green-dried sweet cicely

Brown sugar

2 tablespoons cream *or* top of the milk

Method:

1. Pick over elderberries; wash carefully; allow to drain well.
2. Cut apple into thin slices.
3. Strip elderberries of their stalks with a fork.
4. Boil berries and apple in one pint of water.
5. Smooth cornflour with one-half pint of water and add to the fruit.
6. Bring to a fast boil.
7. Add apple juice, lemon peel, lemon juice, and sweet cicely.
8. Add sugar according to taste.
9. Before serving, add two tablespoons cream and mix well. If too tart, more milk or cream may be added.

Note: Serve hot with a pudding, or chill well and serve with sponge fingers or rusks. May also be served as a cold sweet soup with biscuits.

Herb Jellies

(*a*) Basic Herb Jelly

Herb jellies make a most refreshing change from the usual main-dish accompaniments. Here follows a recipe for a basic jelly which may obtain its flavor from an individual herb or a combination of several.

Ingredients:

2 lbs. tart apples *or* crab apples	Per cup of juice (½ pint):
1 tablespoon red wine vinegar *or* white wine vinegar	1 sprig of the fresh herb used for flavoring
¾ cup sugar per ½ pint juice	*or* 2 teaspoons of the green-dried herb, put in a muslin bag

Method:

1. Quarter the apples and just cover with water; boil until soft.
2. Pour into a jelly bag and leave to drain overnight; measure the juice.
3. Add the herb and red wine vinegar for the strong-tasting herbs, or white wine vinegar for the delicate herbs.
4. Boil all the ingredients together for about 10 minutes.
5. Heat the sugar in a warm oven.
6. Add the sugar slowly to the boiling liquid, stirring until it is dissolved.
7. Boil the jelly until setting point is reached, or the sugar thermometer registers 219°; then remove the herbs.
8. Pour jelly into warm jars and seal.

Note: If desired, the herbs, chopped finely, may be left in the jelly to provide attractive specks of green.

(*b*) Herb-flavored Jellies

Follow basic herb jelly recipe for:

BASIL HERB JELLY: served with desserts, fish, game, poultry, and roasts.

MARJORAM HERB JELLY: served with au gratin dishes and fried dishes; with meat, chicken, game, and turkey.

MINT OR PEPPERMINT JELLY: served with lamb, cold poultry, fish; peppermint jelly may also be used for sweets and drinks.

MULTI-FLAVORED HERB JELLY: a special mint, such as Bowles or Eau de Cologne Mint, may be combined with marjoram and burnet.

ROSE-GERANIUM AND BAY JELLY; mixed with chopped lemon peel, makes an exquisitely flavored jelly.

SAGE JELLY: served with mutton, lamb, pork, cheese dishes; with all dishes for which sage is usually used.

TARRAGON JELLY: served with fish, meats, salad, poultry, and shellfish.

THYME OR LEMON-THYME JELLY: served with cheese dishes, eggs, fish, game, meats, poultry, and shellfish.

Herb Butters

These delicious home-made spreads for so many occasions give the full flavor of uncooked herbs. Use generously on bridge rolls, toast, sandwiches, canapés—which may be garnished with radishes, cucumber, tomatoes—for tea and cocktail parties or picnics. Herb butters kept in the refrigerator will lend the professional touch to steak and fried dishes, particularly if the herb butter is shaped into a roll—approximately an inch and a half in diameter—packed into foil which is twisted at both ends and placed in the refrigerator. Slices of this may be cut when needed.

(a) Mixed Herb Butter

Ingredients:
4 oz. butter
2–4 teaspoons fresh herbs
  or 2 teaspoons green-dried mixed herbs, such as parsley, tarragon, chervil, chives, mint, lemon balm, sweet cicely, marjoram, basil, summer savory, marigold (for proportions, see GUIDE, page 119)
Juice of up to half a lemon

Method:
1. Allow butter to soften at room temperature.
2. Cream butter.
3. Reconstitute two teaspoons green-dried mixed herbs in juice of lemon, but do not use more than the herbs absorb; or use two to four teaspoons fresh herbs, finely chopped.
4. Blend herbs and salt with the creamed butter and set aside at room temperature for one or two hours so that the herbs can permeate the butter.
5. Store in small tightly covered jars in refrigerator. May be kept until required.

(*b*) Tarragon Butter

Ingredients:

1 teaspoon green-dried tarragon	1 teaspoon lemon to reconstitute
4 tablespoons butter	tarragon

Method:
1. Reconstitute tarragon in lemon juice.
2. Blend with the butter.
3. Add salt according to taste and allow to permeate.
4. Keep in a cool place. May be kept in the refrigerator for several days.

Note: Particularly good on grilled steaks. Other herb butters may be made with individual herbs (see GUIDE, page 119), for proportions; and Twenty-four Herbs in a Chest, pages 119–57).

(*c*) Cucumber and Dill Butter (to serve with fish)

Ingredients:

1 oz. butter	Salt
Cucumber	1 teaspoon fresh chopped or green-dried dill
Juice of half a lemon	

Method:
1. Peel cucumber and grate it or mash it in blender.
2. Beat butter until soft.
3. Blend all ingredients with the butter, adding salt to taste.
4. Put into a small pot and keep cold until required.

Chapter 10

Sweets and Desserts, Cakes

Peach Tart (*serves* 6)

An attractive sweet to serve when peaches are cheap.

Ingredients:

Casing:
3 egg whites
⅔ cup sugar
¾ cup flaked coconut
1 tablespoon fresh chopped or green-dried sweet cicely
½ cup cornflake crumbs
⅓ cup chopped toasted almonds

Filling:
2½–3 cups peach slices
1 teaspoon fresh chopped or green-dried sweet cicely
Whipped cream
2 teaspoons flaked coconut
1 teaspoon fresh chopped or green-dried lemon balm

Method:

1. Beat egg whites until stiff.
2. Gradually add sugar, and continue beating until stiff glossy peaks form.
3. Fold in flaked coconut, half of the sweet cicely, cornflake crumbs, and almonds.
4. Spread meringue evenly over bottom and sides of a well-greased nine-inch pie tin.
5. Bake in a cool oven for 50 to 60 minutes or until golden. Leave to get cold.
6. Just before serving fill with peach slices.
7. Sprinkle with remaining sweet cicely.
8. Top with whipped cream and sprinkle with coconut mixed with lemon balm.

Orange Chiffon (*serves 4-6*)

A delicate-flavored dessert to serve after a rich meat dish.

Ingredients:

1 tablespoon gelatin
½ cup sugar
Pinch of salt
1 cup hot water
3 eggs, separated
1 teaspoon fresh chopped or green-dried sweet cicely
2 teaspoons fresh chopped or green-dried lemon balm
6 oz. orange juice
3 tablespoons lemon juice
½ pint whipped cream
¼ cup halved toasted almonds

Method:

1. Mix together the gelatin, sugar, and salt in a double boiler.
2. Stir in the hot water and cook over boiling water, stirring until the gelatin dissolves.
3. Beat egg yolks slightly and stir into gelatin mixture.
4. Add herbs.
5. Return to double boiler; cook, stirring until mixture coats the spoon.
6. Remove from heat and add orange juice and lemon juice.
7. Chill until it starts to congeal.
8. Beat egg whites until stiff.
9. Fold two mixtures together and chill.
10. Top with the whipped cream and almonds.

Cream-Cheese Whip with Berries (*serves 3-4*)

A dish for those who like unusual flavors.

Ingredients:

3 oz. cream cheese
2 tablespoons top of milk *or* cream
1 tablespoon brown sugar
1 tablespoon chopped nuts
1 tablespoon chopped, seedless raisins
Pinch of cinnamon
1 grated eating apple
1 teaspoon fresh chopped or green-dried sweet cicely
1 teaspoon fresh chopped or green-dried lemon balm

Method:

1. Beat cream cheese with top of the milk or full cream until smooth.
2. Combine with all other ingredients.
3. When all is well mixed, add five to seven ounces of washed strawberries or any other berries.

Strawberry Tartlets with Whipped Cream

When strawberries are plentiful, this is a delicious way to serve them.

1. Wash and hull strawberries.
2. Sprinkle with sugar and a little fresh chopped or green-dried sweet cicely.
3. Fill individual pastry cases, top with whipped cream, and sprinkle a little sweet cicely on top;
   or Mix whipped cream with sweet cicely before decorating the strawberries;
   or Decorate with whipped cream, and hand around a small jar of freshly chopped sweet cicely for individual flavoring.

Rhubarb Cream (*serves 3–4*)

All the family will like rhubarb done in this way.

Ingredients:

1 lb. rhubarb
2–3 tablespoons brown **sugar**
Grated lemon peel
Pinch of cinnamon
2 eggs

2 teaspoons fresh chopped or green-dried sweet cicely
1 tablespoon fresh chopped or green-dried elder flowers

Method:

1. Wash and cut the rhubarb into small pieces and cook with a little water or apple juice; sieve.
2. Add two tablespoons brown sugar, grated lemon peel, and cinnamon. Allow to cool.
3. Beat yolks with one tablespoon brown sugar, sweet cicely, and elder flowers, and add to cooled rhubarb.
4. Beat the two whites of egg until stiff and add to the mixture.

   Note: If liked, eight tablespoons double cream, whipped stiffly and folded into the mixture, will improve the flavor.

Fresh Lemon Ice Cream (*serves 6–8*)

An ideal dish to serve as dessert at a party or barbecue.

Ingredients:

1 cup double cream

1 egg

¾–1 cup sugar

⅓ cup lemon juice

2 teaspoons grated lemon peel

1 teaspoon fresh chopped or green-dried lemon balm

Pinch of salt

1⅓ cups milk

Method:

1. Beat, in an electric mixer, the cream and egg, until blended and thickened.
2. Add sugar gradually while beating, until mixture is stiff.
3. Beat in the lemon juice, lemon peel, lemon balm, and salt.
4. Add the milk and beat again.
5. Immediately turn into a large refrigerator tray.
6. Leave in the freezer until firm, about four hours.
   Note: This quantity may be halved for a small family.

Herbed Fruit Salad (*serves 6 or more*)

A fresh-fruit dish for a hot summer's day, to which the herbs give sweetness, reducing the sugar; the extra tang from the lemon thyme replaces Kirsch.

Ingredients:

Juice of 2 oranges *or* the equivalent of apple juice

3 oranges *or*

2 oranges and 1 grapefruit

1 apple, finely sliced

1 pear, finely sliced

1 banana, sliced

1 teaspoon fresh chopped or green-dried sweet cicely

Pinch of fresh chopped or green-dried lemon thyme

½–1 oz. sugar *or* sweetening tablets

Method:

1. Peel oranges and remove all pith; halve each peeled orange across the middle and then cut each half into eight pieces—16 pieces in all. Cover well.
2. Place all other sliced fruit in a bowl.
3. Add oranges and grapefruit.
4. Add sugar or dissolved tablets.
5. Add herbs and juice.
6. Mix gently but thoroughly.
7. Press gently with a plate and keep covered.
8. Allow to permeate for one hour and chill before serving.
   Note: May be served with liquid or whipped cream.

Plum Salad (*serves 4*)

Use dessert plums for this salad; no extra sugar is needed.

Ingredients:

1 lb. plums
1 tablespoon fresh chopped or green-dried sweet cicely
1 teaspoon fresh chopped or green-dried lemon balm

¼ cup cream
¼ cup yogurt *or* sour cream
Lemon juice

Method:

1. Stone plums and dice.
2. Sprinkle herbs over plums.
3. Make a dressing of cream and yogurt or sour cream with lemon juice; mix well.
4. Add to plums.
5. Allow to permeate and then taste; add sugar if necessary.
6. Serve chilled.

Banana Sweet (*serves 3–4*)

A hot party sweet for a cold winter's night.

Ingredients:

4 bananas
2 oranges
1 teaspoon rum *or* curaçao
1 teaspoon fresh chopped or green-dried sweet cicely
or 1 teaspoon mixed fresh chopped or green-dried sweet cicely and lemon balm

Pinch of peppermint (optional)
Piece of butter, size of walnut
1 teaspoon honey
or 1 teaspoon brown sugar
Lemon juice

Method:

1. Squeeze juice of two oranges and add the rum or curaçao—if the oranges are very sweet, add a little lemon juice.
2. Add the herbs to this liquid and allow to stand for 10 minutes.
3. Melt the butter in small frying pan or skillet.
4. Add the orange-juice mixture and the honey or sugar. Bring to the boil.
5. Add the peeled whole bananas and baste with the mixture; cook for 5 to 7 minutes.

6. Serve the bananas straight from the skillet *or* remove carefully onto a hot flat dish and cover with mixture, which should have been left cooking for a little longer after removal of the bananas.

Almond Peaches (*serves 6*)

Peaches and almonds combine to make this a good party sweet.

Ingredients:

6 fresh peaches
½ cup finely ground almonds
½ cup icing sugar
2 tablespoons butter
½ teaspoon grated lemon peel
1 teaspoon fresh chopped or green-dried sweet cicely

1 teaspoon fresh chopped or green-dried lemon balm
½ cup orange juice
⅓ cup granulated sugar
Double cream

Method:

1. Mix with a spoon the ground almonds, icing sugar, butter, lemon peel, and herbs; blend well.
2. Stir in about one tablespoon orange juice to make a good consistency for shaping.
3. Peel, halve, and pit peaches.
4. Stuff center of each peach with the almond mixture.
5. Put halves together again and arrange in greased baking dish.
6. Pour remaining orange juice over peaches; sprinkle with granulated sugar.
7. Bake in a moderate oven (375°) for 20 to 30 minutes, or until tender, basting several times.
8. Serve warm with cream.

Flavored Salzburger Nockerls (*serves 6*)

This famous sweet was invented in Salzburg and is served in coffee houses with variations in flavor. It is a very unusual dessert, but is not a difficult one to make; it should be prepared and served quickly.

Ingredients:

6 egg whites
⅛ teaspoon salt
3 tablespoons castor sugar
2 level tablespoons flour
3 egg yolks
Butter

Milk
2 tablespoons grated orange peel
2 tablespoons fresh chopped or green-dried lemon balm
A pinch of fresh chopped or green-dried lemon thyme

Method:

1. In a large bowl beat egg whites with salt until frothy.
2. Gradually beat in sugar, adding one tablespoon at a time, beating after each addition, until the whites form stiff peaks.
3. Beat egg yolks with flour until thick and light.
4. Grate fresh orange peel into egg mixture and add herbs.
5. Carefully fold egg-yolk mixture into the whites.
6. Melt butter over low heat in large frying pan (at least 10 inches in diameter), until butter bubbles.
7. Spoon egg mixture into pan, piling it into mounds.
8. Cook egg mounds over low heat, until undersides are golden (about two minutes).
9. Turn the nockerls over carefully; cook for a further two minutes.
10. Then place them in a fireproof shallow dish in which there is already a quarter of an inch of boiling milk and a knob of melted butter.
11. Put this dish into the oven (325°).
12. Allow the nockerls to rise; but they should not get too dark.
13. Serve as quickly as possible with a sprinkling of icing sugar; they are very delicate and may fall.

Carthusian Dumplings (*serves 4–6*) (B)

A satisfying sweet for all the family.

Ingredients:

½ small whole-grain loaf *or* French loaf

¼ pint milk

1 egg

1 tablespoon fresh chopped or green-dried lemon balm

1 tablespoon fresh chopped or green-dried sweet cicely

Pinch of lemon thyme

Butter for frying

Sugar and ground cinnamon mixed (proportion: 1 teaspoon cinnamon to 4 tablespoons sugar)

Method:

1. Grate off rind of loaf and keep the grated crumbs.
2. Cut bread into thick slices and then across again (should give squares of two inches).
3. Beat well together the milk with sugar, whole egg, and half the mixed herbs.
4. Allow bread cubes to soak in this mixture.
5. Before frying, take out cubes and place on a plate.
6. Mix well grated bread crumbs and remaining herbs.

7. Cover bread cubes with the bread-crumb mixture on all four sides.
8. Fry in hot butter, turning frequently.
9. Serve with sugar and cinnamon (mixed).
   or
   Serve with wine sauce:

Sauce

Ingredients:

1 cup white wine *or* apple juice
1 egg
1 teaspoon lemon juice
A little grated lemon peel

1–2 tablespoons sugar
2 teaspoons flour *or* cornflour
   (smoothed with a little water)

Method:

1. Mix all ingredients, except the flour, in a saucepan, and bring almost to the boil, beating with an egg beater all the time.
2. When it bubbles, take off heat, let it settle down, and add smoothed flour.
3. Bring to the boil again.

Elder-Flower Fritters (*allow 2–3 fritters per person*)

A delicately flavored sweet to be made when elder flowers are in full bloom.

Ingredients:

Prepare batter (page 289)
Freshly picked elder-flower heads
Oil
½ teaspoon marigold petals

Sugar
or sugar and cinnamon mixed
   (proportion: 1 teaspoon cinnamon to 4 tablespoons sugar)
1 teaspoon fresh chopped **sweet** cicely

Method:

1. Dip the whole heads of elder flowers into the batter, holding them by the short stalks.
2. Immediately deep fry in hot oil until golden brown; drain.
3. Serve quickly, either with sugar, or sugar mixed with cinnamon, or less sugar mixed with fresh chopped sweet cicely.
   Note: Marigold petals should be mixed with the batter. Sweet cicely, green-dried, may also be added to the batter.

Elderberry Dumplings (*serves 6*)

Wild elderberries have been used since the days of the American pioneers. Black currants or blackberries may be used instead, if liked.

Ingredients:

Sauce:
2 cups washed elderberries, without stems
¾ cup sugar
1 tablespoon flour
2 tablespoons lemon juice
¾ cup water

Dumplings:
¾ cup flour
1½ teaspoons baking powder
¼ teaspoon cinnamon
Salt
¼ cup sugar
¼ teaspoon lemon peel
1 teaspoon fresh chopped or dried marigold petals (if available)
¼ cup milk
1 egg slightly beaten

Method:

Sauce
1. Put elderberries in a saucepan.
2. Mix sugar and flour, and smooth with lemon juice and water.
3. Pour over the berries.
4. Bring to the boil.
5. Reduce heat just enough to keep berries hot.

Meanwhile, make Dumplings:
1. Sift flour and mix with baking powder.
2. Add cinnamon and salt.
3. Add sugar and lemon peel.
4. Combine milk and egg.
5. Stir into dry ingredients until blended.
6. Pour elderberry mixture into an eight-inch square baking tin or fireproof dish.
7. Drop the dumpling mixture into the elderberry sauce by the tablespoonful (there should be exactly six dumplings).
8. Bake in a hot oven (400°) 25 to 30 minutes, or until the tops of the dumplings are golden.

Note: May be served warm with thick cream.

Sorrel Turnover (*serves 4-6*)

A most unusual sweet.

Ingredients:

1 cup dry pastry mix (page 288)
3 teaspoons fresh chopped or green-dried sorrel
2 teaspoons fresh chopped or green-dried sweet cicely

1 tablespoon lemon juice (to reconstitute dried herbs)
2 tablespoons brown sugar

Method:

1. Add enough water to pastry mix to make a firm dough.
2. Roll out and cut into two rounds.
3. If dried herbs are used, reconstitute in all the lemon juice; otherwise add less juice.
4. Mix herbs and brown sugar and spread on round of pastry.
5. Wet edges of pastry and put second round on top, pressing down lightly.
6. Place in shallow dish or on a baking tin and bake in moderate oven (350°) for about 15 minutes or until golden.
   Note: If preferred, make individual turnovers.

The following three recipes make unusual tea-time treats:

Rosemary Biscuits (*makes approx. 4 dozen small biscuits*)

Ingredients:

4 oz. butter
2 oz. sugar
6 oz. flour

2 tablespoons fresh chopped or green-dried crushed rosemary

Method:

1. Cream butter and sugar together until light.
2. Add flour and rosemary to butter mixture.
3. Knead well with hands until it forms a dough.
4. Gently roll out on lightly floured board.
5. Cut into small rounds with biscuit cutter.
6. Place biscuits on greased baking sheet.
7. Bake in hot oven 450° for 10–12 minutes until golden and firm.
8. Remove at once to cool on wire tray.

Marigold Sweet Buns (*makes* 20)

Ingredients:

2 eggs
Their weight in:
  Plain flour
  Castor sugar

2 tablespoons fresh chopped or
dried marigold petals

Method:

1. Separate the eggs.
2. Add the sugar to the egg yolks and beat well.
3. Fold in flour and marigold petals.
4. Beat egg whites until stiff.
5. Add to yolk mixture, mixing well together.
6. Divide in greased muffin tins topped with more marigold petals and a sprinkling of sugar.
7. Bake in a moderate oven for about 10 minutes.

Cream-Cheese Cake

Ingredients:

5 oz. butter
5 oz. sugar
6 egg·yolks
¾ lb. soft cream cheese
Grated rind of half a lemon

5 oz. almonds, skinned and ground
2 teaspoons fresh chopped or green-
dried lemon balm
6 egg whites

Method:

1. Cream butter, sugar, yolks, and cream cheese together.
2. Add lemon rind, herbs, and ground almonds.
3. Fold in beaten egg whites.
4. Place in greased sponge tin.
5. Bake for one-half hour at 300–350°.

Chapter 11

Sandwiches, Savories, Herb Breads, and Pastry

Savory Sandwiches

These sandwiches can be made equally well with either white or whole-grain bread, but the slices need to be thinly cut. For figure watchers, pumpernickel or rye bread makes low-calorie sandwiches.

(*a*) Nasturtium Sandwiches

Chop nasturtium leaves finely, butter slices of whole-grain bread, and arrange nasturtium leaves between the slices. Cut neat, small, triangular sandwiches. Prepare shortly before required.

(*b*) Tarragon and Chive Sandwiches

Blend well together a half pound cream cheese, two teaspoons (each) fresh chopped or green-dried tarragon and chives, and leave to permeate for 5 to 10 minutes before putting in the sandwiches.

(*c*) Herb-Egg Spread Sandwiches

Ingredients:

2 eggs, hard boiled	2 teaspoons bouquet for omelettes
2 tablespoons butter	*or* 2 teaspoons mixed of fresh
1 teaspoon yogurt	chopped or green-dried chives,
Pinch of salt	parsley, chervil
	A pinch of fresh chopped or green-dried marjoram or thyme

Mix the finely chopped hard-boiled eggs with the softened butter. Add all the herbs, salt, lemon juice, and yogurt, and mix well until smooth. Spread fairly thick on either whole-grain or white bread.

(*d*) Cucumber and Dill Sandwiches

Cut fine slices of cucumber, arrange on buttered bread, and sprinkle generously with dill before adding the second slice of bread.

(*e*) Chicken and Marjoram Sandwiches

Ingredients:

3–4 oz. minced cooked chicken
¼ cup sour cream
1 teaspoon fresh chopped or green-
dried onion green

½ teaspoon fresh chopped or green-
dried marjoram
¾ teaspoon salt
¾ teaspoon paprika

Blend together well before using as a spread.

(*f*) Tomato and Basil Sandwiches

Cut slices of tomato, place on buttered bread, and sprinkle generously with basil before adding the second slice of bread.

Note: The basil is used instead of pepper and often replaces the salt, but if a little salt is required, this may be added.

Pastry for Herb Recipes

(*a*) Short Pastry

Ingredients:

¼ lb. butter
½ lb. flour
Salt
Water

This makes 2½ cups of dry pastry mix

Method:

1. Sift flour and salt into a bowl.
2. Rub butter into flour until it resembles bread crumbs.
3. Add sufficient water to make a firm dough.

(*b*) Yeast Dough (savory—for Pizza, Rolls, etc.)

Ingredients:

8 oz. flour, 2 oz. of which may be
whole-grain
2 oz. butter

Salt
1 oz. yeast or more *
4–6 tablespoons milk

* In England, yeast is sold by bakers according to weight, but it is a different kind of yeast from that in the United States. Here a standard pizza dough recipe may be used, as shown on the yeast packages.

Method:

1. Sift flour and salt into a bowl, make a well in center, and put in a warm place.
2. Cut the butter into small pieces and dot on the flour.
3. Mix the yeast with two tablespoons milk, pour into well, and mix with a little flour to make a thick paste.
4. Cover bowl with a cloth and put in a warm place till the dough in the well doubles its size.
5. Add the rest of the milk and knead the flour into the dough.
6. Beat dough until smooth and allow to rise in a warm place, covered by a cloth, until approximately double the size.
7. Roll out and line baking tin, or use according to recipe.

(c) Choux Pastry (*makes 14 savory or sweet puffs*)

Ingredients:

2 oz. butter	3 oz. plain flour
¼ pint cold water	2 large eggs
Pinch of salt	

Method:

1. Place the water, butter, and salt in a saucepan, and bring to boil.
2. Immediately add all the flour.
3. Remove from the heat and beat until the mixture leaves the sides of the pan.
4. When cool, beat in the eggs a little at a time.
5. Place dessertspoons of the mixture, spaced well apart, on a greased baking sheet, or press it through a forcing bag in any shape desired.
6. Bake in oven (400°) for about 40 minutes.
7. Split and allow to cool.

Note: Add one tablespoon sugar for sweet puffs, grated nutmeg for savory puffs.

(d) Batter for Vegetable and Fruit Fritters

Ingredients:

4 tablespoons flour	6 tablespoons water
Salt	1 egg, separated

Method:

1. Sift flour and salt in a bowl.
2. Mix to a smooth paste with the water and yolk of egg, and leave to rest for at least half an hour.
3. Then, shortly before using the batter, fold in gently the stiffly beaten white of egg until well mixed.

(e) Easy Pastry made with Oil (*sufficient for 1 crust*)

Ingredients:

¼ cup sunflower *or* corn oil   1 cup sifted flour
2–3 tablespoons cold, creamy milk   ¾ teaspoon salt

Method:

1. Put the oil and the milk together in a cup; do not stir.
2. Mix the flour and salt in a bowl.
3. Pour in oil and milk, mixing with flour.
4. Press into a ball.
5. Place between two sheets of waxed paper (12 inches square).
6. Dampen table top to prevent slipping.
7. Roll out until circle reaches edges of paper and peel off top paper.
8. Place pastry, paper side up, in eight- or nine-inch pan, remove paper, and fit to pan.
9. Prick pastry in several places with a fork.
10. Bake in hot oven (425°) for about 10 minutes.
10A. If used to top a pie, place over filling and bake in hot oven for about 40 minutes.

Note: This pastry may be kept unbaked in refrigerator or deep freeze for use at any time. Wrap in aluminum foil to retain moisture.

Hot Herb-Buttered French Loaf

Easy to prepare, excellent on its own, and one of the best accompaniments to any savory dish. A great standby to eke out the meal, when unexpected guests arrive.

Ingredients:

1 long French loaf   Herb butter (see page 274)

Method:

1. Prepare herb butter.
2. Cut a long French stick across into small slices.
3. Spread herb butter generously all over one side of each slice.
4. Press closely together again.
5. Wrap foil around loaf and seal well.
6. Place in medium oven (350°) for 20 to 30 minutes or until crisp.
7. Unwrap and serve at once.

Cheese-Herb Bread (*makes one 2-lb. loaf*)

Ingredients:

3¾ cups flour
2 tablespoons melted butter
1 tablespoon sugar
1 teaspoon salt
½ teaspoon fresh chopped or green-dried marjoram

1 teaspoon fresh chopped or green-dried thyme
1 cup milk
1 cup grated Cheddar cheese
1 envelope active dry yeast
2 tablespoons warm water

Method:

1. Blend three tablespoons flour with butter, sugar, salt, marjoram, and thyme in saucepan over medium heat.
2. Stir in milk.
3. Cook, stirring until thick and smooth; remove from heat.
4. Add cheese and stir until cheese melts; keep just warm.
5. Soften yeast in the warm water; add to cheese mixture.
6. Gradually add flour, beating until smooth after each addition, mixing to a stiff dough.
7. Turn dough on to a lightly floured board.
8. Knead gently until dough is a smooth ball.
9. Return to pan; grease top of dough; cover with damp cloth.
10. Stand pan in a warm place and allow dough to rise—about 50 to 60 minutes.
11. Return dough to floured board; punch it down and shape into a loaf.
12. Place in greased loaf tin (two-pound size); cover with damp cloth and allow to rise until almost double the size.
13. Brush with melted butter.
14. Bake in moderately hot oven (375°) for 35 minutes.
15. Turn out on wire tray and cool before storing.

Cream-Cheese Puffs

Ingredients:

Savory choux pastry (see page 289)
7 oz. cream cheese
2 tablespoons each milk and cream
3 tablespoons grated cheese
1 tablespoon chopped or green-dried chives

½ teaspoon each fresh chopped or green-dried summer savory and thyme
Salt
Yeast extract, slightly diluted with a few drops of water

Method:

1. Prepare choux pastry.
2. Shape into small but longish rolls; place on baking sheet.
3. Bake in moderate oven (350°) for about 15 minutes.
4. Beat cream cheese until it is of a soft creamy consistency.
5. Add other ingredients and beat well together.
6. Cut rolls in half, lengthways; pipe or fill with stuffing.

Note: A suggestion for a sweet cream-cheese filling is Banana–Cheese Cream (page 107).

Savory Turnovers (*makes approx.* 20)

A savory accompaniment to vegetables and thick soups.

Ingredients:

Full quantity of short pastry (see page 288)
5 oz. cream cheese
1 egg
1 tablespoon cream *or* top of milk
1 tablespoon flour
Salt
1 tablespoon fresh chopped or green-dried chives

½ teaspoon each fresh chopped or green-dried summer savory, basil, tarragon, and lovage
Nutmeg }
Paprika } According to taste
Caraway *or* poppy seeds

Method:

A savory accompaniment to vegetables and thick soups.

1. Prepare pastry and roll out to a quarter-inch thickness.
2. Cut into four-inch squares.
3. Mix other ingredients together and put one teaspoon of this filling on each square.
4. Brush edges with water, turn over to make triangle, and press edges well together.
5. Brush top with egg yolk.
6. Sprinkle with caraway or poppy seeds.
7. Bake in moderate oven (350°) until golden brown.

Note: The filling can be made in a number of different ways—with minced meat, poultry, fish, mushrooms, or cabbage in place of the cream cheese. Originally Russian, the turnovers may be eaten with any meal instead of bread.

For cocktail or party purposes, they are delightful if made smaller (three-inch squares).

Pizza Napolitana with Basil (*makes approx. 10*)

An easy and excellent way to make this traditional Italian dish, for which herbs are of such importance.

Ingredients:

Yeast dough (see page 288)
6 ripe tomatoes, skinned
3–4 oz. Gruyère *or* Cheddar cheese, in slices
1 tablespoon mixed fresh chopped or green-dried rosemary and parsley
Oil for brushing

Pesto:

2 tablespoons grated Parmesan cheese
1 clove garlic
1 level teaspoon fresh chopped or green-dried basil
1 tablespoon sunflower oil
1 tablespoon butter
or Genoese pesto (page 269)

Method:

1. Prepare yeast pastry.
2. Roll out to about a quarter inch thick and cut into rounds four to five inches in diameter.
3. Put on baking sheet.
4. Brush edges of each round with oil.
5. Mix Parmesan cheese, garlic, basil, oil, and butter into a thick paste, or use Genoese pesto.
6. Spread some of the paste thinly on the center of each round where not touched by oil.
7. Put some slices of tomato on top.
8. Sprinkle a little of the other mixed herbs on the tomato slices.
9. Top with slices of cheese.
10. Allow to rise again.
11. Bake in oven (400°) for 10 to 20 minutes.

Savory Herb Pastry to Serve with Soup

(*a*) Parsley Biscuits (*makes 2 dozen*)

These may be made with either lovage or marjoram in place of parsley.

Ingredients:

1½ cups short pastry mix (see page 288)
¼ cup finely minced parsley
or 2 tablespoons green-dried parsley

1 tablespoon onion, finely chopped
¼ cup milk

Method:
1. Mix parsley and onion with pastry mix.
2. Add milk to make a stiff dough.
3. Turn onto a floured board and knead well.
4. Roll out to half-inch thickness.
5. Cut into one-inch squares or diamonds.
6. Place on baking sheet and bake in moderate oven (375°) for 15 to 20 minutes. Serve hot.

(b) Cheese and Ham Twists (*makes approx. 30*)

Ingredients:

1 cup pastry mix (see page 288)
1 teaspoon chopped or green-dried chives
½ teaspoon fresh chopped or green-dried summer savory
2 oz. grated Cheddar cheese

¼ cup milk
1 tablespoon melted butter
2–3 oz. chopped ham
1 teaspoon fresh chopped or green-dried tarragon

Method:
1. Mix pastry, cheese, and herbs (except tarragon) together.
2. Add milk and knead lightly.
3. Turn onto a floured board and roll out a quarter inch thick to a rectangle.
4. Brush this pastry with the butter.
5. Mix ham and tarragon well; spread this mixture over the pastry to within one inch of the edge.
6. Fold lengthwise and pinch-seal the edges.
7. Cut into half-inch strips and twist each.
8. Place on greased baking tin and bake in moderate oven (375°) for 20 to 25 minutes. Serve hot.

(c) Cheese Logs (*makes 16*)

Ingredients:

2 oz. soft butter
1 teaspoon hot water
4 oz. flour

2 oz. grated Cheddar cheese
1 teaspoon fresh chopped or green-dried thyme
Poppy seeds (optional)

Method:
1. In an electric mixer, whip butter with hot water for two minutes at medium speed.
2. Add flour, making a soft dough.
3. Add cheese and thyme, mixing well.

4. Chill in refrigerator until stiff enough to handle.
5. Turn onto a floured board; roll into logs a half inch around and two inches long.
6. Brush with beaten egg, roll in poppy seed, and place on greased baking tin.
7. Bake in a moderate oven (375°) for about 20 to 25 minutes.

Rosemary Ring

Good to accompany vegetables, excellent as a snack, hot or cold, with soup or coffee.

Ingredients:

½ lb. yeast dough (see page 288)
2 tablespoons butter

1 tablespoon fresh chopped or green-dried rosemary
2½ oz. Cheddar cheese, grated

Method:
1. Roll out dough to a half-inch thick; cut into biscuit rounds.
2. Melt the butter and add the rosemary.
3. Brush tops of biscuits with this mixture.
4. Arrange the biscuits in a round cake pan to overlap each other.
5. Brush the tops again with the remaining butter.
6. Sprinkle with the grated cheese.
7. Bake in a hot oven (425°) for about 10 minutes until golden brown.

Meat and Vegetable Pies

For the lunch-box and the picnic basket.

A perfect alternative to sandwiches, these pies provide a complete meal, containing such important proteins as meat, eggs, cheese, and nuts, wrapped in a yeast crust. This means less calories and a better proportion of starch to protein than sandwiches. They may be eaten with the fingers. Heated up, and wrapped well in two or three layers of foil, they will stay hot for several hours.

Pies may also be frozen; thawed pies can be heated in a 300° oven for about 15 minutes. They may be served plain or with a sauce, or as accompaniment to a salad when they supply a whole meal.

Make yeast dough (see page 288) from a pound of flour to provide 18 pies—six each of the three following fillings,
or
Buy a package of bread mix (white or brown) and follow the directions on the package.

Ingredients:
Yeast dough *or* 1 package bread mix   Caraway and poppy seeds (optional)

Method for Pies:
1. When the dough has risen sufficiently, turn onto a floured board.
2. Roll out to about a half inch thickness, making a rectangle of about 16 by 24 inches.
3. Cut the dough with a sharp knife into eight-inch squares.
4. Have ready a choice of three fillings and place 2 tablespoons cold filling in the center of each square.
5. Brush all four edges with water.
6. Bring corners together at the center of the square and pinch edges together to seal, making four diagonal seals.
7. Brush with beaten egg yolk and sprinkle with caraway or poppy seeds.
8. Place on well-greased flat tin.
9. Bake in moderate oven (350°) for 30 minutes or until golden brown.

(a) Beef and Cabbage Filling (6 pies)

Ingredients:
½ medium-sized onion, chopped
1 tablespoon butter *or* margarine
½ lb. minced beef
¼ teaspoon salt

1 teaspoon each fresh chopped or green-dried lovage and summer savory
1 small cabbage head, chopped

Method:
1. Brown onions in butter and add the meat, stirring until redness disappears.
2. Add salt, herbs, and cabbage, and simmer for 45 minutes, covered, stirring occasionally.
3. Set aside to cool.

(b) Egg and Carrot Filling (6 pies)

Ingredients:
½ lb. carrots, cooked and finely chopped
1 tablespoon butter *or* margarine

3 hard-boiled eggs, chopped
2 tablespoons fresh chopped or green-dried parsley

¼ teaspoon salt
1 teaspoon each fresh chopped or green-dried tarragon, summer savory, and basil
½ teaspoon fresh chopped or green-dried marjoram
or 1 teaspoon bouquet for omelettes

Nutmeg and paprika
1 tablespoon thin cream

Method:
1. Sauté the carrots in the butter for five minutes.
2. Remove from heat.
3. Stir in salt, herbs, eggs, parsley, nutmeg, paprika, and cream.
4. Cool and use for filling.

(c) Cheese, Nut, and Eggplant Filling (6 *pies*)

Ingredients:
1 medium-sized onion, chopped
2 tablespoons butter *or* margarine
¾ lb. grated cheese
Salt
1 tablespoon fresh chopped or green-dried onion green

1 teaspoon each fresh chopped or green-dried lovage, summer savory, and tarragon
1 medium-sized eggplant, peeled and chopped
¼ cup nuts or slivered almonds
Nutmeg

Method:
1. Sauté the onion in butter for five minutes.
2. Add onion green and sauté, add the eggplant, salt, and all herbs.
3. Cover and allow to simmer on low heat for 10 minutes.
4. Stir in the cheese and the nuts and nutmeg; then allow to melt.
5. Remove from heat, drain excess fat, and cool.

Savory Bread Mixture (B)

Tastier than sausage mixture or minced meat; to be used for stuffings, dumplings, roasts.

Ingredients:
4 oz. bread
8 tablespoons chopped onion
3 tablespoons fresh chopped or green-dried parsley
4–5 tablespoons fresh chopped or green-dried onion green

Salt
Grated nutmeg
Ground ginger
1–2 eggs

Method:
1. Soak bread (preferably whole grain) in cold water until the crust is soft.
2. Take it out and squeeze well so that it is mashed and fairly dry.
3. Sauté chopped onion in oil until golden.
4. Add parsley and sauté again.
5. Then add onion green and sauté again (a few more herbs such as celery leaves, lovage, and a small quantity of marjoram may be added according to taste).
6. Add to this the squeezed bread.
7. Mix well and sauté, turning over all the time, until all the moisture has disappeared and the mixture is fairly dry.
8. Allow to cool.
9. Season with salt, grated nutmeg, and ground ginger, according to taste.
10. Add eggs and mix all well.

Note: This stuffing may be used for stuffed cabbage leaves, spinach leaves, vine leaves, stuffed tomatoes, marrow, potatoes—in fact all kinds of stuffing.

Bread Dumplings

1. Roll the same mixture between wet hands without pressure, to form small balls.
2. The dumplings should be cooked in salted water or stock.
3. Cook one dumpling, and, if it does not hold well together, add another egg and more bread crumbs to the mixture.
4. Place dumplings in the boiling liquid, allow to simmer—when they come up to the surface, they are ready.

Note: Dumplings the size of a walnut may be served in clear broth; larger dumplings—the size of a plum—should be drained well and may be served with melted butter and fried onions on a heated shallow dish.

Roasted Loaf

The bread mixture may be shaped into a loaf and roasted like a joint in a heavy saucepan or in the oven. To make a full meal, one or two hard-boiled eggs may be placed in the center of the loaf.

Savory Marjoram Rolls (*makes approx. 15*)

Similar to scones for tea or as a snack.

Ingredients:
Yeast dough (see page 288)   3 teaspoons fresh chopped or green-
                                       dried marjoram

Method:
1. Make yeast dough according to recipe, adding the marjoram to the dry ingredients.
2. Roll out half an inch thick.
3. Cut rounds with biscuit cutter.
4. Allow to rise until double the size.
5. Brush tops with water.
6. Bake in a moderate oven (350-375°) approximately 30 minutes.
   Note: Eat when fresh, cut across and spread with butter.

Chapter 12

Herbed Drinks—Alcoholic and Non-alcoholic

Herb-Fruited Wine Cup (*makes 20 glasses*)

Ingredients:

2 bottles sweet white wine, such as Sauterne

1 bottle champagne *or* soda water

2 sprigs each fresh *or* 1 teaspoon each of green-dried lemon verbena, sage, and mint

1 small sprig rosemary *or* ½ teaspoon green-dried rosemary

4 fresh *or* green-dried whole scented rose-geranium leaves

1 lb. strawberries, fresh *or* frozen

2 tablespoons honey (preferably flower or herb honey)

Additional scented rose-geranium leaves for garnish

Method:

1. Lightly crush fresh sprigs and 4 rose-geranium leaves in bottom of a large jar.
2. Cool wine and pour over herbs.
3. Steep for 3 hours at room temperature (covered).
4. Clean and crush strawberries; if fresh, sweeten with honey.
5. Chill for 30 minutes in refrigerator.
6. Add sweetened berries to wine.
7. Chill well and keep chilled by placing jug of crushed ice in center of punch bowl.
8. Just before serving, pour in champagne or soda water.
9. Serve in chilled punch cups with one small rose-geranium leaf floating on top.

Note: If green-dried herbs are used, strain before adding fruit.

Woodruff Cup

If woodruff is available, this makes the best May-wine cup or herb cup, but the fresh woodruff must be dried in a well-covered china or earthenware bowl for two days before using. If woodruff is carefully green dried, and thus becomes available the whole year, approximately one-eighth ounce green-dried woodruff (whole leaves) should be used.

Method:
1. Add ¼ of the quantity of white wine being used to the woodruff (or clear apple juice if wanted for a non-alcoholic cup).
2. Allow to steep for half an hour.
3. Filter and add more wine (or juice).
4. Flavor with lemon juice and rind, and add strawberries or peaches, sugar, and champagne or soda water, according to taste.
   Note: An excellent, even exhilarating drink may be made when woodruff is allowed to steep in clear, undiluted apple juice.

Burnet Cocktail

Ingredients:

Sprigs of burnet leaves   Juice of ½ lemon
A tot of whisky   Crushed ice
½ teaspoon icing sugar

Method:
1. Bruise a sprig of burnet leaves in a well-chilled cocktail glass.
2. Combine the whisky, icing sugar, and lemon juice.
3. Add another whole sprig of burnet to the mixture.
4. Pour into an electric blender with crushed ice and whirl until the ice is powdered. Strain the snow through a fine mesh strainer over a cone-shaped mound of crushed ice in each cocktail glass.
5. Decorate with a sprig of burnet and serve with a straw.

Melissa Liqueur

Method:
1. Place a handful of fresh or dried whole melissa leaves (lemon balm) or 2 tablespoons green-dried lemon balm in 1 pint of brandy or kirsch and leave in a warm place for 24 hours.
2. Remove leaves from liquid and sweeten with ½ lb. sugar.
3. Pour into bottles; seal well.

Miner's Arms Long Herb Drink

A long drink may be made by using an herb decoction which is made up beforehand. This herb mixture should be allowed to steep for at least two days before use and can be kept indefinitely in a screw-top jar for use as required. The decoction may ferment, so the bottle should be opened from time to time to release the pressure; actually fermentation enhances the result.

This is an invention of the host at the Miner's Arms in Priddy, Somerset, England, and produces an excitingly pleasant long drink. He reports that it has an enlivening and exhilarating effect beyond that normally attributable to the brandy.

Herb mixture:
> Equal portions of freshly chopped or green-dried mint and borage with 2 fl. oz. lemon juice, together with the yellow rind of 1 lemon and 1 good teaspoon each of borage and lemon balm.

This drink is made as follows:
1. Put into a large glass (about 8 oz.) a piece of ice.
2. Add about 6 drops of Angostura bitters and the same quantity of the decoction of herbs in lemon juice (see above).
3. Add an even slice of lemon, a large measure of cognac, and top up with a small bottle of Schweppes' tonic water.

Mint Julep

Ingredients (per glass):
3–4 fresh mint leaves
or 1 tablespoon green-dried mint
1–4 teaspoons sugar syrup (according to taste) made with equal parts sugar and water

1 fl. oz. whisky
Crushed ice
Whisky to fill up the glass
2 sprigs of mint for decorating

Method:
1. Place a little of the crushed ice in the bottom of a glass.
2. Add the sugar syrup according to taste.
3. Add whisky and mint.
4. Stir well, crushing the mint.
5. Fill the glass with crushed ice and pack tightly to the top.
6. Slowly fill with whisky.
7. Stick in 2 sprigs of mint to decorate the top; let it stand for a minute or two.

8. When the glass starts to frost, the julep should be served.

Note: Crush the ice—which is important—either (*a*) by a blender; or (*b*) by packing ice cubes in a tea towel or canvas bag and hammering it until flat. This is to keep the ice dry.

Cider Cup with Borage (*makes approx. 3 pints*)

Ingredients:

1 quart cider	½ cup sherry
1 lemon	½ gill brandy
1 pint orange juice	Sugar ⎱ According
1 handful fresh or green-dried	Soda water ⎰ to taste
whole borage leaves	

Method:

1. Finely peel lemon so that the skin remains in one piece and attached at one end.
2. Prick the lemon with a fork and immerse in the cider.
3. Add borage to the cider.
4. Cover and leave to stand for about 2 hours.
5. Add orange juice, the sherry, brandy, and sugar.
6. Chill.
7. Add soda water shortly before serving.

   Note: Remove lemon (optional).

Fresh Mint Punch (*makes about 2 pints*)

Ingredients:

6 good sprigs of fresh mint	¾ pint apple juice
Juice of 3 oranges	6 tablespoons sugar
Juice of 2 small lemons	½ pint cider

Method:

1. Wash and bruise the mint and place it in the bottom of a large jug.
2. Pour over the orange, lemon, and apple juice.
3. Add the sugar and stir well.
4. Allow to stand at room temperature for 1 hour; then chill in the refrigerator.
5. Just before serving, fill up with cider (up to 2 pints can be added).
6. Put layers of crushed ice into bowl and pour mixture over them, or serve in individual glasses containing some crushed ice.

Mint Syrup (*makes 1 cup*)

Ingredients:
6 sprigs fresh *or* 6 tablespoons   3 cups sugar
   green-dried mint *or* peppermint   1 cup water

Method:
1. Select fresh, crisp mint. Wash and dry thoroughly.
2. Crush or bruise leaves and stems in small bowl.
3. Pour water into heavy saucepan; dissolve sugar in water.
4. Add mint.
5. Bring to the boil over medium heat.
6. Boil 5 minutes, stirring occasionally.
7. Remove from heat and allow to stand for 15 minutes.
8. Remove mint sprigs, or strain if green-dried mint is used.
9. When syrup is cool, pour into bottle; cork tightly.
   Note: Use as a flavoring for drinks; also with fresh fruit cups and desserts.

Mint Lemonade (*makes ½ pint*)

Ingredients:
Juice of large lemon   ¼ pint apple juice
Juice of 1 orange   Sprigs of fresh mint for garnish
5 tablespoons mint syrup (see
   above)

Method:
1. Mix together lemon and orange juice.
2. Add mint syrup and shake well.
3. Stir in apple juice.
4. Serve chilled and garnished with fresh mint.

Hibiscus Punch—Hot or Cold

Ingredients (per pint of boiling water):
2 heaped teaspoons hibiscus flowers   ½ stick cinnamon
⅔ vanilla pod   Honey to sweeten
2 or 3 cloves

Method:
1. Place flowers, vanilla, cloves, and cinnamon in a warmed pot.
2. Cover with the boiling water and allow to draw 5 to 10 minutes; strain.

3. Sweeten with honey.
4. Serve hot in winter or chilled in summer.
   Note: Add half of the quantity red wine if desired.

Fragrant milk drinks for those with a delicate palate:

Elder-Flower Milk

Ingredients:

1 head of elder flowers
or 1 tablespoon dried elder flowers
1 teaspoon fresh chopped or green-
 dried lemon balm

½ pint milk
1 teaspoon honey

Method:

1. Pour hot milk (not boiling) over elder flowers and lemon balm.
2. Allow to draw 5 to 10 minutes in a warm place.
3. Strain, add honey, and mix well.
4. Allow to cool. Serve cold.

Orange-Apple Milk Drink

Ingredients:

¼ pint milk
2 oz. orange juice
2 oz. apple juice
1 teaspoon honey

1 teaspoon fresh chopped or green-
 dried sweet cicely
Few drops of lemon juice

Method:

1. Mix all ingredients together, whisking well, or whirl in a blender.
2. Leave to stand at room temperature for about half an hour.
3. Strain and serve chilled.

Raspberry Milk

Ingredients:

 ¼ pint milk
 1 oz. blackberry juice } or 1 tablespoon
 1 oz. raspberry juice } raspberry syrup
 1 teaspoon honey
 1 teaspoon mixed fresh chopped or green-dried sweet cicely and
  lemon balm

Method:

1. Mix all ingredients together, whisking well, or whirl in a blender.
2. Allow to stand at room temperature for half an hour; then strain.
3. Serve chilled.

Note: When fresh berries are available, they may be used freshly expressed with added honey; they are of most value to health.